FISHER OF LAMBETH

The Most Reverend and Right Honourable Geoffrey Francis Fisher, D.D., Lord Archbishop of Canterbury, wearing his Coronation cope and mitre, 1953.

FISHER OF LAMBETH

A Portrait From Life

by

WILLIAM PURCELL

I've often said that the first requisite for an archbishop is to be as strong as a horse. That reminds me that I was told of a prep. school, when I was Archbishop, in which a general paper was set to the small boys. One question was: 'Who is Geoffrey Cantuar?' One small boy replied: 'Cantuar is half man, half horse.' Not a bad description of me, really.

G.F.F.

HODDER AND STOUGHTON

Printed in Great Britain for Hodder and Stoughton Limited, St. Paul's
House, Warwick Lane, London, E.C.4, by The Camelot Press Ltd.,
London and Southampton

Acknowledgments

I am grateful to the following for permission to reproduce copyright material:

Her Majesty's Stationery Office for an extract from *Hansard*.

Longmans, Green & Co. Ltd. for extracts from *The Rise of Christianity* by E. W. Barnes.

John Murray Ltd. for the lines from *Summoned by Bells* by John Betjeman.

The Oxford University Press for extracts from *Randall Davidson* by G. K. A. Bell, and *George Bell* by R. C. D. Jasper.

S.P.C.K. for extracts from the report *Lambeth Conference 1958*.

The Spectator for the letter by Randolph Churchill.

Contents

Contents

Illustrations

The Archbishop robed for the Coronation[1] *Frontispiece*

Between pages 176 and 177

KEY TO ACKNOWLEDGMENTS

1 Topix
2 Tucker
3 Archer Smith
4 Sport and General
5 Graphic Photos
6 Harris & Ewing

7 *The Times*
8 Wandsworth Photographic Service
9 Keystone Press
10 Uganda Protectorate
11 W. H. Rendell

Foreword

Many people have helped to make this book possible, and the names of those who have been kind enough to contribute their own recollections of its subject are mentioned in the text, and are here warmly thanked by the author.

There remain, however, two things for him to say. The first is that he alone is responsible for any opinions he has expressed in this book. The second is that he wishes to express to the Most Reverend Archbishop Lord Fisher of Lambeth, and to Lady Fisher, his profound gratitude for their help, their patience, their confidence, and their hospitality. In other words, and in the style of a former age, he would wish to subscribe himself as their most humble and obliged servant,

WILLIAM PURCELL

Foreword

PART ONE

Prologue

WHEN the singing of the last hymn died away, rain, flung by a wild wind, could be heard dashing against the windows of Canterbury Cathedral. It had been blowing and gusting throughout the service. As six sergeants of the Buffs, the East Kent Regiment, stepped forward to shoulder the coffin of William Temple, late Archbishop of Canterbury, there was a moment when only wind and rain, and the movements of the men getting their heavy burden into position, could be heard. Then they began their journey out through the choir, through the screen, out into the nave, while the organ played Bach's choral prelude 'Hark! A Voice Sayeth All Are Mortal'. Here and there, as the coffin passed, people in the vast crowd could be seen falling to their knees. And then, at the West Door it was taken out into the rain, and away to the crematorium at Charing.

For the great soul who thus passed there was surely no cause for grief. In his last address to the clergy of the Canterbury diocese, made shortly before his death, he had quoted the words of Arthur Hugh Clough:

> It fortifies my soul to know
> That, though I perish, Truth is so:
> That, howsoe'er I stray and range,
> Whate'er I do, Thou dost not change.
> I steadier step when I recall
> That, if I slip, Thou dost not fall.

It was enough, in such a context, to give thanks for William Temple, and rejoice for him.

But left behind in the Cathedral was a sense of almost irreparable loss, a microcosm of the emotion, the world extent of which had already been reflected in messages coming in from all sorts and conditions of people, from the captains and the kings, from the President of the United States, from workers in industry, to a schoolboy of fourteen who wrote home saying, 'This is the first time in my life that anyone has died whom I knew really well.'[1]

Also left behind in the Cathedral, on the high altar, was the pastoral staff of the late archbishop. During the service, it had been removed from the coffin by the archbishop's chaplain and handed to the Dean. Now it lay there, testifying to the fact that the office, one of the greatest in Christendom, and so lately occupied by one who had adorned it as few ever had, if only for two and a half years, was vacant. The date was 31 October 1944. There were some, at least among those in Canterbury on that day, who, as they dispersed, shared a moment to wonder, if a trifle grimly, who would—whoever could—be found with the gifts and the courage to take it up.

There had been other obsequies for other archbishops, of course, in that same place down the centuries. Indeed, he who had just passed had been the ninety-eighth. But there were, at that time, quite special reasons why the death of William Temple seemed to all men of goodwill the cruellest of blows, even in a dark time of war full of adverse fortune, and to Christians in general one of the most inexplicable acts of God. It is necessary to be clear what some, at least, of those special reasons were if some idea is to be had of the magnitude of the tasks facing whoever was to be his successor.

'Temple's death,' wrote an old friend of his, R. H. Hodgkin, Provost of Queen's, 'seemed to shake the Western world as if one of its pillars had been removed.'[2] President Roosevelt, in a cable to the King, had said that the Archbishop had 'exercised profound influence throughout the world'.[3] Another public man expressed the opinion that only two other sudden happenings in his memory—the postponement of the coronation of Edward VII and the loss of Lord Kitchener in the cruiser *Hampshire* in the First World War—had had comparable shock effects.[4] Such sentiments, related to such a death, were by any standards unusual. If, all these years later, a parallel and an explanation are to be sought, there may perhaps be

---

[1] F. A. Iremonger, *William Temple* (O.U.P.).   [2] *Ibid.*   [3] *Ibid.*   [4] *Ibid.*

found to some extent in the death of Pope John XXIII and more sharply and more poignantly in that of President Kennedy. John went in the fullness of years; the President in comparative youth. In terms of age, Temple was somewhere between the two. But in one significant particular he may be held to be with them as one of that select few which humanity invariably recognises and mourns as the Lost Leader.

Here, then, is one of the special reasons why it was going to be so difficult to follow Temple.

True, he had not been young. He was, in fact, sixty-three at the time of his death. But he had been undoubtedly and with cause, sensed to be a different kind of archbishop from almost any of his predecessors. To those who had followed his career, and knew of his life-long involvement in the pursuit of social justice, or his tremendous influence at such long-remembered and seminal conferences as that on Politics, Economics and Citizenship, in 1924—'Copec', as it was named—or the Malvern Conference on the Social Order in the early years of the Second World War, or with his writings in the same field, this element in his archiepiscopate, at York as at Canterbury, was no surprise. But to the general public, the impact was considerable, and it seemed that a new champion of social justice had arisen from a part of the Establishment not generally expected, in popular opinion, to be notably productive of such. When the artist Low, in the London *Evening Standard* could devote two of his cartoons to showing the Archbishop as a kind of people's advocate against economic reactionaries, it was clear that something of considerable import had occurred. The term 'the people's Archbishop', often used of Temple, may be said to have derived more from this aspect of his manifold activities than from any other. Now he was dead, and the blow was severe indeed.

But many others felt it—and they had been for years a growing number —who were concerned with the issue of church unity or, more accurately, with church disunity. 'I believe in the holy Catholic Church,' Temple had said once, 'and sincerely regret it does not exist.' And two and a half years before, when Canterbury Cathedral had been full for his enthronement, he had stated that 'as though in preparation for such a time as this, God has been building up a Christian fellowship, which now extends into every nation and binds citizens of them all together in true unity and mutual

B

love . . . Almost incidentally, the great world fellowship has arisen; it is the great new fact of our era; it makes itself apparent from time to time in world conferences such as in the last twenty years have been held at Stockholm, Lausanne, Jerusalem, Oxford, Madras, Amsterdam.'

'In the last twenty years . . .' If the Ecumenical Movement, as it was called, did not begin with Temple, as appeared to be sometimes supposed, its debt to him was enormous. That massive head, those gold-rimmed spectacles had been familiar at all those conferences and at many others besides. The development of the Movement, from the Edinburgh Conference of 1910 through 'Life and Work', 'Faith and Order', to the World Alliance of 1914, followed by a break in the war years until the next great ecumenical gathering had become possible at Stockholm in 1925, had been complex but continuous. A net of international inter-church contacts had been woven, and often maintained with moving fidelity, even in times of dictatorship and war, by the time of Temple's enthronement. At the centre of the web, to a considerable extent, was Canterbury, both by history and the long identification of Temple with the movement, ideally placed for leadership in the great steps forward towards the ancient goal of the prayer 'That all may be one', which, in many lands, by many people, were felt to be a necessary part of reconciliation once the war was over.

Nor was the sense of loss confined only to these special areas, vast as they were; or to the private griefs of the thousands who had known and loved Temple. It was felt also, and with understandably special intensity, by that particular part of the church universal, of which he was the head — the Church of England. By 1944, it was a long, long time since he had given up the rectorship of St. James's, Piccadilly, to devote himself entirely to campaigning for the Life and Liberty Movement. It had, to some extent, served its purpose and at any rate, laid the foundations, by no means yet complete, of opportunities for the Church to attempt to reform its own structures.

So, therefore, to his own Church as well as in far wider areas of national and, indeed, international life the blow was staggering. Different people took it in different ways. Some fell on their knees as the news reached them, just as some fell on their knees when the coffin passed in Canterbury Cathedral. One who did so when the news reached him was the then Bishop of London, Geoffrey Francis Fisher. Asked long afterwards what his reaction had been at the news of Temple's death, he said that as it happened he was in the House of Lords at the time. He went to one of the Bishops' Rooms and knelt and prayed a long time, 'not thinking of myself or the future at all, but wondering about the ways of God which could have taken so great a man as Temple from the world at a time when he was needed so sorely.'

Yet there it was; the great man had gone and for these reasons already given a quite unusual degree of interest attached to the question of a successor. He would, like Fortinbras at the end of *Hamlet*, march on to a stage littered with dead although in his case with dead hopes. The question remained as to how many of them he might be able miraculously to revive, how many he would bury and how many, if any, of the tasks of his great predecessor he might be able to carry on and develop.

A great many people, therefore, outside as well as inside the Church, waited for the announcement of the name of the man who had been chosen, by that mysterious and involved process, nicely involving Crown and Prime Minister, and as elusive of definition as the British climate, to be ninety-ninth Archbishop of Canterbury. That there were some strong candidates was a fact. Bell, of Chichester, was certainly one; wise, saintly, experienced and, very importantly, a man with many international contacts, some of them riskily maintained through the fog of war. Bell, as was well known, had been outspoken on the subject of the mass bombing of open cities, and this, it was felt, might well not recommend him to a Prime Minister who had been an ardent advocate of that very policy.[1] And then there was Winchester, Mervyn Haigh, of whom not so much was generally known except that he was intellectually powerful and physically ailing. Garbett, of York, might have been ideal had he not been within sight of his own retirement, so that for once translation from York to Canterbury did not seem very likely.

[1] Further light has subsequently been thrown on this matter by the production of Hochhuth's play *Soldiers*, where Bell is shown as confronting Mr. Churchill on this issue. Later, the Ven. Lancelot Mason, a former domestic chaplain to Bell, wrote in *Crucible*, the journal of the Church Assembly Council for Social Responsibility: 'The substance of the Bishop's argument against the policy of the War Cabinet is not unfairly presented.' Whether this attitude of Bell's was an element in keeping him at this time from Canterbury is not inferred. It is suggested, however, that in later years it may have kept him from York. (See also p. 109.)

But nothing happened. Two months passed before an announcement was made, and when it came the surprise it caused seemed to equal the indignation the delay had occasioned. This had been considerable. Garbett of York described it as a scandal, saying of the Church: 'They are like a government without a prime minister.' That may well have been so. But the real government of the day did have a prime minister, and there were, to put it mildly, ample reasons for supposing that Mr. Churchill had at that time other matters on his mind, besides the appointment of a new Archbishop of Canterbury. Nor was he the man to delegate even such a responsibility as that. However, he got round to the task in the end. The man upon whom the choice fell, asked later of his memories of a preliminary interview with the Prime Minister, recalled that Mr. Churchill was genial. One of his questions to the Archbishop-designate was whether he had read Renan's *Vie de Jésus*. Answered in the negative, he expressed surprise.

Soon afterwards, on 2 January 1945, two months and two days after the funeral of Temple, the new archbishop was named. He was the man who, hearing of Temple's death, had felt moved to pray alone in the Bishops' Room at the House of Lords: Geoffrey Francis Fisher, Bishop of London.

'Thus there succeeded to the throne of St. Augustine one of the least-known archbishops for many years.'[1] It is a surprising statement. Fisher had been before a sizable section of the public as Bishop of London throughout the war years, even if his episcopate at Chester before that, or his headmastership of Repton, the great Midland public school, for many years before that, had not in themselves brought him into prominence. His time at London had been prophetic in one respect at least, in that he had brought administrative order out of chaos, and his activities in that direction had at times been matters of some general interest. So had his resolute leadership of a diocese passing, especially in the early days of the bombing, through severe trials. More importantly—although the public could not be expected to know this—he had been seen by Temple himself as a natural successor. 'I must give up in time to let Geoffrey have his whack,'[2] he had remarked to his wife once, when they had been discussing

[1] Roger Lloyd, *The Church of England, 1900–1965* (S.C.M. Press).
[2] F. A. Iremonger, *William Temple*.

plans for retirement. And the new archbishop had already made his debut in the ecumenical field as chairman of the joint standing committee of one of the earliest acts of Anglican-Roman joint activity—the co-operation towards the end of the war between the Religion and Life Movement (which was Anglican and Free Church) and the Sword of the Spirit (which was a Roman Catholic body), dedicated to the same broad purpose of showing where Christian insights could be brought to bear upon modern complexities. Anyway, known or unknown, there he was. And at two o'clock on the afternoon of Thursday, 19 April 1945, with the Allies within sight of victory in a shattered Europe, Geoffrey Francis Fisher was enthroned with much pomp in Canterbury Cathedral, as ninety-ninth Archbishop. So that pastoral staff which had been left behind by Temple, passed to his hands. His investiture with it was, indeed, the first act of the service, and after that everybody sang:

> Put thou thy trust in God,
> In duty's path go on;
> Walk in His strength with faith and hope,
> So shall thy work be done.

It was exactly what the new archbishop intended to do, and the words 'duty', 'strength', 'faith and hope', 'work' seemed to spring out of their well-worn context and fit with particular accuracy the *persona* of the man. They represented the characteristic virtues of the stock from which he came, Victorian clerical upper middle class, nurtured on plain living and high thinking against a background of country life and public school. They seemed to accord even with his appearance; stocky, strong, oak-like, with an imperial nose, a formidable mouth and chin, and eyes which could twinkle or glare according to the demands of the moment. They were to do both, and frequently, during the next sixteen years.

The public was to get to know this man well, or at any rate to become familiar with his image to a remarkable degree during that time, and the Anglican Communion in particular, as well as the Church at large, was to see and hear more of him, more directly, by their own firesides often enough, than of any of his predecessors. Two technological developments were to make this possible; television and the long-range aircraft. Here, in fact, was the first Archbishop of Canterbury whom millions could see and hear burying a king, or crowning a queen, or being interviewed on this or that public issue. Here was the first Archbishop of Canterbury who could descend from the skies upon New York, or Rome, or Istanbul, within hours of leaving London, and who did so. When the wide-ranging activities of Fisher as Archbishop of Canterbury are praised, as well they may be, the technological bases of them should not be overlooked. They gave the opportunity; he seized it.

But there is another aspect of this matter which may also be usefully borne in mind. It is that we have scarcely yet begun to realise the very considerable extent to which television appearances and rapid air communications have increased the impact of the characters of public men upon their public. They are under personal scrutiny as never before. Nor has the degree to which both have speeded up and increased the tensions of being a public figure yet been recognised. It follows that these factors have now, for the first time, to be taken into account when assessing the careers of public men. In the case of Archbishops of Canterbury, the exercise becomes fascinating. What, for example, would have become of the cautious diplomacy of a Randall Davidson had he been faced with a television interview often, and at short notice? How would the dignity, if not the pomp and circumstance, of Lang have stood up to trans-world flights, disarranging both calendar and clock and ending, as like as not, with a press conference at the airport on arrival?

We don't know; they didn't have to face up to these things. But Fisher did. That he was at times infuriated, often pleased, and almost invariably intrigued by these exercises is some measure of the many-sided character of the man, and of the vigour and openness with which he approached these new challenges. It is also some measure of the resilience with which a character such as his, to whom public relations as professionally practised were virtually an unknown field, adjusted himself eventually to so novel a situation. It is true that his relationships with the press suffered from what some regarded sometimes as an appalling frankness. When asked once to make a pronouncement on the future of mankind under the shadow of the H-bomb, it might have been unwise to offer the view that the physical survival of mankind cannot necessarily be regarded as the will of God. But it was utterly honest; the natural reaction of a man who had never been able not to say what he meant. 'Let your yea be yea, and your nay nay.' Such was his principle; he abided by it and the fact is highly relevant to the image which, for better or for worse, he created as one who was before the public, for reasons already stated, more often and more directly than was the case with any of his predecessors. In the humble opinion of this biographer, at any rate, that image did far less than justice to the true nature of the man, or to the vast labours and achievements of his archiepiscopate.

But this matter of the image he created is, after all, quite peripheral. It is the quality of his achievement which is central to any picture of his work. That his achievement was great, especially as regards ecumenical initiatives, becomes more apparent as the consequences of them begin to emerge, as others build where he laid foundations. After all, to take two outstanding instances, it was Fisher who was the first Archbishop of Canterbury to break the Roman ice, just as he was the first to make significant and practical approaches to the Methodists. And, in another area altogether, his labours towards making the Anglican Communion, perhaps for the first time, really conscious of itself as a world entity, were as considerable as they were successful. So were his efforts towards reform in the administrative machinery of that part of the Anglican Communion which is the Church of England. In view of all this, and of much else besides, such a verdict as Roger Lloyd's on this archiepiscopate seems almost ludicrously inadequate: 'If he was not one of the most spectacular, he was certainly one of the better Archbishops of modern history. The Church took little hurt from his hands and gained much from his leadership.'[1]

The time for any such evaluations may, in any event, not be yet. Such judgments belong rather to the historian than to the biographer, and require years before they can be attempted, if only because the results of what a man does in his time and generation can be seen in relation to other events only when they too have become history.

So this particular book does not set out to be a biography in the accepted sense. This is a portrait from life. The Most Reverend Archbishop

[1] Roger Lloyd, *The Church of England, 1900–1965.*

23

Lord Fisher of Lambeth was very much alive when this book was made, so the story of his life comes in part from him direct; and the great events of his archiepiscopate here touched upon come, not at second-hand from the recollections of others, or from written records (although, indeed, reinforced by both) but from conversations with the Archbishop himself. This is the first time, so far as this writer is aware, that such a record has been possible, and the relationship between the great central figure of it and his present biographer may be summed up in some words which Boswell used in his preface to the life of one who was at once his subject and the object of his profound admiration: 'As I had the honour and happiness of enjoying his friendship . . . as I had the scheme of writing his life constantly in view; as he was well apprised of this circumstance, and from time to time obligingly satisfied my enquiries, by communicating to me the incidents of his early years; as I acquired a facility in recollecting, and was very assiduous in recording his conversation, of which the extra-ordinary vigour and vivacity constituted one of the first features of his character; and as I have spared no pains in obtaining materials concerning him, from every quarter where I could discover that they were to be found, and have been favoured with the most liberal communications by his friends; I flatter myself that few biographers have entered upon such a work as this with more advantages; independent of literary abilities, in which I am not vain enough to compare myself with some great names which have gone before me in this kind of writing.'[1]

Such, then, is the nature of this book. One unusual circumstance made it possible, and two general considerations add to its interest. The unusual circumstance was that in 1961, at the age of seventy-four, with an un-expectedness which appeared to take the public by surprise as had his appointment sixteen years before, Archbishop Fisher resigned. The ap-parent suddenness concealed careful thought and cogent reasons—both will appear in their due place in this narrative—which lay behind the action. But resign he did, receiving, it is true, many honours and a title, and going with the utmost content to the humble position of priest-in-charge of a Dorset village. That is what Roger Lloyd means when he says: 'Humility seasoned all . . . it was to enable him to lay down his great

[1] James Boswell, *The Life of Dr. Johnson.*

office without any fuss, with no pangs because he was no longer at the centre of things, with none of the backward-looking regrets such as most of his predecessors had voiced. He laid himself quietly on the shelf of dispensability, and became the cheerful assistant curate of a West country village.'

The place in fact was Trent, a straggling, pleasant village some few miles out of Sherborne. The rectory is opposite the church. Rooks caw in elms; occasionally a tractor goes by and in the silences sometimes, in summer, the woodpecker can be heard in the garden.

Will there be another quite like him? The question leads to the first of those two general considerations which are roused by a narrative such as this. The fact is that the British, by immutable historical processes to which praise or blame are equally irrelevant, have shrunk.

> Far called our navies melt away
> On dune and headland sinks the fire . . .

It follows that some of the characteristic types of men and institutions which were formed by an era of greatness, when Britain was not an over-crowded offshore island looking for a place in the world, but the centre of an empire, will become fewer as time goes by. They will have their successors, of course; but other times, other manners. The new men will be different kinds of men, operating in different situations. Nor is there any reason to suppose that this process of change and diminution will pass by the throne of St. Augustine. So the primacy of Canterbury within the Anglican Communion, long taken for granted, may come to be no longer assumed, and one of the fruits of that ecumenical endeavour in which Canterbury has played so notable a part, may well lead to the absorption of Canterbury into a greater whole. It may equally as likely lead to an internationalising of the primacy itself, so that the time may come when some future archbishop may hail from Texas, or California, or elsewhere. And meanwhile, and largely since Fisher's day, the theological ferment, long simmering, has come to the boil and not a few old certitudes are melting therein.

It may well then be that we have in Fisher of Lambeth the last of the

Archbishops of Canterbury who could deal in certitudes from a position of authority, having behind it the prestige of a materially great power. That alone is enough to lend a nostalgic fascination to the study of such a character. When headmaster of Repton, the public school which occupied so many of his years, and clearly so much of his affections, he drew up a rule book. In his own words: 'Rule 1 was perfectly clear: "Any breach of common sense is a breach of these rules." The boys were tickled by this. They realised it was fair; but one or two of them would say to me, "But sir, who is going to decide what is a breach of common sense?" The answer was quite obvious. "I decide, and nobody else." '

Such certitudes, and the strength that goes with them, are no longer possible. Many would applaud the fact, and not only circumstances, but also not a few persons, especially the professional denigrators of so much that Britain once stood for, and indeed achieved, have worked to that end. They may care to congratulate themselves on the fact that the old lion appears now to be in reduced circumstances. But there are others who may view the matter differently, seeing a shaft of golden sunlight playing upon the end of an era. It will not be difficult for such to see the ninety-ninth Archbishop of Canterbury, Geoffrey Francis Fisher, as regards background values and character, outlined against it, strong as a rock, honest as the day. And they may well wonder if his like will ever be seen again and, if not, what will replace it.

One other general consideration remains to be mentioned. It is the question of how far Fisher, who took up the pastoral staff of Canterbury from where his great predecessor laid it down, was able to fulfil some of the expectations which William Temple's genius had aroused. Only the tale of what actually happened between the April day of 1945 when Fisher was enthroned, and the day in 1961 when he retired can give us as much of an answer as is yet possible. But one thing is clear; whatever Fisher did was decided by what Fisher was, and to make that clear it is necessary to go a long way back, to a little village in the English Midlands, in the year 1887 when he was born.

I

Scenes from Clerical Life

There is no mathematical equality in a family between different children: only the equality of love, which is a very different thing.

G.F.F., in an address delivered at Brisbane, November 1950

THE village was Higham-on-the-Hill, Leicestershire, in that flat Midland countryside which Hilaire Belloc once described as 'sodden and unkind'. It would be fairer, maybe, to speak of it as undistinguished, with its own reticences, so that its beauties, and there are some of a quiet sort, right there at the heart of England, have to be sought for, but can be found. Today, power-lines festoon too much of it, and heavy transport is thick upon the roads. But in 1887 Higham-on-the-Hill was quiet enough.

The name of Fisher had been associated with it a long time, even then. When Geoffrey Francis was born, his father had been the rector twenty-six years, and was to stay for forty; his father had been there a similar period before him, and his father—the new baby's great-grandfather—had an equally long reign. When George Eliot published, in 1858, the three tales which make up *Scenes From Clerical Life*, about the only cleric of the area she felt able to speak of with unqualified approval was, in fact, the grandfather of Geoffrey Francis. The rest were an indifferent lot, and something of the isolation, and even barbarism, of those mid-nineteenth century Midlands comes through the pages.

A mile away from Higham was the Watling Street, and two miles beyond that road was Nuneaton, the country town of the area, with its fine church, grammar school, square with the shops around, and an inn, the Newdigate Arms, speaking of a coaching past. But already beyond lay an area possessed by coal mines, stretching away to Coventry, eleven miles away.

The future archbishop grew up in what he described as 'a country rectory of the proper kind'. Behind were portions of an old manor-house. The front part was all Georgian, roomy and very comfortable, with a red-brick front and steps down to a drive, and a tennis court the other side. The family was large, mother and father and eight surviving children: two elder sisters, Edith and Katie, then twins, Lucy and Legh, of whom Lucy died early. Next came the brothers Harry, Herbert, Leonard and, five years junior to Leonard, Geoffrey, who was thus a good deal the youngest, and therefore lived his earliest years somewhat apart from the rest.

They were all people of distinct personality, having the capacity to live together in harmony, nonetheless, so that the life of that country rectory was happy. Soon, however, the older brothers went away to school; Katie went away to be a nurse; Edith remained the constant feature of the home. The subsequent fortunes of these two women may here be mentioned, the exercise having the interest which always attends the turning of pages of a family album in order to see what becomes of this person or that.

Edith, then, stayed at home, always helping her mother, almost unpaid curate to her father; but yet a person of shrewdness and gaiety in spite of this self-immolation. Her views were at times regarded as peculiar, as when she became a British Israelite, so that much argument with her sister Katie ensued. But this phase passed, and Edith may be regarded as one of the many Victorian daughters who also served by only staying at home. She and the little Geoffrey, in fact, were the only two children regularly there for some time.

The destiny of Katie was very different. She became, in her brother Geoffrey's words many years later, 'one of the heroic women of the world' who had gone from this country to other countries and there become out-standing figures. So Katie went out as medical missionary in 1901. Geoffrey remembered going to London, to the Dismissal Service, when that batch of C.M.S. missionaries was sent out. There, for the first time, he realised the power of corporate prayer, when this very large gathering said together the Lord's Prayer. His sister went out to Palestine, to a hospital the other side of the Jordan, under a Canadian doctor. After some years, the doctor went and Katie was left, the only white woman the other side of the Jordan, with Bedouin as her chief patients. She was happy there, and always she was quite fearless.

Of the rest of this rectory family of Higham-on-the-Hill, Legh became a robust and vigorous parish priest, Harry became a doctor, Herbert a Colonial civil servant and Leonard, gentle, philosophic and devoted, after service in England and Africa became Bishop of Lebombo and finally a greatly beloved Bishop of Natal.

So there they were; argumentative, talkative as a family, and all deeply involved in the social life of the village community with which their name had so long been associated. The origin of two characteristics of the Archbishop who was to come from this family may here be noted; a strong sense of community, in school or church, manifesting itself, whenever he was in a position of high authority in either, in a sharp indignation wherever he felt that the wholeness of the community was being disrupted by irresponsible activities. This was combined with a genuine classlessness. This last, in later years, was often greatly misunderstood, especially by the press, still associating with Canterbury the fixed idea of prelatical pomps. Fisher's position was much simpler; he was never bothered with his position because he knew what it was. And he knew what it was—knew where he stood in the scheme of things—because he came from a village life where everyone else did the same. The point had better be made in his own words: 'If I sum up my childhood to the age of eight, the first and greatest thing I can say is that the community was the background and the life-blood of everything. Everybody in the place knew us as a family attached to Higham, and we knew all the ramifications of the village families, too, and we were really, in one sense, a classless society because we all belonged to one another. We each knew our own station and our own place. We weren't jealous of each other; we weren't working against each other; we were combined in a community of friendship and mutual help. It was a grand thing.'

What then of the parents of this vigorous family in the rectory at Higham-on-the-Hill? The father, the Rev. H. Fisher, belonged to a family which had lived a long time in that part of the world. Furthest back in traceable origin was a John Fisher, at Burton, Prior of Burton

Priory. There was at the same time a Richard Fisher, otherwise known as Richard de Stapenhill, who rented the fishing of the Trent from the same prior. From that origin, Richard de Stapenhill, otherwise the Fisher, the family continued. In the fifteenth and sixteenth centuries they were yeoman farmers at a little place called Foremark, a mile or two from the village of Repton. Later in time, they became chiefly a family of clergymen.

The Rector of Higham-on-the-Hill, Geoffrey's father, was a spare man; keen, engrossed in whatever was before him at the moment, as later his youngest son was to be, full of interests of every kind, with the instincts of a scholar, never idle. Geoffrey remembered him preparing his sermons, working on them right up to the moment when the last bell began from the church across the fields; scratching out sentences, writing in little bits, inserting new words, unable to leave it until the last possible moment. He was a model landlord, with two glebe farms, and he was knowledgeable in farming ways, and a devoted member of the local Board of Guardians. A busy person, constantly about his parish and beyond, he was not expansive but universally respected and enjoyed.

It was the mother who was the presiding genius of the whole family. We may see her most clearly in her son's own words: 'My mother was a very lovely, very handsome woman, with a great presence. She moved in any society with an air of distinction, and at the same time, in herself, she was simple, natural, unaffected, shrewd, able and everything except well-read. Like many girls, her education had stopped short when she married my father as a young girl. She once told us that, having come under a triumphal arch back to the rectory as the Rector's bride, she led a very lonely life for some little time, my father engrossed in his work and in his reading, and she herself, to break the monotony, used to do little mathematical sums to keep her mind engaged. Yet she had a great deal of relevant knowledge of all kinds, and could use it, and control a situation by the shrewdness, the quietness, the gentleness, and the understanding of her judgment.'

Her background was more distinguished than that of her husband. Born Katherine Richmond, she could include among her forbears that Reverend Legh Richmond (1772–1827) who became widely known in his day by having the triple distinction of having been chaplain to the Duke of Kent, a notable rector of Turvey in Bedfordshire, and author, in an age when moral tracts were the thing, of one of the best-selling of all, *The Dairy-man's Daughter*, which, translated into many languages, sold two million copies. Another forbear was Dean Close, sometime Rector of Cheltenham, founder of the public school there which bears his name, and later Dean of Carlisle.

A brother of Katherine's, Douglas Richmond, at one time Fellow of Peterhouse, became Controller and Auditor General. A product of his first marriage was Bruce Richmond, founder and for many years editor of *The Times Literary Supplement*. From a second marriage came Oliff Richmond, scholar of Eton and King's, later Fellow of King's and professor of Latin elsewhere.

Geoffrey, as her youngest child, was with her about the house a great deal, and the sight of him then, as he recalled it, gives another clear picture of a Victorian rectory in the eighties. There were three servants in the kitchen, all from the village, their families and the rectory family sharing in community of interests. Beyond the kitchen was a room where the laundry was ironed, and there, every Monday morning came up two old ladies from the village who did the washing and ironing, and occasionally allowed the child to help. There were three cows; and pigs. There were fields and a pond, and a great walled garden looked after, among other occupations, first by one William Knight, a rather old and sour man, and then by Sam Smith, a very fine-looking, commanding person, who not only ran everyone but also sang in the choir and whose able son, Fred, became the organist of the parish church.

This was a tight village community. Only one place in it spoke to the child Geoffrey of even the possibility of other worlds. This was the station, half a mile across the fields, on a line which ran from Nuneaton to Burton and beyond. One vivid memory of this line remained with him always. It was of his eldest brother's going off to school at Glenalmond and, late in the evening, starting by train from Higham and down to Nuneaton, there to get the Scottish express from Euston. Geoffrey thought the same train took him all the way, and would thrill at the moment when the fireman would open the furnace and onto the darkness would gleam the glow of fire.

Then there was the village school, where Geoffrey began his education and experienced the discipline and good teaching of Miss Boot, its headmistress. And then, too, there were village events, strengthening the community spirit. Notable among these events was the annual Harvest Festival, when all the farmers and their workmen met first in the church for the service, crowding the place. Thence all went to the school for the Harvest Supper, followed by songs that had come down from father to son, probably all through the nineteenth century. The church itself had an ancient Norman tower, with a useful, but entirely undistinguished, modern nave and side aisle. The Sunday morning scene here, as recalled by the Archbishop, has the clarity of a photograph turned up in an album long unopened. In the chancel was the reading desk and the choir was at the west end, over which the Rector's wife presided, Geoffrey sometimes with her or, as he grew up, sitting in the rectory pew three-quarters of the way up the church.

The Rector read the service in a very reverent, simple and devout manner; Mr. Lea, headmaster of the local preparatory school, read the lessons in an austere, commanding voice. Then there would be a sermon, long and somewhat prosaic. A youthful parishioner, in after times to be a notable war mayor of Chelsea, said of these sermons: 'When I listened to them, I knew I was getting something out of them in a way of cultured discourse about a reasoned theme, even though it didn't particularly appeal to me.' As for Geoffrey himself, it was perhaps in character that the only times he became worried was when his father became emotional, leaving his text, and holding forth with vehemence. Then Geoffrey was disturbed, knowing that his father, as he put it, 'was too vehement and violent to convey the balanced judgment which he usually displayed'.

At eight years of age, Geoffrey went as a boarder to Lindley Lodge, the local preparatory school, although for two years previously he had attended as a day boy, walking a mile across the fields morning and evening. That daily walk to and fro did a great deal for him, planting in the child a seed of independence and teaching him to face a daily duty cheerfully. It also laid the foundations of a love of country walking which never left him.

Meanwhile, in these early days, the influence of both parents played constantly upon the gradually-forming personality of their youngest child.

Three incidents remained with him permanently. Two concerned his father. One day, talking in general, the Rector revealed the fact that he had lived through the Crimean War. That opened to the boy the truth that past history was a reality to be reckoned with; not a mere story of the past. It was real; it happened; and it reached through to the present. The second arose from the apparently trivial discovery that, although once his father had taken the *Morning Post*, at a certain point he had changed from that to *The Standard*, then a daily. The fact thus revealed was that it was possible to change one's political outlook, for the *Post* had been rigidly Conservative, whereas *The Standard* was notably less so. A further revelation was that his father reckoned himself now a Liberal-Unionist. The conclusion, never to be changed or forgotten, was that it was necessary to watch politics to see where they were going, and to decide for oneself and according to one's principles, and in the light of whatever information one could come by, whether they were going in the right way or the wrong way.

Out of such toy-like bricks of childhood experience are the foundations of character laid. All have their significance; some can be found still present years later, however far the character concerned has travelled from his point of origin. So it may be said that the boy who feared for his father when he became too vehement, in case his judgment should thereby be clouded, was himself not at his best when, if rarely, in after times he himself did the same thing. Coolness and judgment suited him best, as they suited his father. And then again, who can say but what the sense of history, as a living thing, and of the consequent importance of continuity in human affairs—a marked feature in Geoffrey Fisher—may not have begun with that humble discovery that his own father had lived through the Crimean War? 'We are one with our fathers in quality and spirit,' he said in a sermon in St. Paul's at the time of the death of King George VI, 'inheriting a tradition, and ourselves responsible for it, which is stamped and sealed with great truths of man's well-being, not made by man but received of God.' And, speaking of the changes affecting most of human society through which the world had been passing in the late King's time and before, he said that 'The very changes in expression have only served to enhance the sense of continuity, of cohesion, of purposeful direction for which the Crown stands in our midst.' The discovery that vigilance and personal judgment, rather than the acceptance of preconceived attitudes, were essential elements in a democracy, may well owe something to that revelation of a change in the political opinions of the Rector of Higham-on-the-Hill long ago.

Altogether different in nature was one supreme service which, by accident, Geoffrey's mother did for him. One day, in the holidays, rummaging about in the house he found a row of books and, in the middle of them an unused little penny notebook which attracted him, so he took it to school at Lindley Lodge. Then one day, in term time, he came home and, as usual, after morning service, went home for lunch. As he walked across the orchard, he produced this notebook, saying it had been given to him by a boy. His mother took it, looked at it, and found in the middle of it some writing of her own. She said, 'You've taken this from the house!' The whole of her son's world at that moment fell to pieces. He knew he had told a flat lie, and that to no purpose at all. The consequences struck home with all the force which such events can generate in childhood. And so he felt that, while hitherto he had been an untroubled follower of Christ, in an ordinary healthy way, he had, in a single moment, destroyed himself in the presence of his Lord, his mother and himself, with no possible hope of recovering. It was a character-forming moment; 'the grandest thing' as he afterwards described it with the hindsight of age, 'that ever happened to me. For I then realised that, in the end, after you have discovered anything that has been wrong in your life, there is no hope for you at all except in the fact that God, and those who are your friends, forgive you. From then onwards, I never again tried to hide myself from myself. But I had an innate sense that you do what you do as well as you can, and if you fail, you fail openly and honestly before Christ, and look only for his forgiveness to restore you. I remember reading somewhere that repentance follows forgiveness, and does not precede it. How true that is! I realised how true it was as early as this little incident, that my repentance for lying about that book did not begin until my mother had faced the fact and forgiven me for it.'

The move as a boarder to Lindley Lodge was not a vast adventure for a boy of eight; but it was his first involvement in a situation not solely that of home and village. The headmaster, Mr. Lea, a tall, venerable, rather forbidding person, strict in his morals and evangelical faith, inspired a certain amount of fear. But he treated Geoffrey generously, and amongst other things introduced him to the idea of the responsibility of authority, perhaps because he was intelligent and able, and to undertake special tasks such as paying special care to one boy or another who had trouble of some kind, or who was not holding his own. From this Geoffrey learned early to be a responsible person, and that it was 'a good thing to be in support of authority, so that authority could use you for good ends'. The words are his own. The worthy headmaster of Lindley Lodge can scarcely have been aware of the importance of what he was doing in this regard.

But it was important, and anyone who cares to follow the progress of Geoffrey Francis Fisher through life will find this characteristic running as a continuous thread all the time. Whether it was at school, or university; as headmaster or as bishop, or as archbishop, this regard for authority, almost in the spirit of 'the powers that be are ordained of God', is marked. He was never a rebel: once convinced that authority was good—and his general disposition appears to have been to agree to such a supposition— then authority was to be supported. It followed, logically, that enemies of authority were to be opposed, not infrequently with considerable vigour and severity. Thus, far away in the future, there were to be the battles to restore discipline at Repton after the less observant ways of Temple's headmastership: or order to the diocese of London after the too generous ways of its former bishop, Winnington Ingram. And beyond that again, there were to be his labours over Canon Law and the attempts to pin down, define, and generally make sense of that notoriously elusive concept of 'lawful authority' as applicable to the Church of England. The list could be extended.

The writer of these words once asked the Archbishop, shortly after he had retired from Canterbury, what happened to this instinct of bringing order and authority into any given situation when he found himself confronted with one in which his writ did not run; one in which, in fact, he was not a headmaster, or a bishop, or even an archbishop. His reply was to tell a story against himself. At the beginning of the Second World War, when Bishop of Chester, he returned one night to his house to find that some seventy evacuee children from the slums of Liverpool had been moved in. Later still that night, as he was sitting in his study he heard uproar in the bedrooms above. Thinking of this as a familiar situation, calling only for the technique of a headmaster in dealing with a noisy dormitory, he went upstairs and appeared in the doorway. Instant silence, however, did not ensue; the chaos continued and when he accused one of the children of causing the disorder, the reply was 'It wasn't me, it was *him.*' It was a salutary reminder of the difference in confronting not a school, or the Church, but the world.

However, all this was, and is, a long way from Lindley Lodge preparatory school. There, Geoffrey was happy, and the teaching was at least sound, though it was not inspired. It was certainly not tuned up to scholarship standard. One result was that, though he tried for a scholarship at Rugby he did not get it. But in the December of 1900, Marlborough College gave him a Foundation Scholarship and there he went, for the first time out into the great world which lay waiting, far beyond the village of Higham-on-the-Hill.

II

Marlborough to Oxford, Return

Education begins and ends in an enthusiasm of joy, conviction, satisfaction and peace which passes both understanding and expression, which cannot be communicated in rational language at all, but which can be caught, and is caught wherever anyone at all, young or old, comes alive in the capture of some reality of beauty, truth and goodness.

G.F.F., from a sermon preached in Westminster Abbey,
9 June 1956

GEOFFREY FISHER was a boy at Marlborough from 1901 to 1906, a master there from 1911 to 1914, headmaster of Repton from then until 1932. This gives a total of some twenty-six years, just over a quarter of a century as boy, master, or headmaster, lived within the atmosphere of the English public school. He married the granddaughter of a famous Victorian headmaster—Dr. Pears of Repton. Two of his six sons were to become headmasters. He was one himself, of great experience and expertise before ever he appeared on the episcopal scene as Bishop of Chester in 1932. It follows that this prolonged association with a particular kind of school may be regarded as an important formative element in the character of the man who eventually became Fisher of Lambeth.

It also imparts to his schooldays, in whatever capacity they were lived, whether as boy or master, an importance far greater than is usually the case with any ultimately public figure. For that reason, while this part of Archbishop Lang's life, for instance, could be dismissed by his biographer in a paragraph, and Temple's in a few pages, Fisher's needs to be looked at in some depth.

The fact that he had been a headmaster so long was often offered, not always with approval, in after times as explanation for what some saw as authoritarian and high-handed methods. Thus it will be alleged that he disciplined the Anglo-Catholics in the diocese of London, when bishop there; or kept the Church Assembly in order when Archbishop, or dealt severely with recalcitrant individuals, such as Bishop Barnes of Birmingham, from time to time, always in the interests of good order and discipline, much as some Jovian headmaster of a former day might dispense the law. Even his approval was occasionally referred to by the wits in public-school terms, as when, after the late Richard Dimbleby had comported himself well in a long-remembered interview with the Archbishop at the period of the Princess Margaret and Group-Captain Townsend affair, they said that 'Dimbleby would get his House colours'.

The picture is inaccurate, omitting as it does so many other quite different qualities in a very strong character—among them kindness, humility, wisdom and judgment in difficult situations, and always a great love for ordinary people. It also omits the fact that, as he himself once said in a conversation after his retirement, if he had appeared thus to be authoritarian, the plain fact was that he had continually over the years been placed in situations where authority was necessary. The pattern, when carefully looked at, is extraordinarily uniform. The boy who had, as prefect, to deal with two disorderly rugger toughs, in the Adderley Library at Marlborough, as will shortly be told, became the headmaster of Repton who had to take drastic measures to clear up a situation left there by Temple. The headmaster of Repton became the Bishop of London who had to clear up a situation left by the indiscreet judgments of Winnington-Ingram. The Bishop of London became the Archbishop of Canterbury, who had, among a host of other demands for strong action, to tighten up the central administration of the Church. Fate placed him, over a long span of years, in authority-demanding situations. To state that he exercised authority within them is true. To complain that he did so is scarcely, to use one of his own favourite expressions, common sense.

But the criticism of him, often heard in his day (but wisely not in his hearing) of being 'headmasterly' had other roots. The soil in which these grew was surely that of the curious love-hate relationship which has for so long existed between the English mind and one of its most characteristic national institutions—the public school.

It may be allowed that the history, never mind the nature, of such places has been extraordinary. They began as public; they developed in some cases into exclusive enclaves, each riddled with its own customs and traditions. They began for the education of the poor; they developed into the preserves, within certain limitations, of the better off, although it needs to be said that this was a later and not necessarily universal development. They have produced many great men, and some bad ones. They have been imitated in other lands. They virtually officered an empire, in the days when the British had one. They have been productive of a special genre of literature, ranging from the panegyric of the *Tom Brown's School-days* type, Farrar's books and H. A. Vachell's *The Hill*, to the somewhat different *Stalky and Co.* of Kipling, the bitterly critical and in its day highly influential *The Loom of Youth* of Alec Waugh in the early twenties, to the comic world of Billy Bunter and the *Boys' Own Paper*. They have changed their nature. They have been criticised and reviled; loved, admired and envied. The debate on their educational and social desirability has led to at least one Royal Commission, notably that of 1964, and to a debate which still continues.[1]

Much more could be said of them, but only one thing must as strictly relevant within the context of this narrative. It is that, broadly speaking, they have often been places where the weaker, or the non-conformist, tended to be unhappy. Thus the delicate Dick Sheppard, later to be a notable vicar of St. Martin-in-the-Fields, was so miserable at Marlborough that he deliberately induced pneumonia by sleeping between wet sheets, in order to get away from the place.[2] The highly non-conformist John Betjeman spent a lot of his time in the same school in a condition of acute apprehension.

> Those few who read Dean Farrar's *Eric* now
> Read merely for a laugh; yet still for me
> That mawkish and oh-so-melodious book
> Holds one great truth—through every page there runs
> The schoolboy sense of an impending doom

[1] E. C. Mack, *Public Schools and British Opinion, 1780–1941* (Methuen and Columbia University Press).
[2] R. Ellis Roberts, *H. R. L. Sheppard.*

Which goes with rows of desks and clanging bells.
It filters down from God, to Master's Lodge,
Through housemasters and prefects to the fags.[1]

But the strong could survive: the strong and the able could be happy:
the strong, the able and the natural supporters of authority could be very
happy indeed; fulfilled, content and, in the end, impressive testimonials to
the system which had moulded them. So also could those who, if gentler
and shyer, happened to fall into the hands of benign authority. And insofar
as Fisher was strong and able and a natural supporter of authority, it need
not be surprising that the record of his schooldays, both as boy and man, is
one on the whole of much happiness.

To use another of his favourite expressions, it was grand, all of it, this
period of his life, from beginning to end. And it began with a wholly
characteristic gesture of independence. His father had proposed to take
him to Marlborough as a new boy. But he refused, saying: 'No, you can
come as far as Birmingham. From there I shall go by myself.' And so he
went off, bracing himself for what might come. What in fact came was a
temperature, developed that evening as he sat in the common-room of the
Junior House, to be duly taken thence to the sanatorium, there to spend
his first week of his first term.

As he lay there, the life of Marlborough College, into which he was so
soon to be plunged, stirred about him. Marlborough was not one of those
venerable institutions, like Eton or Winchester, with a history stretching
far back into time. No new public school had been created for more than
two hundred years, until Cheltenham appeared in 1841. Thereafter, to
meet the needs both of an expanding empire and upper middle class, the
appearance of new ones or the transformation of old grammar schools into
public schools became a frequent occurrence. Marlborough emerged in
1843, founded for 'sons chiefly of clergymen of the Church of England',
although in fact its personnel covered a far wider field. Into the world of
this school, nearly half a century old by the time he got there, Fisher
entered as soon as he emerged from the sanatorium.

He soon encountered three types of individual who will be familiar to

[1] John Betjeman, *Summoned By Bells* (Murray).

anyone who has delved much into public school literature. There was, first, the terrifying master or super-tyrant. This was the redoubtable P. W. Taylor, a clergyman and master of Remove A, a notorious figure for his harshness, sternness, some part of which was, perhaps, a pose, for he had a genuine pastoral heart. All moved in terror of him. Yet his house was the best in the school, and he ruled it entirely through his leading boys. Before he retired, he had lost all his terrors, and after he retired, went to a country parish in Dorset. When he died, he had a tremendous funeral, all the people of the village pouring out to pay their respects because, underneath his stern exterior, was a devotion to the ordinary person, men and women in their daily work, to which all had responded.

Next in order of encounter came the Eccentric Headmaster. This was G. C. Bell, known as 'Tup'. When Geoffrey arrived, he had been at Marlborough twenty-six years. To the boy he looked a very old man, with long beard and drooping eyes, a patriarch, with whom one rarely had personal dealings. When one did, they tended to be odd. Meeting a boy he did not know, he would say 'Hey, boy who are you?' The youth would say that he was Jenkins, or whatever. Then would come the question: 'Are you the son of your father?' If that left the boy speechless, as not infrequently happened, it was because he did not realise that Bell had known the fathers of many boys in the school, and that this was his way of enquiring whether the boy before him was the son of the Jenkins he had known many years before. Another story of him told of how, once when he was taking Sixth, a workman arrived outside the window and erected a ladder, whereupon Bell addressed to him the long-remembered words: 'Hence, ingenious artisan, and come back some other-when.'

Thirdly, and far more momentously for the development of Geoffrey Francis Fisher, there arrived on the scene the young headmaster, the Great Man, to the growing boy the pattern of many excellencies. This was the celebrated Frank Fletcher, who arrived as Master of Marlborough when Geoffrey was a junior member of the Sixth. Once again, authority was met which, because it was highly intelligent and constructive, could with enthusiasm be supported. How this man appeared to Geoffrey, and what he owed to him, can best be given in his own words.

'Frank Fletcher was thirty-two at the time, slim, not impressive to look at, with rather a strange voice. He did not make a good impression. I remember the first time that he came into the Sixth to greet us all, shaking hands with each one. He had no ready conversation; he was a little awkward; we were all a little awkward and thought: 'This won't take us very far.' How wrong we were! He very soon established himself amongst us by his character and by the brilliance of his mind, and it was not long before some of us learned that we had only to observe what he was doing and how he did it to benefit from him immensely. He made changes, and I, by nature rather a conservative person except when I saw that changes were necessary, had not yet learned from him the art of changing effectively when change is needed. I did learn it from him; as I learned very many other things from him. He was a brilliant teacher, especially of the things that he loved. Like William Temple, his passion was for Plato, Browning, St. John, and St. Paul's Epistles. When he preached from them, boys didn't much take to his sermons. But they were very good, if you would give your mind to what he was trying to say in his rather strained and ineffective voice. I learned from him the one great art of saying to myself what he said openly to any statement—'Why? Why is this? Why does this person say that? What does he, or it, mean?' And thus he taught us all, or those of us who learned it, never to be content with a superficial impression, never to take a thing at second-hand, but to work through it until we found the underlying and satisfying reason, so far as there was one to be found . . . Those who were taught by him learned never to be content with the second-rate, the ambiguous or the obscure. I responded wholeheartedly, the more so because I had the instincts of a mathematician, which he lacked. So I was trained always to look for the real thing, the real answer, the real value.'

Other masters pass across that distant scene, of whom two may be mentioned because of their particular contributions to the moulding of the character of Fisher as a boy. One was F. B. Malim, afterwards headmaster of Sedbergh, then of Haileybury, then of Wellington, who impressed with his teaching, especially of the Old Testament. There was also the Rev. Charles Wood, who preached in an enthralling way. There poured out of him the most vivid presentations of Isaiah, or Amos, or another of the prophets. One consequence of this may be again quoted in Fisher's own words. 'It penetrated the heart. I've always had something of the Old Testament prophet in myself ever since, a kind of moral fervour born from hearing him.'

But always it was Frank Fletcher who was the dominating and beneficent influence. Geoffrey was entirely of his training. Years later, when he came to read Fletcher's biography *After Many Days*, he learned for the first time how carefully the Master had prepared him to be his first wholly congenial Senior Prefect. The discovery was salutary, because he had long been of the opinion that he had thought it all out for himself!

So the boy grew securely and happily up the school. He reached the Sixth when he was fourteen, and was asked there whether he would like to become a mathematical specialist; but chose to remain with the classics. He was a good athlete; he adored Marlborough, approving of it all. Even so, he had his trials. Characteristically, two of the best remembered were both of a disciplinary nature. The first arose from the fact that the really big people in the school were the athletes, not the school prefects chosen from the Sixth. Fisher felt this to be unhealthy, and when he became Senior Prefect he started to reverse the order and make the prefects the prevailing power. This included starting a Prefects' Roll, with a ceremony in which new ones signed, and were admitted into office, to enhance their sense of responsibility. Many, many years later, visiting Marlborough, he found the same book and the same ceremony still in use.

A second disciplinary crisis which came his way as a prefect arose in a room called the Adderley Library. There, every evening, the senior boys from many houses used to come to do their evening prep under the supervision of a school prefect, normally the Head Prefect. Fisher, a year junior, shared this duty with him. One evening, in the absence of the Head Prefect, Fisher observed that the captain of the School Fifteen and one of the school half-backs, powerful persons both, had begun piling big volumes one on top of the other. The pyramid mounted higher. The higher it got, the more all work in the library stopped, and all present stared, hoping that sooner or later it would topple over. This was a crisis. Geoffrey knew that if he sat and watched it, he was ruined. If he went and asked them to desist, he was in a weak position. There was only one action left that any prefect in charge could, in his opinion, take. He could go to the two and turn them out of the library and send them back to their own houses, and after that to report them to the master in charge of Adderley. He did not relish it, and as it happened he was playing for the School Fifteen at the moment but very uncertain of his place. But he did it, and his battle was won, and his position established. In one form or another, there were to be many similar situations in the unguessed at years ahead.

And all the time, behind these schoolboy dramas and joys and stimulations stood the two supreme influences. One was the master, Fletcher; the second influence was the chapel, the focus of, as he put it, 'a very personal and real religion. It took the form of an unquestioning acceptance of Christ as the Master of the good life, and of myself as a disciple, learning from him how to lead the good life as valuable for its own sake. I knew the New Testament pretty well and I loved studying, as we did in the Sixth, St. Paul's Epistles in detail. But what I chiefly got was a real approach to my daily life. Taught by the New Testament and the chapel services, I was learning how to tackle everything that came along in what I now recognise was an intelligent Christian way, not consciously borrowing from Christ, not precisely trying to follow his example, but translating into my daily duties and occupations and pleasures and sympathies the spirit which flowed from his revelation of the Kingdom of God.'

When the time came for him to leave Marlborough, after these full and happy years, he took a moment to kneel in the chapel for a while in a very rare moment of outward expression of thankfulness to God and dedication to his service. He felt it necessary to add, however, when recalling the moment sixty-two years later, that it had never been, in principle, his custom to concentrate his devotions more in one particular place than in another and that, on the whole, he disapproved of the practice.

A finished Marlburian, loaded with prizes and honours, he went up to Oxford on a scholarship in the October of 1906.

.   .   .

His college was Exeter, and it was an interesting time to be up at the university. Yet no extraneous influences, now or at any other time, seem to have shaken Fisher's foundations. Doubt, in fact, in the religious sense, does not at any time to have appeared to have been among his experiences though questioning the known in order to clarify it was constant. Temple was troubled, at one time, over the Virgin Birth, and there were some initial difficulties over ordination. But such hesitancies were not for Fisher. A growing certitude in matters of faith seems, so far as the observer may presume to judge, to have been a natural part of him always, and the distinction between lively intellectual speculation and personal conviction, based on the experience of life, does not appear at any time to have presented the difficulties which the exercise has posed for some.

As to the relevance of the contemporary scene to his character, here the position would seem to be entirely different. He was always a man of his time, in the sense that he was always acutely aware of what his times were, and of what they demanded of him. He was indeed, on several notable occasions, ahead of his time, as his ecumenical initiative bears witness. The visit to Rome, so many years after these Oxford days of his youth, was a case in point. And his utterances from time to time on education, gambling, marriage and divorce, the Wolfenden Report, and a host of other questions, all show this continuing awareness and grasp of contemporary issues. Perhaps the whole matter may be summed up by saying that he was always a Christian statesman rather than a professional theologian, and a Christian whose faith continued throughout his life to find satisfaction in the forms and the manners which had their beginnings in the calm certitudes of a country rectory and public school chapel.

In the summer vacation before going up to Oxford, he held a private consultation with himself on a typically practical issue. This was whether to smoke or to drink when he got to the university, as socially suitable habits. The question was decided empirically. He decided against drinking because it burdened one with the sometimes tricky labour of deciding when one had had enough. Smoking was to be permitted because it did not. One result was that he smoked a pipe heavily for forty years. Then, one evening in Lambeth Palace he felt sick. Going away next day for a fortnight, he left all his smoking materials behind, and never used them again.

So much for that, as he would say. As to his Oxford career, this also was marked by that same total content, total absorption in all that was going

45

on and total loyalty to the institution of which he was a part—in this case Exeter College—which had characterised his schooldays at Marlborough. He was a faithful attender at college chapel, a helper with its choir of boys collected from all the purlieus of Oxford, and had a part in the Sunday School which the college, with the active support of one of its dons, ran for them. But now also began to emerge a level of competence, an array of powers in so many varied directions, that their very multiplicity, as well as the casualness with which long afterwards he recalled them, disguised the fact that this scholar of Exeter was already, by then, a remarkable person. The non-drinking, pipe-smoking sharer in all sides of the college life, available for such social duties as assisting incapacitated companions to bed after a bump supper, became, in due course, President of the Junior Common Room. The young man who took up rowing because a broken collar-bone, badly set, kept him from the rugger he had played at school, became Captain of Boats and rowed in the university trial eight; and in his fifth year went back to rugger and won his college colours at it. But these were all part of the busy life. Academically, he read Mods and Greats and enjoyed it very much, taking a First in Mods in 1908, a First in Greats in the following year, and a further First, this time in Theology, in 1911. This last, however, he found child's play after reading Greats. A remark he once made in this connection is revealing of a life-long attitude: 'There was the evidence before me, indeed much of it already known well enough, all to be found by the detailed study of the Old and New Testaments and of the history and doctrine of the first five hundred years of the Church; and there one could follow rival interpretations of critics who exploded evidence, or twisted it, or interpreted it to support their own views, or humbly sought for truth. It was a grand study to make one's way through the thickets of controversy and schools of thought, and to get back as far as one could to what was the true view and so to test and try the doctrine of the Church of England as I had come to know it. All my life I have been perfectly clear that there was a clear and reasonable doctrine of the Church of England by which all other doctrines must be judged. This doctrine was not, finally, enshrined in any documents or any formulae. It was indicated, it was grounded first in the New Testament and then in the Book of Common Prayer and in the living

Church. But always it is the living tradition which propagates itself, active and growing, and yet resistant to the insertion of some foreign matter. I have always found, throughout my life, that I had to start from the Church of England doctrine as I knew it, and then judge whether it was properly adjusting itself to some new facet of truth, or some new impression of reality, but never to admit anything unless it was congruous with the fundamental lines of Church doctrine.'

His reaction to some of the personalities engaged in those days in the theological battle, as well as his own predilections in this field, have a special interest. There was, for instance, N. P. Williams, very much later to be Lady Margaret Professor of Divinity. When he arrived as a don at Exeter, he was 'a very shy, frightened man, who crept about the college. When you talked to him, he kept his eyes almost shut, and had a queer way of speaking as though he was saying prunes and prisms all the time. He was a marked Anglo-Catholic, and shocked the college by walking about in rather stylised clerical dress, with silver-buckled shoes. His sitting-room had a resemblance to a drawing-room, richly furnished, while at one end of it was a little wall altar with candles and the like. It was all a queer mixture. But I came to know him well as my tutor, I learned a great deal from his brilliant mind and I came to regard him with great affection as a friend. As we talked theology, he always kept so far up in speculative clouds that he had little relation to the practical theologies of the living Church. He wrote great books, one especially notable, *The Ideas of the Fall and of Original Sin*. Like the theology he read, this sort of thing was in sharp contrast to the "lively, vigorous, searching for truth" by people like Streeter and William Temple and Ronnie Knox and others.' Fisher worked for a time with Ronald Knox and shared with many others in the brilliance of his many-sided wit and insights: but he later confessed to finding more wit than wisdom in him.

A great influence in his life came from the Student Christian Movement, at that time at the peak of its power. It had great leaders, for these were the days of J. R. Mott and of J. H. Oldham. Never an officer of this body in the university, Fisher yet drew much inspiration from it and its leaders, graduate and undergraduate. What was the dominating religious influence upon him in these years at Oxford? The answer, in the first place, is bound up with the fact that while it was a vastly enjoyable time, full of endless interests and activities, Oxford did not make the kind of enduring impression on him that it has made on so many other people. The cause, in his own view, was that Oxford and its community life developed, stabilised and enriched the same attitude to life that he had already acquired before leaving Marlborough. This meant that the religious attitudes which he had acquired there, persisted. The basis was, in his own words: 'A religion, such as a public school at its best encourages, includes an enormous love for the ordinary services of the Book of Common Prayer, a quite different and far more personal devotion to Christ in the Holy Communion and a very high interest in intelligent discussion of preaching of the Christian faith and a consequent direction of life to good purposes. I am sure,' he added, 'that those things stand as the best way of leading people to live according to the kingdom of God. The Holy Communion was an essential thing, but never in any kind of isolation from the rest of one's life. As a boy I had grown from going to Communion once every three weeks to going every Sunday; and to go to Communion every Sunday remained a constant and constructive feature in my life. I never particularly wanted, except under special circumstances, to go more often than that, and certainly I felt no doctrinal necessity to go more than that. As to preaching; I have never yet heard a sermon out of which I did not get some interest, if sometimes no profit; but almost always profit as well.'

.   .   .

Various attractive offers came his way at the end of his five years at Oxford, among them approaches from Balliol and University College, as to the possibility of his going as chaplain to one or the other. But Frank Fletcher offered him a mastership at Marlborough, and this he accepted without hesitation. He passed rejoicing to be a chaplain and a schoolmaster at Marlborough, so far as he knew or intended for the rest of his life.

His three years as an assistant master proved again to be a sunny time. He loved teaching, with its challenges, its opening of one's thoughts, its opening of perspective, above all the community life which it offered.

During this time, also, an important event took place in his life. He was ordained. The adjective is carefully chosen. Ordination is always important; but anyone who would seek justification for using such terms as 'life-changing' or 'dramatic' in this instance would seek in vain. Neither the intellectual hesitancies which Temple passed through, however briefly, nor the highly-dramatised moment of decision which Lang said he experienced in Cuddesdon Parish Church as a prelude to ordination, are to be discovered in the case of Fisher. Here all is matter-of-factness and inevitability. He had always ordination in mind. It was as inevitable in his life as becoming a schoolmaster. Both to that profession, as to his religion, he gave as of habit total concentration, the totality of himself. It was, for him, the natural continuation of the way of life of a schoolmaster. He felt it as a fulfilment and as an enrichment which would enable him to do more with, and for, boys than hitherto he had been able to, and on a deeper level. Pressed once on this point, he added that he was, in any event, suspicious of undue emotion in connection with ordination, or of any 'waiting for the moment', or listening for 'the call'.

So he went to Wells Theological College for one term in the long vacation of 1911. His brother, he who afterwards became Bishop of Natal, had been there before him. Fisher enjoyed—the word is his own—Wells; but was there too short a time to do more than get a sense of liturgical routine, and the pastoral experience of one of the College Missions at the top of the Mendips. Wells also interested him in providing a contact with the distinguished patristic scholar, Armitage Robinson, sometime Dean of Westminster, then of Wells. But theological college life never 'possessed him'. He was ordained deacon in 1912 by old Bishop Wordsworth at Salisbury, and priest the following year by Bishop Ridgeway.

Meanwhile, there were, as so often in Fisher's life, the disciplinary situations to be cleared up. He was appointed, for instance, to share with a rather less forceful master the task of bringing good order and discipline in the Upper School, the daily home of a mob of boys in a barn-like Hall. This was duly done. There was a notable occasion when he went in to take Upper School prep and found the whole floor covered almost knee-deep in every kind of waste paper, including toilet rolls. Obviously, some of the bigger boys had been enjoying themselves. His own description of this incident calls for quotation, since it presents, if unconsciously, a mini-version of the kind of action of which he was capable in great events as well as small, and which sometimes caused people, in after times, to wish that they had not clashed with him.

'It is the kind of crisis at which you either win a victory or are sunk for-ever. I at once did one thing. It was the custom that in the first minutes of prep the junior boys had to pick up paper. I ordered the senior boys to pick up paper instead. That took them back a bit, but they had to do it and so far I'd won, but I didn't think that that was quite enough. I there-fore ordered that all the senior boys should come in on the following Saturday afternoon. I then had the problem of settling what to do with them for two hours. I went to my friend, the chief mathematical master, and said, "How can I keep these people occupied, with no problem to myself, for two hours?" He replied: "Set them on to multiply one by two, and the result by three, and the result by four, and the result by five, and the result by six, and so on indefinitely, and I will give you a check so that you can see what is the right answer when you get up to ten, and what is the right answer when you get up to twenty, and nobody will get beyond that!" It was magnificent because there they were, doing this menial task of multiplying, and I would walk round quietly, and just from the check scratch a notebook and say 'Wrong! Begin again from the beginning!' They all knew that they'd been thoroughly had, and that in this battle of wits it was, on the whole, better not to engage in open conflict with me. Our personal relations were always cordial and in all ways enjoyable.'

This happy and contented, if formidable, assistant master at Marl-borough had no ambitions. It was enough to teach, to get to know boys, to love the place. But boys have a curious habit of asking prescient questions. One he happened to remember: 'Sir, will you be a headmaster one day?' His answer was 'I don't know. If ever I did, perhaps one day I might become headmaster of Ashby-de-la-Zouch grammar school.' The name attracted him, and the place was some fifteen or twenty miles from Higham rectory, and the question had received an answer. But that was not to be. One day, Wynne Wilson, then Master of Marlborough, stopped him and said that he ought to apply for the headmastership of Repton. The idea seemed ludicrous. But Frank Fletcher, written to for advice, told him that he ought to apply. So did William Temple, whose desire it was, as it turned out, that Fisher should succeed him. Fletcher had, in fact, been approached earlier by Temple as to whether he knew of a suitable successor to himself at Repton, and Fletcher had named Fisher; but said that he was too young. To this Temple had replied on a postcard 'Fisher we must have.' And so he applied. There followed a rather daunting interview with the elderly governing body of Repton in the now long-vanished Westminster Hotel in Victoria Street, looking towards that Abbey where, in years to come, the candidate for the headmastership of Repton was, as Primate of All England, to experience so many great occasions of Church and State.

The result was that he was elected. He was twenty-seven. When the news reached him at Marlborough, he went to the rooms of his friend, the chief mathematical master, a person not much older than himself, and together they shouted with laughter. The whole thing seemed absurd. Even so, the Reverend Geoffrey Francis Fisher was headmaster of Repton. The date was June, 1914.

III

Repton

'Mark my words,' observed a well-known dignitary of the Church of England, who had been closely associated with the Primate at one stage of his career; 'when Geoffrey was headmaster of Repton, everybody said "What a good school Repton is", but nobody ever said "What a great headmaster Fisher is!" When he was Bishop of London, everybody said: "How well the diocese is running" but nobody said "How admirably Fisher is running it!" And it will be the same all his life.'

Charles Smyth, *Repton, 1557–1957* (Batsford)

. . .

Here is the most exhilarating and the most exciting and exhausting task in the world—to introduce each single pupil in our care to the world around him, to God and so to himself—that he may find his usefulness and godly service and true enjoyment here and hereafter. Glorious it is, this task.

G.F.F. in an address given at St. Gabriel's Training College, Camberwell, 1953

Where staid and silver Trent
Once wound in deep indent,
By those rich fields that Hotspur claimed and won . . .

So wrote A. C. Benson in one of those romanticised and nostalgic school songs which were once composed for schools. The River Trent is not often silver, and not always staid. But if the lines are inaccurate in that respect, they are at least true in that Repton village is not far from the Trent, between Burton and Derby, and that at the heart of the place is Repton School, giving the village distinction now as it has done for four centuries, as it was doing when its new and youngest ever headmaster arrived in the unpropitious year of 1914.

Repton was, as it still is, a great school. Even in appearance, with the Priory and Hall, to which Benson makes reference elsewhere in his verse, and the beautifully spired parish church in the middle, it looks so much the archetype of its species, as to have been used for the filming of a once celebrated film of public-school life, *Goodbye Mr. Chips*. Its history, too, was typical of its kind, stemming back to the dissolution of the monasteries. Repton's share in this was the loss of its Augustinian Priory, itself built in the vicinity of Christian foundations dating back to the earliest days of the conversion of Mercia. What remained of the Priory was eventually bought by the Executors of Sir John Port, a neighbouring land-owner who, typifying by his action a Renaissance tendency to favour educational enterprise, left in his will provision for a 'grammar school in Etwolle or Reptone'. The will became operative in 1557, from which date the school came into being. Thereafter, through varying fortunes and changes, it continued through the centuries, gradually extending itself in importance and in the area from which it drew some of its boys.

But it was the coming of one who has been called Repton's second founder, the Rev. Steuart Adolphus Pears, from Harrow, to be head-master in 1854, which set the school on the path of its renown. Here again the pattern is familiar in public-school history: the appearance of that tremendous figure, the Victorian clerical headmaster around the middle of the nineteenth century, a person possessed of impressive qualities of character and dedicated, among other things, to enlarging the scope of education and to setting his own moral mark upon his school. It happened elsewhere in much the same period. The result at Repton was that after twenty years of Pears Repton was indubitably a great school, and continues so.

To become headmaster of such a place at the age of twenty-seven was likely to be daunting. But two other circumstances, one general and the other particular, added to the difficulties. The general circumstance arose from the outbreak of the First World War in the August of 1914. That was a convulsion which was to destroy many things, and to change almost all. But that it hit the public schools hard—those sources of so much officer material—may be regarded as incidental, except indeed by the masters and by the parents of boys whose names eventually appeared on their school war memorials. Three hundred and fifty-five of them did so on Repton's, eventually. But the immediate consequence for Fisher was greatly to complicate his task in the initial stages.

Before he got to Repton in September 1914, sixty boys had left to join the Army, six masters had disappeared and the first thing to be done was to produce a new timetable with a new allocation of work to the staff for a school where he knew not a soul, except one or two of the senior masters. In that manner, Fisher spent a good deal of the summer holidays. In odd moments, he was furnishing the lovely house in which the headmaster of Repton lives. There he was established when the school returned, and immediately the difficulties arising from the second circumstance, particular to Repton, presented themselves. The fact was that William Temple, who had every other virtue, was not a good disciplinarian, chiefly because he was too innocent. Such, at any rate, was his successor's judgment. He could not live down to the level of ordinary school discipline, and this had been having some disastrous consequences.[1] This had to be dealt with straight away, and it was done. The result was a transformation, and the matter was cleared up speedily. Once again, the disciplinary challenge which seemed to face Fisher wherever he went was presenting itself. That he responded to it always with a necessary degree of severity does not mean at all that he was severe in himself. He was, on the contrary, a genial and friendly person, though without ever imperilling the proper dignity of his office. He rarely had to think about discipline. Before long, good discipline had just taken its place as a natural feature of the school, including the famous rule-book mentioned earlier.

It remained always true that retribution of some severity could descend upon offenders. But such occasions became fewer and fewer. When such things did happen, they could, at times, be spiced with wit. One such instance was long remembered. One of the rules of the place was that no boy might have a motor cycle at school. But one term, on the last morning, when the boys started leaving very early, Fisher heard a roaring up and down the village street. Enquiries revealed that someone had not only

[1] 'Yes—the Hall has had a fearful crop of failures. I expect Fisher will be better than I was in these ways.'—Temple in a letter to D. C. Somervell, quoted by Iremonger in *William Temple*.

broken the rule, but was parading the fact. A telegram was immediately sent to the boy's home: 'Return before midday'. The boy returned and the headmaster had, as he put it, 'the extraordinary experience of caning a boy in plus-fours'.

There was an occasion of a very much more serious kind, which may be told because it is a brush-stroke, at least, in the portrait of Fisher. There was a senior master, much respected for his athletic powers, not a man used to opposition, who became the central figure of an early trial of strength. Sometime during the war, an old Reptonian, no doubt in the Royal Flying Corps, droned out of the sky and landed his aircraft in a field quite close to the main playing fields. The school, of course, spent a great deal of time watching and admiring the pilot. Fisher was told that the young man was going to fly away again at ten-thirty the following morning, an hour at which all would be in school. Asked whether boys could be let out to see the take-off, he declined. But he himself went out to see the flier off. Standing there, he observed this master leading his science class straight towards him across the cricket field. It was a moment when all might be won or lost for the headmaster, young and new. The boys foresaw the crisis. Fisher walked straight to the master and told him bluntly to take his class back immediately. The order was obeyed without a word. The matter was never referred to. But a lesson was learned by all present.

Yet these were small matters. In a while there arose a great matter, a problem which tested and exercised Fisher's powers of statesmanship to the full, which gave him much anxiety, which spilled out into the world outside and has left an echo which can even still be heard. This was what came to be known as the Somervell–Gollancz row. One side of it, set out at great length, can be read in Victor Gollancz's first volume of his *Letters to Timothy*, written when he was a highly successful publisher. The other side of the matter—Fisher's—can be read here.

Gollancz throughout his account referred to Fisher as 'the old man'. The facts are that he himself was at that time twenty-four, while Fisher was thirty, and certainly as flexible in outlook as Gollancz, as events eventually showed. Fisher, needing a good classical master in a time when masters of any kind were difficult to come by, heard of Gollancz, an officer in the Army. As he was confined to home service, however, the War Office was ready to release him for teaching work. Gollancz was then just at the end of a distinguished university career. He was indeed a brilliant man, and remained so to the end of his life; full to overflowing with an exuberant imagination, responding sensitively and emotionally to every form of idealism and art. But he did not know how to adapt himself and his enthusiasms to such a community as a school. D. C. Somervell, the other protagonist in this affair, was nine years his senior. An admirable master, he had been a particular friend of William Temple's. His abilities were great; he was a finished historical scholar, and the best kind of liberal.

He came with Gollancz to Fisher one day and suggested that they should start a Civics class, designed to give boys some idea of the national and international background out of which the war had arisen, and of the problems to be faced in the future. Fisher at once entirely agreed, and gave permission to Somervell and Gollancz to proceed. The resulting Civics class was the first of its kind and a great success. It appealed to Fisher's liberal instincts without disturbing his equally valued conservative common sense. But after a while the younger man began to take the lead from the older, and enthusiastic idealism began to outrun discretion. Dangerous tensions arose.

Anything which suggested some lack of patriotic fervour was liable to arouse hasty suspicion and antagonism. The antagonistic element was led by two masters, who gathered a following among masters and boys.

Gollancz enjoyed the situation, seeing himself as waving the flag of true liberalism against the enemy. All this was now becoming highly dangerous as well as offering an excellent example of how dire consequences can sometimes arise from the best of intentions. This was a period of great anxiety for Fisher. It would be easy to suppress the Civics class. On the other hand, to do that would seem to be sacrificing a valuable piece of liberal thinking, on great national questions, to reactionary forces, wherein had been displayed tempers equally indiscreet and unjustifiable. But the moment had not yet come when suppressive action had to be taken.

Then, world events offered a way out. The German offensive of March, 1918—the last fling of the German Army in that war—imperilled for a time the whole Allied position. They were desperate times. They were times when all should stand together. Instantly, seeing his moment, Fisher gathered the school together and told them that it was unthinkable that, at such a moment, there should be any cause of division among them. The Civics class ceased, to be revived after the war with great profit and under wiser leadership.

For Fisher, the experience had been invaluable, in view of the many instances in the years ahead where, on a far larger scale, statesmanship was to be necessary. It was the first time he had found himself up against a problem of immense difficulty and importance, in which it was his duty not to suppress a liberal attitude, and yet not to encourage reactionary forces. He consulted no one in the school. Discussion could not help: only he could judge precisely when the decision to end this experiment could be made. And when the moment came when he could act he seized it with both hands, and was perfectly clear what the action should be. The lesson lasted him for the rest of his active life. When there was a difficult situation the thing was not to make up one's mind too quickly, not to apply any fixed principle or any fixed rule, or any fixed attitude, but to weigh and consider the liberal and the conservative, the two great forces always at work. Then, when one was quite clear what kind of action was required and when one was feeling inside oneself that the moment had come for it, to act. To the recorder of such an affair long afterwards, two brief reflections may be allowed.

The first, that the idealists of this world, so often by their extreme and aggressive attitudes, spoil their own case. And the second that, as a consequence, those in authority, though lovers of liberality and balanced judgment, may often be forced into action which appears illiberal.

But professional matters, however involved and sometimes anxious, were not the only ones which occupied the young headmaster of Repton at this time. He married, and laid the foundations of that strong family life which ever afterwards were so marked a feature of his background. His bride was Rosamond Forman, daughter of a former master at Repton, and granddaughter of the 'second founder', Dr. Pears, her mother being his youngest daughter. She herself was the ninth of fourteen children, all born at Repton, and all with their names in the same register as her mother, who was also born there. Subsequently, her own six sons were to be in the same register at the parish church. Rosamond Forman's father died when she was fifteen and, he being a housemaster, the family had to leave their house and move to their holiday home at Minehead. But she used to go back nearly every year to visit friends in Repton. In 1916, aged twenty-six, she returned to pay a final visit before going off to train as a missionary, having made an offer to S.P.G. On this visit, she saw her future husband for the first time. They met in the art school, which thereafter remained rather a special place for them. He said: 'Repton belongs to you more than to me, really, and I know all about your father and grandfather.' This was a pleasant beginning, and by the Thursday of that week, they had fallen in love with each other, and he had said to his sister—this was the Katie of Jordanian missionary renown, then keeping house for him—'If I marry at all, I shall marry Miss Forman.' In the October he asked her to marry him, and the rest may be told in her own words.

'I had previously been worried about this, because I had committed myself to go to S.P.G. and I felt I had put my hand to the plough and was looking back. I couldn't ask my mother's advice about this, because I knew she was so Reptonian that she was bound to be biased in favour of giving up the missionary idea in order to marry the headmaster. So I wrote to the principal of my college in London, Miss Helena Powell, and told her that I had met a man, that I had fallen in love with him, that I thought he had fallen in love with me, and that if I saw him again, I should almost certainly not become a missionary. What ought I to do? Should I go and see him again? She wired back and said "Go", and so I went, and did not become a missionary. And he always said that he had sent back to the mission field a wonderful missionary in his sister, and saved the mission field from a very bad missionary in me, so that was all right.' They were married the following April.

The first child was born in 1918. The six sons who were to make the family were born within twelve years exactly. The fortunes of all of them, as the years unfolded, may be mentioned here. The first, Henry Arthur Pears, scholar of Marlborough and Christchurch, cut short his university career to go to the war, and was in the Army for seven years, becoming G.S.O.I. to General Slim in Burma at the age of twenty-six. After the war, he went to the Bar, was also elected a Fellow of All Souls and in due course became Chairman of the Bar Council. He is now a judge of the High Court.

The second son, Francis Forman, went to school at Repton after his father's time there. He became head of school, captain of cricket, and then went on to Cambridge. After a year, he also went to war and served seven years, being a prisoner in Italy for two. While being transferred to Germany, he escaped and reached the advancing Allied army. He came back to receive the Military Cross, went later to Repton as a master, and thence to be Warden of St. Edward's School, Oxford. He is now headmaster of Wellington.

Then came Charles Douglas, who also went to war and afterwards to Oxford. Later he was on the staff at Harrow, and is now a headmaster in Australia.

Humphrey, the fourth son, went to school at Repton but had an accident when he was just seventeen, falling off his bicycle and breaking his neck. This did not prevent him, eventually, from getting into the Army for a time, before going up to Oxford for a year, then into films, and then into the B.B.C., of which for three years he was the Representative in Australia. He is now head of a B.B.C. Division at home.

Geoffrey Robert Chevallier, born in 1926, chose, at an early age, to be a doctor and to be a general practitioner where the opportunities properly called pastoral are at their greatest. The youngest son, christened Richard Temple, but known as Tim, was born in 1930 and is now housemaster at the Hall at Repton—the same house in which he was born.

Rosamond Fisher had always had very much her own life and personality and interests from the beginning. The total life of a headmaster's wife, with the ninety boys in the Hall also within her care, was exacting. She had also a natural position in the village, her mother and grandmother having been leaders in the life of the place, as well as in the life at school. So Mrs. Fisher was soon involved in the Mothers' Union. Added to this she became president of the Women's Institute, and she also ran the Sunday School.

Thus the years passed, happy and full for both of them. Fisher made great changes at Repton. The change of house names, which endures to this day, was one of them; the restoration of the ancient Priory as a war memorial—a very notable piece of work carried out by local craftsmen—was another, and all the time the vivid, variegated life of the place continued. Characters abounded, of whom the great Harry Vassall was one, an elder statesman among masters and a splendid man in himself. He had a laugh as vast as William Temple's. When the two of them laughed together the sound, it was said, could be heard far and wide. It was also a cause of irritation to an elderly retired master, named Gurney, who lived in a house full of strange pieces of apparatus and whose hobby was weighing the world. The combined laughs of Temple and Vassall, he was alleged to mutter, upset the balance of the globe and threw out his calculations.

But these were details. What really happened in Repton is now written, consciously or unconsciously, in the hearts and minds of boys and masters who were there at the time. One story in this connection may be mentioned, exactly as Fisher recalled it. 'At the end of every term, the leaving boys, on the last day, came down to say goodbye to me. They came in, one by one, into my study, and I would try and think of some suitable thing to say to them, knowing a little about their careers, about some of them knowing a great deal. It was always an exciting thing trying to think of the right words for each. I can remember to this day one boy. As I waited for him to come in, I said to myself: What on earth can I say to this boy? He's utterly blameless, he's utterly colourless, he's gone through his career here making no impact, no impression, so far as I know, on anybody. What can I say to him? Well, in he came, and we talked for a few minutes, and then I said: "Well, So-and-so, I think you'll be able to stand on your own feet all right." Many years afterwards, when he was a professional man of good standing, I ran into him. He said to me suddenly: "I don't suppose you remember it, but in fact the thing which you said to me when I was leaving changed the whole course of my life. I was a very diffident boy, very frightened of everything, unsure of myself, and unsure of what life would do with me. I came down to say goodbye to you, and you shook me by the hand and said: 'You'll be able to stand on your own feet.' That gave me a confidence which changed the course of my whole life." No one can ever tell what may be the effect of a word or two casually spoken to another.'

But, always, it was contacts with the boys as persons which mattered most. 'My abiding interest the whole time was in each boy, and it was my delight to try to get to know as many as I could. Whenever I passed a boy, I'd stop and say "Who are you?" and ask him a question or two, and get something out of him. The chiefest delight I had was trying to win the confidence of the rather slow, shy, rather eccentric boy who didn't just fit in to the ordinary pattern. That was a constant challenge and joy. I began from the individual always. At the other end of the school were the clever boys, or the middle boys who were going to be up at the top, and they were a joy because they were so easy to talk to if you were prepared to discuss anything with them without embarrassment or pomposity. It meant endless argument and all the fun of the chase, and I learnt how always to hold my own, knowing just a bit more, though not necessarily much more, than they about whatever had come up, and enough, if they got too conceited, to put them gently in their place. And out of this kind of atmosphere, with free discussion with anybody who was competent to discuss, and gentle encouragement of everybody who was shy, or thought he had little to say (though often he had a lot to say)—out of this excellent relationship between boys and masters, and out of the admirable skills of most of the latter, we produced a fine tradition of intelligent and good behaviour.'

The subsequent careers of some of those of Fisher's day would certainly seem to bear this out. Ashley-Clarke became a distinguished ambassador in Italy, Roger Allen became ambassador in Greece. Another boy, Humphrey House, became a Fellow of Wadham; Vernon Watkins, 'a queer little oddity of a boy', became a considerable poet and a friend of Dylan Thomas; Noel Hunter became a playwright; A. A. Cooke, a composer; Christopher Isherwood a novelist and a collaborator with Auden. On the science side, Edward Bullard became a physicist, Wigglesworth a distinguished medical research worker. In the aircraft industry, Verdon Smith became a distinguished name. Among artists, Anthony Devas, Anthony Gross and Rupert Shepherd, a Professor of Art in South Africa, made a place for themselves. In the Services and in industry and in other walks of life were those who became distinguished and who, along with those already mentioned, held special places in Fisher's affection and esteem. To the ministry of the Church went, among others, Charles Smyth, now a distinguished ecclesiastical historian. There was also a boy called Michael Ramsey, in the fullness of time Fisher's successor as Archbishop of Canterbury.

There is one more matter which may be mentioned before these Repton days are left. It concerned the school chapel. What did Fisher make of that—nowadays such a sensitive point of controversy, like everything else where an element of compulsion is either involved, or thought to be? His comments on this matter once again belie the aura of heavy authoritarian-ism associated by some with him. 'We tried to keep the chapel services alert and alive and fruitful and joyful. Of course, boys got bored with parts of them. That didn't worry me; I've never known anything good that I've enjoyed that hasn't had its boring aspects as well, and there's certainly nothing in the life of the school in which there's not a liability to boredom. Take cricket, for instance. Even in my day, this was boring for some boys and nowadays, I should think it's boring for a great many more. In my day, of course, there was a public feeling about cricket that kept it as a thing that everyone ought to support. In my day also there was still a universal feeling that the Christian faith was something which everyone ought to support, ought to be interested in, and ought to absorb something from. And thus there was very little feeling against the chapel services and the like. The time came when I was perfectly aware that the ordinary routine of services was too much for the ordinary boy, with a voluntary celebration at eight every Sunday, an hour of divinity, at eleven Matins and then in the evening, Evensong for the whole school with the sermon. I knew that most of these boys, if they went to church at all in their holidays, would go once on a Sunday and no more. Therefore (I think we were the first school to do it) I made an arrangement by which any boy who went to the early service need not go to the half-hour Matins at eleven which followed the divinity hour: but to make it rather more of a special effort, I put the celebration at a quarter to eight instead of the normal eight o'clock. Thus it required a deliberate purpose to go to communion, and no one could feel that he would be getting off something of much moment later on in the day. That system worked very well, and it certainly helped to secure that, all through my time, the attendance at

our Holy Communion was very good. There was no undue pressure in
the system. From time to time there were Saturday night preparation
services, which I took myself, and I tried to make it obvious how serious
and how sensible the communion service was, not to be undertaken lightly
or wantonly, but only with a true Christian purpose. I don't think there
was any abuse of this arrangement. I think that the services all through
were reasonably enjoyed, the communion service was properly respected,
the boys grew up in a disciplined sense of Church membership and Church
worship and the preaching by the staff and, I hope, by myself, was such as
to engage their interest, or, when appropriate, their amusement.'

Of his own preaching, he had this comment: 'Charles Smyth and
Michael Ramsey told me that they both spotted that my sermons were
good and worth listening to when they were boys. But I dare say a few
others did. For the most part, I think boys and other people thought they
were suitable and even interesting at times. But they were not converted by
them. Indeed, I am not aware that I've ever converted anybody, particularly by anything I've had to say.'

The end of these eighteen years at Repton came in 1932. That summer
William Temple came to the school for a Governors' Meeting. When it
was over, in the afternoon, he and Fisher went for a walk in the grounds
and, as they walked, Fisher unburdened himself. He had begun to feel, he
said, that he had been there long enough. He did not want to leave; but
thought he should. When Temple asked why, the reply was: 'When a boy
gets seriously ill, I can't stand the strain. Once I could; but now I cannot.'

Temple asked what he would like to do. Fisher replied that he would
like to be a country parson. Temple first suggested he should write to
various bishops whom he knew, to say so, and then, without a pause,
named the man whom he would wish to succeed Fisher. And that was all.
What Fisher did not know, and what Temple could not tell him was that,
at that moment, his name had been put forward for the Bishopric of
Chester, by Archbishop Lang and himself. A fortnight later, a letter
arrived from the Prime Minister with the offer. Fisher read it, and then
sought his wife to consult her. They could see no valid reason for not
accepting. And so he accepted, and Repton and all the long years there fell
into the past.

An old Reptonian summed them up, as regards Fisher, during the latter's time at Canterbury. 'When all is said, it is chiefly the impression of complete integrity, and of ordinary human friendliness that abides: and perhaps no one who has never, as a boy, felt the boss put his arm around his shoulders, and heard him chuckle and utter his familiar "Well done!" can fully relish the late Canon Leonard Prestige's characterisation of the present Primate of All England as the greatest schoolmaster—and the greatest schoolboy—who has ever sat upon the chair of Saint Augustine.'[1]

[1] Charles Smyth, *Repton, 1557–1957.*

IV

Chester

Every day is a new day. Act as though it were your first and last.
Choose! Decide! Have the humility and the trust to take St. Peter's
simple, saving advice—be sensible: say your prayers: do your straightforward duty honestly and by the grace of God: do all as for his laws
and give him the glory.

> G.F.F. in a broadcast from Old North Church, Boston, U.S.A.,
> 7 September 1952, on the text I Peter iv 7

．　　　．　　　．

This is a true saying, if a man desire the office of a bishop, he desireth a
good work.

> I Timothy iii. 1

IT could be said that this schoolboy element in Fisher, possibly more
accurately described as a zest and humour which would keep breaking
in, was well illustrated by an incident which befell very soon after his
arrival at Chester. He was shown a parish magazine in which the vicar
had said he could not quite understand why the new bishop had been
appointed. He had no parochial experience, nor apparently any qualities or
abilities to suit him for the job. He added, however, that as they had been
praying about the matter, and as this was apparently the answer, they
had to make the best of it. Fisher included this episode in his address
at his first diocesan conference, winning many hearts at once and getting
off to a good start. But the same evening he was rung up by a Manchester
paper and asked if it was true and, if so, how it affected his views on the
efficacy of prayer. His answer is not on record; but the incident was an
indication of the difficulties sometimes posed—and in after years and on a
greater scale they were to be many—by questions put to him by the press,
requiring a whole philosophy for an adequate answer.

However, on the whole, the transition from being a headmaster to being a bishop did not prove difficult, in spite of the forebodings of the clergyman in his parish magazine. It turned out to be, in fact, much the same thing in a rather different setting. In both places, and in both roles, the man concerned was part of a living and vital community, and in both reacted, as was his wont always, in interesting himself in every aspect of the community life, in all the agents doing the job, in all those who were trying to help. Other duties as he saw them were to try to remedy anything that seemed to call for remedy, to improve anything that seemed to need improvement, and to give himself fully to encouraging an active, cheerful, intelligent, purposeful spirit. He went, moreover, with three factors in his favour. The first was that of never having been identified with any particular ecclesiastical controversy or party interest. His was, as it ever remained, 'the ordinary working faith and practice of a straightforward, theologically-minded, scholarly churchman'. The words are his own. The second advantage he began with was the handy size and geographical cohesion of his diocese. Chester, as he found it, was a lovely diocese. There was every kind of thing in it—Birkenhead and Wallasey at one end, Stockport, Altrincham, Sale and the rest at the far end. There were country towns like Sandbach, Lymm, Congleton, Nantwich and several others. In the middle were country parishes and, beyond, Macclesfield and the beginning of the Derbyshire hills. All were within one county, and it was Fisher's experience that the fact of diocese and county being co-terminous meant a very great deal to both. It was a point he was to recall long afterwards when Anglican-Methodist relations were much in his mind. He had learned in his friendly dealings in Chester with Dr. Stafford Wardle and other leading Methodists what an advantage for fruitful co-operation it would be if the administrative areas of the two Churches should be made to coincide as far as possible. Indeed, so strongly did this impress itself upon him that, when Archbishop, he caused his chaplains to begin to try to see how this co-ordination of large administrative areas could be worked out. But they got nowhere, and the matter lapsed.

A third advantage he had was that of following a man who had been both revered and loved. Bishop Paget was indeed saintly and devout, and at the same time abounding in odd stories and even odder pieces of advice.

One story arose from the fact that there was supposed to be a rivalry as to whether he or his brother, Francis Paget, of Oxford, was the ugliest man in England. Each vied for the distinction. Bishop Paget, as Bishop of Stepney, going home late at night in a bus in which he was the only passenger, overheard the conductor going to the driver and saying: 'See that man? He's the ugliest one I've ever seen!' Upon which Bishop Paget said: 'No, you haven't seen my brother!' As to advice, it was Paget who taught Fisher a rule about saying grace. He said: 'We say grace only for meals at which there are potatoes. That means we don't for breakfast or for tea.' Another piece of advice to his successor was: 'You will know a great many people. Please see to it that you are worth knowing.' Even so, Paget approved of the new bishop because, he said to Mrs. Fisher at a later meeting, 'Nothing succeeds like successors.'

Paget was a high-churchman. A remark which Fisher heard him make early in their encounter he found revealing. A clergyman from the diocese came to see Paget who, before the audience, confided to Fisher: 'I've got to go and see Mr. So-and-so. I don't know what to say to him. He's a very, very low-churchman. I suppose he does some good, but I cannot conceive that he's ever saved any souls.' Fisher's reaction, as later recalled, is important in view of conflicts he was to have, especially when Bishop of London, with the same viewpoint. He said that this 'did reveal a weak spot in Bishop Paget's mind, and one that is often present, I find, in the minds of quite reasonable Anglo-Catholics. They cannot believe that the conservative evangelicals do any good, or save any souls. Later on, I got to know that particular clergyman. I went to his church. It was desperately low, but all the same, I took a confirmation there, and the atmosphere was first-class, the attitude of the candidates was first-class, and the whole thing was full of evangelical commitment to Christ, of a kind that only evangelicals can really produce. For, to put it very bluntly, evangelicals do produce people committed to Christ; Anglo-Catholics produce people committed to Christ through the Church, and the two are not the same. They are sometimes regarded as contradictory; they are, in fact, deeply complementary, provided that, of course, the holders of these views never allow themselves to become militant or political. That destroys everything.'

Fisher was consecrated in York Minster on 21 September 1932 by

William Temple. Mrs. Burne, wife of a future Archdeacon of Chester, recalled the occasion. 'There was a special train from Chester, and as it was a very foggy day on the Pennines, it arrived at York half an hour late and the ceremony in the Minster had to be held up for half an hour. The nave was full of people—about three-quarters of one side with those from Repton, and the other side with people from Chester. When we returned to Chester that evening, Archbishop and Mrs. Fisher were on the train, and walked all down it talking to people as they went.' This warm family sense was to be a marked feature of the Fishers' time at Chester, as the same writer also recalls. 'When the Fishers came, it was quite a new experience for the diocese, to have this young bishop and his wife with six sons, and of course there was a good deal of excitement among the clergy, who had young families too. Mrs. Fisher used to give parties from time to time. I can remember one occasion when she asked thirty children from all over Cheshire, and had a lovely party in the Bishop's House.'

The Fisher boys were not always so pleased. When the sons came back from their respective schools, they told their mother that she mustn't accept invitations unless she had asked them first. She said, 'Very well, I'll remember that in future. But you must go to these parties that I've accepted for you now. It'll look very rude not to.' At the end of the holidays, one of the boys said in a casual manner, 'By the way, you can stop bothering about parties. They're not so bad, after all!'

The new Bishop seemed to spark with energy, although he sometimes shook people a little, in a time when it was much easier for clerics to shake and to shock than it is now. To get out of his car and jump on the activating strip in the road, in order to turn the lights green, as he was once observed doing in Wallasey, was one thing; but to play a barrel-organ in the streets was quite another. He had an operation in the hospital, and the chairman of the hospital board, in those days long before the Health Service, asked Fisher if he would play the instrument to help raise hospital funds. The Bishop said he would, and the Bishop did; but it led to a good deal of comment on the grounds that it was not a very dignified thing for a bishop to do.

Less reprehensible was a misunderstanding of which he was the cause. An old lady who lived near the Cathedral said she saw the Bishop wearing a strange vestment, which appeared to her to be a kind of magenta stole, together with white trousers. The strange vestments were, in fact, a blazer, white trousers and a Leander scarf, for the Bishop was at the time on his way to play squash.

'During the seven years they lived in Chester,' wrote Mrs. Burne, 'the impression one got of Bishop's House was that it was a real home, especially in the holidays when the boys were there, and Mrs. Fisher. Young and old could turn to her. The Bishop himself was a great family man, with the gift of being able to work in a room where other people were. He could enter and sit down and get on with something, and yet at the same time have half an ear open in case some of the boys got quarrelling or something like that.' It was in these years that Mrs. Fisher became prominent in Mothers' Union affairs, becoming diocesan president in Chester, a work which she did excellently. 'She had her own car, and was able to go out and about in Cheshire visiting all sorts of parishes, and becoming known all over the diocese.'

Another picture of Fisher at this time comes from Archdeacon Burne. 'When we heard that the headmaster of a public school was going to be our new bishop, we naturally wondered whether he would continue to be the headmaster in governing and managing the diocese. We were soon reassured; he was so friendly and kind and affable. But there was one trait which revealed his origin. Sometimes he forgot, when a visitor came to see him in his study, to ask him to sit down. The headmaster was still interviewing the boy! And this, I believe, happened with some quite important people in the diocese. Bishop Fisher was very popular with his clergy. There was nothing undignified, there was nothing cold or stand-offish in his dealings with them; he was friendly and spoke to them as man to man. In fact, on one occasion—and this is a story I had from him—he was interviewing an incumbent who came to him with some complaints, and not for the first time. He was bewailing his hardships in the Bishop's study when, said the Bishop to me, "I took him by the lapels of his coat and gave him a good shaking, and said: 'Be a man!' "

'I chiefly saw him at institutions and inductions to vacant benefices. He drove himself, and always gave me a lift. After the service, there was always some refreshment served in the local school or in the village hall, to which he always stayed, and there was never any suggestion that he was anxious to get away. This was not acting on his part; it was genuine. He enjoyed himself, so that he couldn't tear himself away. I remember on one occasion, when I thought the time was up, I got my hat and coat and sat by the door ready to go. He came along and said: "Come on, Burne, it's time we went. Hallo," he said, turning aside to a party of boys and girls, "how're you?" and he became engaged in conversation with them while I stood waiting. Then he left them and came nearer the door and said, "Come on, Burne, come on. Are you ready? Oh, how are you?" and he turned aside a second time to speak to another party.'

This ease of association was to be with Fisher always, combined with an astonishing memory for names and places. It was to prove a valuable asset later, in dealing with the all sorts and conditions of people with whom an archbishop must come into contact. Perhaps the essence of it was an un- feigned and apparently inexhaustible interest in individuals. It is in human nature to react favourably to such warmth, as a flower to the sun. In after times it was observed that he could make the Queen laugh, when maybe the atmosphere of the moment was unpropitious, and when it did not seem the royal wish to be amused. The choir-boy in the Chester diocese who said: 'I know our bishop; he spoke to me when we had our new vicar,' was voicing a common and very valuable reaction to this character- istic.

But there was always another side to this geniality. The sun did not always shine, as many discovered. And when it did not shine, it was likely more to give place to thunder and lightning than merely to retire behind a cloud. Opposition, in fact, brought out opposition.

His going to Chester involved him making a debut in two places where, as time passed, much was to be seen of him: Church Assembly and Con- vocation. A quite fortuitous circumstance gave him the opportunity of making his mark in the former. It so happened that, in those days of financial stringency, it was adjudged necessary that three training colleges should shut at once. Chester was to be one. Immediately, strong pleas were made to the new Bishop that the college within his own diocese, at least, should be saved. Although having some doubts about the efficiency of that institution at that moment, but at the same time being convinced of its valuable history and good intentions, Fisher reacted in a manner typical of that in which he was to face greater issues often in later years. First, to use an expression he was fond of, he did his homework extremely thoroughly, studying with the relish and ability of one who was always, as he said, 'good at figures', the finances of the matter. He then made ready in his mind a speech compounded of facts, adroit argument, and wit, under the last heading making use of the convenient fact, brought to his notice by Canon Thomas, head of Chester College, that the lesson for the day of the debate in the Assembly contained the phrase 'A partridge sitteth on her eggs and hatcheth them not', when the name of the Church Assembly's chairman on the Board of Finance was, as it happened, Partridge. He then delivered his speech, being called on at exactly the right time for a good hearing, and won the day.

It was a good opening for a new bishop, who had never seen the Church Assembly in action at all, and knew nothing about its finances. It also made his name in the diocese as the saviour of its training college, a fact long remembered.

Unlike some, then and thereafter, Fisher enjoyed Church Assembly, though it would no doubt have astounded him to know that one day he would himself be its chairman.

Travelling to London for the Church Assembly, or Bishops' Meetings, he would get a detective story at Chester station going up, and another coming down, going carefree because he had no intention of making any speech or taking any part in the business of the Assembly. But he did get involved in the Missionary Council, in which John Campbell, an old school friend, was trying to reorganise and revitalise the direction and the effect of the missionary work of the Church. Thus eventually Fisher found himself becoming vice-chairman of the Missionary Council of the Church Assembly, and having to present a statement once a year. It was a modest beginning of involvement for one who was to be in the post-war years the invigorator, remoulder and, indeed, moderniser of much of that body's life and shape.

The northern Convocation, meeting at York, brought Fisher for the first time into the heart of the episcopal scene. Here, among other things, was to be discovered the difference between reality and fiction as regards episcopal deliberation. Bishops have rarely been held in high general esteem. Hensley Henson, when Bishop of Durham, once remarked of a gathering of his colleagues that 'we were an assembly of bishops, and that circumstance alone sufficed to immerse us in much popular suspicion'.[1] This suspicion Fisher now encountered. It was William Temple's custom, as Archbishop of York, to have all the bishops to stay at Bishopthorpe the night before Convocation, and it was commonly supposed that there the bishops arranged what should happen the next day. In a sense, that was true, as Fisher recalled. But he found that what it really meant was that the bishops compared notes. There was never any attempt to unify their thoughts, or to suppress differing opinions. It did mean that they all knew how they should tackle the subject the next day, and who would be likely to be speaking on it, either on one side or another. It meant a very friendly atmosphere in the Upper House. In the Lower House of Clergy there was the same friendly atmosphere. The discussions were friendly, direct and immediate, and there was no gulf to be bridged, no dividing point, so that the business was done quietly, effectively, smoothly and with common sense, a unity possessing all. Most of the business was done with the Upper and Lower Houses sitting together; but every now and then the Upper House withdrew to their own chamber to deal with some subjects which particularly concerned them.

A picture of William Temple emerges here illustrative of one aspect of his extraordinary mental powers. Fisher observed how on one occasion when, as usual, it was the duty of the Registrar to open the convocation in full form by reciting a rather lengthy formula which denounced any persons who were present without leave as contumacious, and so forth, in a form of words which had come down from long past, the Registrar had forgotten to bring the necessary documents. Embarrassed, he said to the Archbishop that he could not proceed, as he had not the form to hand. Without hesitation, William Temple said: 'I think I can remember this.' Then and there, he recited the thing word for word, precisely, without any preparation.

But there were far more serious matters than these, arising out of the continuing life of the Church, which inevitably made their appearance in

[1] H. Hensley Henson, *Disestablishment* (Macmillan).

these gatherings from time to time. One notable debate arose from the fact that the then Bishop of Liverpool, David, had invited a Unitarian to give an address on a weekday in Liverpool Cathedral. The Unitarian was a distinguished man and those who, at this distance of time, may find it curious that such an action should lead to the sharp dissension which did in fact follow, may reflect not only upon the change in ecumenical temper which has taken place over the years; but also upon the fact that the mind of the Church is a continuing, many-sided thing, each age with its own burning issues. In the thirties, the tension between high-churchmen, such as Lord Hugh Cecil, and the Church at large—a tension with a long and complex history—was certainly one of them. So Cecil made a great demonstration against this action, as being, in his view, nothing less than utterly destructive of the character of the Church. He moved protests, and these came to Convocation, where the Bishop of Chester was an interested participant. The Bishop of Liverpool defended his action. There ensued a debate which at least took the sting out of the controversy, and ended, as such things so often fortunately do, in a position in which disapproval had been voiced, but without inflicting reprimand.

Another great event was the presentation, by Bishop Williams of Carlisle, of the Report on Doctrine in the Church of England, which had been produced after fifteen years of solid work by the Church's best theologians. But it never got off the ground. The times were against it, for by 1938, the year of its appearance, there were more pressing matters to engage the attention than the connection between the Fall and the Incarnation, or the relation of modern christology to the formula of Chalcedon, or even the psychological aspects of sin. 1938 was the year of Munich, and the whole report was overlooked. A decade later, when it was so much needed, to guide doctrinal thinking, the report was virtually forgotten.

All Fisher's years at Chester, 1932–1939, were, as regards the world at large, times when crisis followed crisis, when hopes constantly deferred made many hearts sick. The dictators arose: the democracies appeared to be abased. Nazi Germany was born. The concentration camps opened, and the Jews began their most fearful time of persecution. The League of Nations died of ineffectiveness; the Spanish Civil War was fought, and lost by the nobler cause. British Government was weak; the country was divided; its King abdicated in 1936. Only a few, and they unheeded, warned of the gathering storm.

Unless such facts are born in mind, it is not possible to keep such a narrative as this in historical proportion. The manner in which any man reacts to his times always has some significance as to the nature of the man himself. And insofar as the normal environment of man in the thirties was one of crisis and anxiety, and insofar as the whole tone of Fisher's reminiscences of his time at Chester is one of cheerfulness and industry, it follows that a resolute hopefulness was a part of him. The complaining clergyman whom he seized by the lapels with the adjuration 'Be a man!' was not the only person to receive such treatment. He must often, like anyone in a position of leadership in such terrible times, have, metaphorically speaking, done it to himself. So his diocese liked him. He was a good Bishop of Chester and is still remembered as such by those who knew him there.

The same consideration regarding the time and the hour bears with equal relevance on the picture of the Church at any given time. If its doings be recorded solely from the inside, with reference to this or that ecclesiastical issue, the impression can only too easily be given of some kind of ecclesiastical ritual dance, taking place without any particular relevance to contemporary events. But such an impression is misleading. Convocation, for instance, in Fisher's Chester years might have debated the propriety of a Unitarian minister preaching in Liverpool Cathedral, or had presented to it an enormous report on doctrine, which ran like water off the duck's back of graver events. But it was concerned with these also, and with a whole host of social problems, and in so doing mirrored the concern of the Church in general. How these concerns were reflected in debate can be found in the *Chronicles of the Convocation of Canterbury*, as no doubt of York. And how these debates on various issues—questions of housing in particular and the social order in general—emerged onto the public scene can be found reflected in the press of the day. These inter-war years were difficult times for the Church, as they were for the country in general. But to suggest that the Church was indifferent to the nation's needs, or moribund in itself, is to be very wide of the mark. As to the first, the concern of the Church in general, and the involvement of church people, to take one issue alone, as citizens, in the problems of unemployment, were both very real, and can be amply documented from the literature of the day. Who now remembers the Cathedral pilgrimage of 1934, when tens of thousands of people went to cathedrals on pilgrimages, both to make offerings for the unemployed, and to give witness to their own concern in their plight? Probably very few. But it happened, and was one among many manifestations of the anxieties which were occupying not a few Christian consciences in that distant day.

It needs also to be remembered that these were the years, not only of the continuing search for Christian unity; not only of the search for a Christian social order; not only of significant theological thinking; but also of the emergence of a new kind of Christian communicator. The great majority were Anglican. Along with William Temple, Dorothy Sayers, C. S. Lewis, T. S. Eliot and others did a fine work of Christian communication. In another sphere, too, that of mysticism and the devotional life, Evelyn Underhill was at this time making her mark. And in W. H. Eliot, the Church found a broadcaster who, in that emerging means of mass communication, could command an attention never equalled before or since.

All this varied life of a by no means moribund Church can be found reflected in the Chester years of Fisher.

The first big task he was faced with, for example, was an Industrial Christian Fellowship mission in Birkenhead, in the days when the I.C.F., under the leadership of P. T. R. Kirk, was still living within the glow of the memory of Studdert Kennedy, its greatest missioner. Nothing could have been more remote from Fisher's experience up to then. As a boy at public school, at Oxford and then at Repton, he used to go to the Oxford and Bermondsey Mission, as it was then called. But that had been his only direct contact with industrial urban life. Now he had to face it. And, as ever, he plunged into it heart and soul, being given a programme of going from stand to stand in the evenings in the Birkenhead slums, to speak. His essential humility comes out in his own memory of this endeavour, which had also a personal sequel.

'How much I made real contact with the people I addressed I don't know at all. But they were quite friendly to me and I was friendly to them, and I hope I did no harm. Anyhow, the mission went very well, and I made friends with the missioners, who seemed to have no particular complaints. A year or two later, there was another I.C.F. mission at Northwich, and that, too, I led. That is to say, I was the figurehead of it and I took as active a part in it as I could. That went well as far as I know. But the chief memory I treasured from it was that there I met Hussey, a vicar of Salford, in Manchester, as he remained almost all his life. He was a most witty person; full of stories, full of good humour, full of wit. We enjoyed each other at that meeting. I never met him again until I was Archbishop, and found him as a member of the Church Assembly. There at once we struck up a queer kind of alliance. In churchmanship, he was pretty high, and he can't have thought all that well of me; but we at once became allies. We both listened intently to what was being said in the debates; when a thing got difficult, I would always want to do something to relieve the tension; but again and again it was not I that had to do anything, for Hussey stepped into the breach. He would rise and make some brief speech, beginning with a witticism which swept the House, and obliterated all the ill-feeling and tension that was growing up.'

In a quite different sphere of activity, Fisher encountered in Chester, in the person of the Dean of its Cathedral, Frank Selwyn Macauley Bennett, a man whose genius for that aspect of the Church's ministry brought a change not only to his own, but to all English cathedrals which has lasted until now, and shows every sign of continuing. Under Bennett, the greater part of whose pioneer work had been completed by the time that Fisher arrived, Chester Cathedral had become a place of pilgrimage. It had become a thing of beauty and a joy for ever, rather than the place of cloistered mystery with no particular function, which some cathedrals had long been. Benson, at Truro, in the nineteenth century, and Hensley Henson at Durham in the twentieth had struggled with the problem, each in his time and place. Bennett in the twenties made a breakthrough by imagination, by drive, by throwing open his Cathedral to all and sundry and delighting in seeing them there. The details of how this was accomplished do not belong to this particular narrative. What does is the fact that Fisher was able to meet Bennett at the culmination of his achievement.

'Dean Bennett,' he recalled, 'was a great man. It was he who freed the Cathedral. When he came to Chester he threw it all open. He was always there, he lived in it and would go round with people, talking to them, and now and again he'd assemble them round the pulpit to give them a short address on the Cathedral, and then say some prayers for them. He was rapidly turning the Cathedral into a lovely house of God. Attached to it was the Refectory, and there meals were provided and all sorts of meetings were held.'

The two did not necessarily see eye-to-eye on all points of churchmanship; but they were both wise men and co-operated happily, and backed each other up wholeheartedly.

There were a few very high and a few very low churches in the diocese; but Fisher got on well with them and never tried to interfere or cut them out in any way, provided that when he went to officiate in them, they did not attempt to order him about. But these were details and, in the diocese as a whole, there was no worry about churchmanship, but rather a general acceptance of a good range of lively traditions. And the diocese was relieved to find in Fisher 'a straightforward, central churchman, with only one principle: to be faithful to the doctrine of the Church of England.'

The life of the Church is not made up of matters of distinctions between various kinds of churchmanship, however, or of collections of persons rich in character, as though the whole thing were some esoteric internecine battle. Larger issues also occupy the stage, and Christian men and women are to be found in every place and generation, giving them-selves to the kingdom of God. So it was in Chester. There was there, for instance, a very distinctive body of persons devoted to evangelism, led by the women messengers with, at their head, Mrs. Ffoulkes, a splendid woman, the sister of Sir Philip Baker-Wilbraham. These organised missions in parishes, assisted by lay people who worked with them. A team would go, missioners and lay men and women, and live in a parish for some days and do their work. Mrs. Fisher was in her element here and was much involved. All that side of Church life was thoroughly awake, and there were many people taking their part in various aspects of it with special emphasis on the missionary cause, efficiency in Sunday-school teaching and the contribution of youth, greatly inspired by Anne Rollins, a young and brilliant youth-leader; charming, Irish, shining in her vivacity and in her Christian devotion.

Here, in short, was a diocese—and that in a period commonly regarded not only as one of national ineffectiveness, but of religious indifference to a notable degree—which had, in fact, its full share of happy community life and vitality, and deep Christian commitment. It would scarcely have been in character for Fisher not to revive and improve its administrative machine. This he duly did, with much benefit all round. In his time the old order, with a diocesan office under one devoted but elderly man, was replaced by a new diocesan secretary, Canon Walker. The office became a new thing, and the administrative side became active, up to date and progressive. And Fisher inherited a splendid group of laymen, devoting much time and great ability to working the diocesan machine. Outstanding among them was Mr. Bevan, a member of the Church Assembly and the chief financier of the diocese, who held the entire confidence of the diocesan conference, and won from everyone affectionate trust in his leadership.

Thus the years passed at Chester, full and happy ones in Fisher's domestic as in his public life, in spite of the fearful developments which were, step by step, bringing successive crises towards war. After Munich, no one knew what would happen. After the invasion of Poland, everyone knew what had to happen. And so the day came when 'the British Government instructed its ambassador to present its ultimatum to Germany on the morning of September 3rd, and to request a reply before noon. There was no reply. On Sunday morning, September 3rd, crowds gathered in Downing Street and Whitehall and heard through the loudspeakers Chamberlain's declaration of war. A moment later the sirens screamed. It was a false alarm; but it added its own dramatic touch to that tense moment of history. The hectic, frivolous, frustrated, puzzled, frantic period of "between the wars" had come to an end.'[1]

So, for Fisher, had the long, active years at Repton; the satisfying years at Chester. For he, who had gone to Repton at the beginning of one war had, by the beginning of the second, been translated to London. As Bishop of that capital of an empire at war he was soon to hear, and often, those sirens sounding in earnest.

[1] James Laver, *Between the Wars* (Vista Books).

V

London

An Anglican, as it seems to me, is one who above all does not desire or wish that any one element shall part company with the others: that any one shall prevail over or suppress the others. He cannot be a partisan, in the sense of thinking he is right and the others are wrong.

> G.F.F. in an address given to the Joint Session of the General
> Convocation of the Episcopal Church of the U.S.A.,
> Philadelphia, 12 September 1946

· · ·

This is a bad time for all who would cling to their lives: an invigorating time for all who would spend them for true ends, truly seen and faithfully pursued.

> G.F.F. in a sermon preached in Westminster Abbey at the
> Dedication of the Battle of Britain Chapel, 10 July 1947

HE had no wish to go to London, nor had ever expected to do so. It was a foreign place to his thinking: he had no wish to go near it, and the idea of being involved in the ecclesiastical controversies for which, by that time, the vast diocese with its six hundred parishes was famous, or notorious, according to viewpoint, really horrified him. In London, apart from grievous questions of diocesan politics, were to be found the headquarters of many Church Societies and, outstanding for its influence and efficiency, the Church Union, the head and front of the Anglo-Catholic movement. In its notable history, it had claimed the allegiance of some fine men and been productive of some heroic ministries, especially in the East End of London. Nonetheless, it posed severe questions of Church order and ecclesiastical discipline upon anyone who, as bishop, had to concern himself with these matters. The problem was large and complex and it will be necessary to return to it.

But first, since this is the story of Geoffrey Fisher as a person, rather than a chronicle of his times, it does seem necessary to note here how yet again, with that curious consistency which dogged him in this respect throughout so much of his public life, he was called upon to face difficult tasks in difficult times. He had gone to Repton at the beginning of one war: now he was to go to London at the commencement of another even more terrible and, as it affected that diocese, infinitely more testing. And as one of his first tasks at Repton had been to tighten up a discipline which had become too loose, so now in London the same quality was to be called for, and on a very much larger scale. In London he succeeded the beloved Arthur Foley Winnington-Ingram, Bishop of London 1901–1939, who, with many excellent qualities, lacked some of those which are needed for the oversight and discipline of such a vast and varied diocese as London. And any weaknesses there had repercussions all over England.

Winnington-Ingram had been an outstanding character in his day: in terms of personal appeal and evangelistic power a very great bishop. But the situation left by him was such as to confront Fisher with acutely difficult problems from the start, and it therefore seems logical to begin with this situation.

Winnington-Ingram was one of those personalities who flourished and did great work in the period leading up to 1914. By his ever-youthful charm and goodness he came to hold a unique place. Handsome and young at his first bursting upon the public scene, in personality highly attractive, in faith simple, in energy boundless, he took the social situation of his day —poverty living alongside wealth, privilege with under-privilege—and applied the full force of his energies to redressing some of its injustices.

Fisher himself had been captured as a boy at Marlborough by Winnington-Ingram. 'He came down in 1901 when I was a new boy, to introduce himself as an Old Marlburian. He came down every year, and his visit was a highlight in the life of the school. He was then a young man, full of grace and charm, and we all fell for him. Each year, when he preached in chapel, we hung on his words, winged as they were by his manner of speech and shining sincerity. On my last Sunday as Head Prefect, he took me out for a walk in the afternoon, up on the cricket field. It was a very memorable occasion for me. After Oxford, I went back as master to Marlborough, and on my last Sunday as a master there, before going to Repton, again he took me out for a walk. I never forgot these two events and he would almost always mention them whenever we met later. At Oxford, his annual preaching at St. Mary's on a Sunday evening was always a notable event. It was necessary to cut Hall and queue for an hour or so before the service began in order to get a seat. His sermons were always of the same pattern and quality, and held an undergraduate audience spellbound, not so much by what was said (it was difficult to recall what had been said) as by the fascination of his personal eagerness, and power to attract, and patent goodness. But as time went by, it became clear that there was not behind this glowing fervour of spiritual light and fire sufficient intellectual power, sufficient understanding of the arts of discipline and direction, to control the disorders of the diocese, or through years of considerable strain in the Church at large to provide effective leadership, except on such matters as evangelisation and youth.'

Winnington-Ingram had retired in a rosy glow of sentiment. But in terms of the true condition of his diocese, he had by then long parted company with reality. His successor recalled that, when he stayed with him, having been appointed to succeed him in the June of 1939, Winnington-Ingram, having said nothing so far upon the matter, remarked one afternoon: 'Let's now walk round the garden, and I'll tell you all you need to know about the diocese of London.' They set off and all the Bishop had to say was: 'We are just one gloriously happy family. Of course, you and I are both Marlburians, and we are used to meeting unusual situations. But that will be all right, my boy; just carry on and all will be well.'

It may readily be seen, therefore, how such a disciplined and organised body as the Anglo-Catholic clergy in the diocese were, could go its own way undisturbed by a diocesan leadership which had always been gentle, and had become virtually ineffective. There existed also, it needs to be said, a Protestant extremist fringe. Between the two, any bishop whose charge included responsibility for the maintenance of Church order and respect for lawful authority, was bound to be in a difficult position. In London it was particularly so, and this was one of the first problems which faced Fisher on his going there. But first he had to settle himself into his

F

new surroundings, in the midst of many anxieties both personal and public which increased as the war progressed, but of which few, if any, ever appeared in his public face or appeared to affect the steady performance of his manifold duties.

Domestically, the London years were times of much stress for the Fishers. Four of their sons were in the Army. During the course of the war, one, Frank, was posted missing for a fortnight. Life at Fulham was difficult, with Mrs. Fisher terribly anxious about her sons at the front. In normal times, Fulham Palace was a lovely country house, entered through an archway into an old Elizabethan forecourt, surrounded by Elizabethan chimneys. Then followed an inner doorway, past a hall on the left dating from early days, and a passage to the chapel on the right. This was followed by another passage running round an inner little court to the Bishop's study and the Chaplains' room on the right-hand side and, beyond, to a gracious drawing-room with French windows looking out on to a beautiful garden, and a great dining-room with the portraits of former bishops around.

In normal times, it was an ideal place to live, within four miles of Hyde Park Corner. On the right-hand side of the garden was the Thames, at the far end All Saints Church, while between the garden and church lay a large walled garden, in which there was a peach-house and a wonderful wistaria screen. But these were not normal times. The gardeners soon disappeared, and a barrage balloon section appeared nearby. Soon also, when the bombing started, it was found necessary to abandon the great rooms and to take shelter in the Elizabethan wing. Various portions of the Palace from time to time suffered from bomb blast, and each time that happened the family had to move their quarters and adjust themselves to an undamaged part. In the end, all were sleeping almost entirely in Morrison Shelters on the ground floor, except for the chaplain, F. C. Synge, who chose to sleep on a camp bed on the lawn, saying that he preferred the risk of being hit by shrapnel to that of being buried alive beneath Fulham Palace.

Everyone in those days had their personal bomb stories. Fisher's, insofar as they were incidents which affected him personally, were few, because it was not in his nature to recount or recall them. But he did remember one bad moment: 'Just after lunch we heard flying bombs approaching . . . I came from the upstairs dining-room in the Elizabethan forecourt to the front door, where I expected to find the car to go out. But the chauffeur had disappeared. I turned round and went down the passage towards the Morrison Shelter. When they went off, I was at a point at which, on the left hand side, was the passage leading to another part of the Palace, behind were the windows which were all smashed to smithereens, on my right was a heavy oak doorway leading to the Chaplains' room. As I observed them afterwards, the door and door jamb had been sucked bodily into the inside of the room, while immediately in front of me, only a yard or two forward, was the lofty staircase-well, and there the whole plaster ceiling from the top of the house had fallen. If I had been a few yards further, it would have killed me.'

More to his taste were two stories which he always liked to tell. The first was of an old lady who lived at the top of a high building in Stepney. All the other inhabitants had left but she refused to move and the authorities were very worried. They appealed to her to move but she refused. Her reason was always the same: 'I don't see why I should move. Here I am, I say my prayers and I go to sleep, there's no reason for the two of us to keep awake.' The two would be herself and God. The other story concerned a woman who was talking about a bomb which fell just further down the street: 'I heard the bomb coming,' she said, 'and I prayed to God as hard as I could to push it a bit further down the street, and he did.'

What was Fisher like as a man in these times? Since no bishop is likely to be a hero, either to his secretary or to his chaplain, it seems reasonable to start at those points for an answer.

Marjorie Harry, now Mrs. Salmon, came from Chester with Fisher to London as his secretary. 'I cannot imagine,' she records, 'anyone for whom it would be easier to work, though the word "easier" must not be taken to denote a minimum of work. Quite the opposite: he himself was a very hard worker and expected his staff to be the same. From a secretary's point of view, his most appreciated characteristic was, I think, his clarity in issuing work and in the dictation of letters. I never had to ask him twice what he meant, or how he wished the work to be done. This was due to his own clearcut, methodical and penetrating approach to every subject with which he dealt. At the same time, his relationship with staff was so good-humoured that, however great the quantity of letters or documents to be dispatched, one never thought of him as a hard task-master. Once the work was dictated, there was no fussing over it; he was quite content to leave it to the secretary's discretion as to how and when it was done. These may sound small points; but in fact they are very important in maintaining a happy relationship between a chief and his secretary.

'The Bishop's recreations were few. A vigorous walk round the Palace grounds seemed to keep him physically fit. Of an evening, he would retire to the family sitting-room after dinner and listen to the nine o'clock news on the B.B.C. More often than not, as soon as that was over, he would return to his study, there to prepare for the next day's work, on some occasions until a very late hour.'

Mrs. Salmon also gave a description of life in the Palace. 'As to the blitz, when the bombing began, various buildings were designated first, second or third lines of defence Rest Centres. Fulham Palace was in the third category, and in general had not much done to it in the way of reinforcement against bomb damage. It so happened that one day both the first and second line Rest Centres were put out of action by the presence near them of unexploded bombs, and so the Palace had to be used. Into it there came some two hundred or more evacuees from neighbouring roads, where houses had to be emptied. This was in the time when many people originally sent away from London into the country had returned to their London homes, so those who came to the Palace for shelter were of all sorts and conditions, ranging from young babies in their mothers' arms to the very elderly. It was a harrowing experience to see them huddled against the walls of the large reception rooms, and all along the corridors, and to know that in the event of a direct hit their chances of protection or survival were slender. Of course, Civil Defence workers and residents from the local Settlement, Bishop Creighton House, came to help in caring for the temporarily homeless people, and the Bishop continually moved amongst them, talking to them and reassuring them. The regular bombing which commenced in 1940 continued without a break for some time, and life at the Palace was adjusted accordingly. The bombers' time of arrival varied very little, beginning in the early evening. So the family evening meal became a high-tea, and thereafter the Palace residents retired to various corners which had been strengthened with girders and sandbags. The Bishop, Mrs. Fisher and Miss Forman spent many an evening in an old pantry which had been so protected. After eleven p.m. Miss Forman and I slept there, to the accompaniment of guns outside. The Bishop slept in an underground shelter beneath the Porteous library, while Mrs. Fisher was in another part of the Palace. That was planned so that, if a direct hit were received, the risk of both parents being killed was at least halved.

'Miss M. C. Forman, Mrs. Fisher's youngest sister, was responsible for all housekeeping and domestic staff, and we all owed her an immense debt of gratitude for her skill in providing for our needs in a terribly difficult period.

'Of course, the one who made Fulham Palace a home, not just a church headquarters, was Mrs. Fisher. In addition, she found time for a number of outside commitments, Moral Welfare work, Mothers' Union, G.F.S., the local Settlement and other things. Her particular work might be said to have been her deep concern for the activities of the Church's Committee for Women in the Forces, of which she was the chairman. For the much-tried clergy wives, in those war-time days, Mrs. Fisher had a special concern, and on numerous occasions had groups of them at the Palace to give them an opportunity of quiet and spiritual refreshment. Nor were the W.A.A.F., who manned the barrage balloon in the Palace field forgotten. A group of them lived in the lodge at the entrance gates, and they were often invited to Sunday tea and made welcome in the Palace.'

A more critical, if no less affectionate and domestic account, comes from the Rev. F. C. Synge, Fisher's chaplain in those London years, now Canon Synge, Principal of Christchurch College, New Zealand:

'Like anyone else's daily routine, his contained a certain number of invariables, most of them unremarkable. But there was one which deserves attention. His passage through the house was marked by the slamming of doors, and his entrance into his study was heralded by the slamming of the door and then, almost immediately, his impetus having carried him to the fireplace, by the tapping of his pipe on the grate.[1]

'He was, I think, quite unaware of this slamming of doors, but it reveals one of the sources of his strength, one of the roots of his unfussability. This period (breakfast) was over—slam—this new period, undisturbed by anything that might have gone before, now began—slam—this watertight compartment is shut—slam—I can concentrate on what lies before me with a clear mind—slam.

'After lunch, out came *The Times* crossword, in which his absorption was complete, and then slam went the drawing-room door, slam any intervening doors, slam the study door, and he was ready for the afternoon's work.

'The strain of one interview did not outlast the interview. The labour of dictation, or of chairing a meeting, was absorbed by a remarkable resilience. He would come back home after a long day almost exhausted, the extent of his exhaustion indicated by the length of his face which used to grow, so we said, about three inches longer. But after a night's sleep it was back to normal and his progress, to and from breakfast, measured by the slamming of doors, would indicate the fact.

'He was completely unfussable. I do not know what went on in his mind as he slept during the blitz of 1940 on the ground floor, and under a shelter during the flying-bomb era in 1944; but I should think that, as he slammed the door before getting into bed, he shut out in some degree the danger that beset us, and so slept.

'He possessed equanimity and magnanimity. Small things are often more significant than large, so I recall a small incident. He was to attend a Masonic dinner as the chief guest and was to make the main speech. It was the time of the blitz and the message came through that the dinner was to be at six-thirty. Whose fault it was, mine or his secretary's, I have never been clear about, but the message as it was delivered to him gave the hour of the dinner as seven-thirty. So shortly after six-thirty the host rang up to enquire whether the Bishop was on his way. He wasn't. He dressed and got there very late, and made his apologies, and charmed everyone by his geniality and his speech. This illustrates his equanimity. His

[1] Fisher's abandonment of smoking came later, when he was Archbishop.

magnanimity is shown by the fact that he did not seek to blame anyone else for his lateness.

'As I have said, he was unfussable and, one would have said, supremely self-confident. Therefore an unlikely incident has stuck in my mind. In the course of his Enthronement at St. Paul's, it was required of the Bishop that from his throne he recited alone the Lord's Prayer. He asked me to be sure that a prayer book, open at the Lord's Prayer, rested on his desk. I attended to this, well aware that, for myself, such precaution would be most unnecessary. But the better I came to know Fisher the more notable the little incident became. What it reveals, I do not quite know — perhaps that he was not as sure of himself as he appeared to be, perhaps that he was unfussable precisely because he took every precaution to avoid assaults upon his composure, perhaps that he wanted to read, on this occasion, with a verve that would open up new depth in what he had to read, both to himself and to the congregation.

'Bishop Fisher's daily session, (daily rapture, one might almost say) with *The Times* crossword may serve to illuminate his character. Here was an artificial darkness waiting to be brought into order. Here was something which brought into play those faculties the exercise of which were his delight and his calling. The crossword was the supreme recreation in that he was exercising them without responsibility. In his daily work he excelled in, and delighted in bringing order to disorder, throwing light upon dark confusion, organising, rearranging, making machinery work smoothly, solving problems of manpower or finances, confident that (like the crossword puzzle) the solution was there to be found.

'Here were both his strength and his weakness. Winnington-Ingram left behind a liturgical chaos which he thought an ordered and happy liberty. Fisher set about providing guidance to a liturgical conformity quite unaware, it seems to me, that there was then and there, stirring, that enormous upsurge of liturgical reform which future historians of the Church will regard as the most exciting and rejuvenating feature of the period of his episcopate. I do not know whether it ever occurred to him that liturgical conformity was never again going to be obtainable within the framework of Cranmer's scholarship and presuppositions. To him, the framework, as in a crossword puzzle, was stable, and profounder knowledge would enable a wise and lasting solution to be attained. So there went out a series of edicts—Bishop's Regulations—which were eirenic and Anglican and shrewd, and which yet never got anywhere near to understanding that the liturgical ferment which he hoped to constrain was something which could not be constrained, but which needed to be blessed.

'No longer could the task of a bishop be likened to the solving of a crossword puzzle; but Fisher was unaware of this. For him, I think, the studies of Bible and of Theology provided a fence to boundaries, police-men who prevented heresy, the clues to the crossword. That such a study should be a stimulus, blowing the framework of the crossword askew; yeasty stuff, was not within his comprehension.

'He was a very English Anglican; full of common sense and wisdom and kindness and prudence and shrewdness: a lover of smoothly-running diocesan machinery. Law, rather than Gospel, was the stuff of his sermons —sensible, balanced, reassuring.

'He possessed a natural dignity of bearing, which enabled him to play his part in ornate occasions without pompousness, without embarrassment, admirably unfussable. Such a bishop was an asset at the time of the blitz on London , a bishop who could legislate calmly for the present confusion and for the future stabilisation. But what if the future would not be stabilised? I doubt whether it was in his nature to grasp the opportunities of heroic and dangerous experimentation.'

Another assessment of Fisher comes from W. R. Matthews, Dean of St. Paul's before, during, and long after Fisher's London days. As an assessment, it reaches in fact beyond London to Canterbury, viewing Fisher in both. But all of it has its place here as a portrait of the man even then, in London, emerging.

'I first met Dr. Fisher when he was Bishop of Chester, though I didn't know him very well then. When he was offered the bishopric of London, he wrote to me before he accepted, to ask me what I thought was the chief quality required in a Bishop of London. I can't remember what I said altogether, but I remember that I said, first and foremost, the quality required was toughness; toughness of mind, body and spirit, and that, I think, is true. The diocese of London was so large, and had got into such a confusion of administration that one had to be tough even to make a beginning of getting it into some kind of order.

'And then I think that toughness of administrative ability was required, because any kind of discipline was strangely absent from the diocese; everybody could do just as he liked. It was chiefly, of course, the extreme Anglo-Catholics that were blamed for this situation, though they were not the only people who went on regardless of every kind of episcopal direction. I think it required toughness to keep one's head and persevere in the general situation in which he occupied the See of London, and also while he was Archbishop of Canterbury, because undoubtedly that period was one of acute crisis, political but above all spiritual. That crisis is still very much with us, and one can say, I think, perhaps no more than this, that Fisher carried the Church through its crisis at possibly its height, and never lost heart, and left it more unified and in fact, I'm sure, less lawless than when he took over the reins.

'In all my contacts with him, I was amazed at his resilience. Nothing seemed to depress him for more than a short time, even under the most crushing disappointments and labours. He was always smiling, and always had some kind of jest. He was a very good speaker at dinners and meetings of various kinds, which made him very much liked in the City of London. In this respect, he was in rather striking contrast to his predecessor, Cosmo Gordon Lang, who was himself one of the most able and attractive after-dinner speakers, as well as being a great preacher. The difference between Fisher and Lang, as after-dinner speakers, if I might be so bold as to say so, was that Lang, though often amusing and always interesting, was always very conscious and always made his audience conscious, that he was in fact the Lord Archbishop of Canterbury, Primate of All England, whereas when Fisher spoke after dinner, if you shut your eyes, very often you might not have thought he was even the curate! I think that sometimes he was not quite as dignified on those occasions as he might have been, but on the whole what he did in the City, and the friendship that he evoked, and the cheerfulness that he exuded were all very great assets.

'I think it worth recalling that when he wrote to me, and I had a talk with him, he said: "I'm not a spiritual leader." I think that was a mark of the humility that was one of his characteristics. I remember that I wrote a rather impudent thing in *The Sunday Times*—they were doing a series of what I think they called "Profiles", and I was asked to do one of Dr. Fisher. I remember I started my profile with saying: "Dr. Fisher is constantly surprised that he is occupying the seat of St. Augustine, for he is a humble man; but he would confess that when he considered who might have occupied that seat more worthily than himself, it was not easy to think of who it would be." He was conscious of his ability, but he was never proud of it. And I think to be aware of one's capacity and to say all the time: "What hast thou, thou didst not receive?" is the true, not the false humility. And I think that is what Fisher had.'

War conditions in London from the beginning naturally profoundly affected Fisher's pastoral activities. For one thing, he found that nobody wanted him on their weekday evenings. The whole population disappeared to shelters, and no parochial life was possible. He would visit the East End shelters or he would appear at some place where there had been an 'incident', as a bomb hit was called in those days, and find himself on occasion involved in rescue operations.

At the beginning of the war, Sundays soon assumed a pattern. On some he would go to a church in the East End and find, most probably, a little handful of people, very likely with their church destroyed, waiting in some church hall, and there he would do his best to encourage and help them, and try to encourage the clergy in their melancholy task of looking after the little residue that remained. On other Sunday evenings, he would go to churches on the outer fringe of the capital, up to Harrow and north London and the like, and find crowded congregations, all very much moved by the circumstances. He found it a joy to meet them and to preach to them. It would not be typical of Fisher, though, if he did not discover it necessary, in recalling these 'old, unhappy, far-off things, and battles long ago', to detect the comic side. Thus: 'There was only one occasion I remember when, as I was preaching at a church, I think, in North Kensington, I heard a flying bomb approach. I suddenly noticed that the whole congregationn had disappeared under their seats. After a time, the bomb went on and they resumed their seats, and I could see whom I was preaching to again.'

Fisher himself long remembered—and the tale may be taken to round off this aspect of his London days—a curious encounter which took place in the early part of the battle of London. There had been heavy bombing of the City and the docks, and he had been invited, after that awful night, to a luncheon at the Mansion House, to welcome the American Ambassador, Mr. Winant. Although the whole City was in chaos, he told his chauffeur, who knew his way about, to try and get him to the Mansion House. This chauffeur, whom Fisher remembered with warmth, was John Binley. His father had been coachman to Winnington-Ingram for long years and, when he retired and cars came in, John Binley became chauffeur. He was the best kind of Cockney, with inexhaustible wit and an invaluable knowledge of London and all its ways. They went by back lanes, driving over hosepipes and shattered glass, and finally managed to get to the Mansion House. There Fisher rang, and the door was opened. He said: 'I won't bother the Lord Mayor.' But the reply was: 'I am sure he'd like to see you.' So he went up, and there were Sir George Wilkinson and Lady Wilkinson in their drawing-room. The Bishop apologised for having come, saying that it was only just to greet them and see that they were all well. But they pressed him to stay, saying that lunch was about to be served, for which they had sent out for some beer and sandwiches. At least it enabled Fisher to claim that he was the only Bishop of London ever to have gone to lunch at the Mansion House to be given only beer and sandwiches, a claim slightly marred by the fact that, as of habit, he did not drink the beer.

Such was one side of the matter. The administrative problems arising out of keeping a diocese running in such conditions was very much another. Fisher's power of attention to detail and indeed enjoyment of administration generally, stood him in good stead here. But he was also ably served, finding soon how much he owed to the wisdom of his suffragan bishops; Bertram Simpson, of Kensington—until his translation to Southwark in 1942—Henry Montgomery Campbell, Guy Vernon-Smith, and Robert Moberley; to his archdeacons and to Stanley Eley, later Bishop of Gibraltar, who was Diocesan Secretary and had an enormous command of the whole situation. The procedures adopted Eley recalled clearly.

'Sometime before the war, it was realised that unless there was a radical change in the political situation, we should probably have to face an upheaval of our diocese, which was bound to be the centre of activity, and also enemy activity from the skies. The consequence was that some of those responsible for the administration put their heads together and tried to see what plans could be made, so that we might face, if necessary, this complete upheaval. In 1938 there was, of course, the fear aroused by Munich. But by that time we perhaps were far from having plans as clearly made as they were twelve months later. But in early 1939, the surveyor to the Diocesan Fund and the Diocesan Secretary had many consultations as to how it would be possible to deal with war damage if it occurred, and consequently a fairly clear-cut plan for the inspection and first-aid repairs of any buildings damaged was ready to put into operation when the blitz broke out in 1940.

'With regard to the outbreak of war, here again it was felt that fairly clear direction would be necessary if the personnel of the clergy was to be properly used to the best advantage, both for the Forces and for the parishes. And so the suffragan bishops and archdeacons decided what instructions should be issued to the members of the clergy, and also what advice should be given to them as to their duty in the event of war breaking out. For example, some of the young men were told quite clearly that, if that happened, the best thing would be for them to volunteer for service with the Forces. These instructions and general directions with regard to the parishes and the personnel were all ready for dispatch about six weeks before war broke out. Meanwhile, we perfected plans as far as we could before the outbreak of real hostilities. During the quieter period, things went on reasonably and normally, during the months between September, 1939 and May, 1940. A great many of the younger men left, some of the older men, too, who happened to be chaplains to the Forces in the Territorials, and so on, and arrangements had to be made for looking after their parishes.

'Then came the blitz, and the scheme which had been put into operation immediately did, in fact, with Dr. Fisher's help and encouragement, work extremely well. The buildings were surveyed as soon as possible after the damage, first-aid repairs were put into operation, and throughout the next four years we went on—some of the things needed not once to be repaired but four or five times. One or two churches which had been almost completely brought back into full use were only in full use for a few weeks before they were practically destroyed. It was a heart-breaking experience for the Bishop and for all who were concerned in it. From the personal side, his own kindly sympathy and his fatherly care of those who were in that kind of situation were quite beyond praise. All of us who worked with him knew perfectly well that the encouragement was there, ready for us, and those of us who were unfortunate enough to suffer repeated damage to our buildings knew that our Father in God, who also suffered damage at Fulham, was fully understanding and sympathetic and willing to help in any way possible.

'Then, when we had the lull in the bombing, for a very considerable period during that time, people were thinking about how it would be possible to plan the reorganisation of the Diocese of London when the time came. When the war broke out, the general administration of the diocese from the financial and practical point of view was, I think, reasonably sound. But, of course, Bishop Winnington-Ingram had continued to rather a considerable age, and as a result some of the strings had become a little loose, and the new Bishop of London had to face a good many problems in that direction. I was concerned primarily with the prospect of what could be done after the war, in view of the great change that had taken place.

'In all of this, Dr. Fisher exhibited his extraordinary capacity for grasping almost instantaneously the detail of a thing, and the implications of it, and it was a great privilege and experience to work closely with him in all this work, because he had this eagle eye for the defective detail, which is a most valuable contribution in a chairman in work such as that.

'For example, he realised that in London it was not merely a matter for the Church of England to co-ordinate its plans and resources. It was much bigger than that. He set up what was known as the Metropolitan Area Reconstruction Committee, which included all the churches, Roman Catholic, Anglican, the Free Churches, the Salvation Army, the Jews and the Quakers. So questions of sites would be co-ordinated, and the Ministry of Works could issue licences for repairs, not on the application of any one parish, or any one church, but on the recommendation of the Committee. That sort of work Fisher encouraged continuously.'

Bertram Simpson, Bishop of Kensington and later of Southwark, one of those working closely with Fisher in those days, formed a clear picture of him. 'I think he was extremely well received from the very beginning. He was equable; I very rarely knew him to get irritated. As a man, I found the Bishop very friendly, very clear-minded and balanced. I can't remember an occasion, outside the Church Assembly, when he was really irritated or annoyed. I loved the sort of scholarly approach that he brought to things. It was, of course, entirely free from the much more sentimental attitude of his predecessor, and it was almost—and he liked to exaggerate this—the approach of a schoolmaster to his staff. But it was a very friendly headmaster and we always, I think, liked the feeling of the grip that he had on the whole situation. As soon as he really got time, after all this formal getting of things straight, and as far as allowed by the War Commissions, he began to get round the diocese, and I think he was very well received and welcomed at the various parishes to which he went. He had a clear, definite way of speaking and knew his mind. I should not have called his approach at all emotional, but with his scholarly background whatever he said was sensible and understandable, and he had a very pleasant, friendly way with the clergy as he moved among them.

'He left London a much more orderly diocese than he found it. I think the diocesan clergy, as a whole, felt very loyal to him. He was popular in a sense; but not with the popularity that a man might have achieved who made a more emotional approach to his clergy or his people. There was such a definite intellectual basis to all that he did, and I think that that may have mitigated a little the popular element of his appeal.'

Such, then, being the man and such being the extraordinary circumstances in which he was called upon to be Bishop of London, it falls now to consider some of the principal tasks which faced him there, both diocesan and in the wider field of the Church in the world.

First among the former was undoubtedly the Anglo-Catholic question. Winnington-Ingram had said that the diocese was a happy family. It was, of course, a very divided and depressed diocese in actual fact. The Anglo-Catholic group had a very firm hold. Its leaders were perfectly good in helping with the political administration of the diocese. But when it came to questions of doctrine, or the conduct of public worship, there was a fortress inside which no bishop was allowed. There was no pretence of obeying the directions of the Prayer Book, or even the Revised Prayer Book; and for many years past episcopal directions had been ignored. How was Fisher to attempt to restore some kind of respect for order and discipline? He pondered on this question. He found some few leading men, such as Dom Bernard Clements at All Saints, who were willing and even eager to co-operate with him in private to find a solution. In the end, he issued to the diocese a document in which he stated precisely what departures from the order of the Book of Common Prayer he was able to authorise as having the assent and the approval of the bishops. He also particularised two or three deviations which he had no authority to authorise; but which he would not attempt to stop as things were. This scheme was, he felt, a reasonable proposal. It had, nonetheless, little effect. The dissentients had no desire whatsoever to return to an ordered Church life. But the diocese did know that there was a norm of lawful behaviour which had the authority of its Bishop to support it, and in appointing to vacant livings, he tried to secure that where there had been extreme practices, there should be a return to those which had diocesan authority.

Such, then, was the situation on this front which faced Fisher and which he attempted to deal with by his Bishops' Regulations. It was his view that, had he been the Bishop of London for twenty years, by the end of that time he could have achieved a more orderly and homogeneous diocese, in which would have been represented the full range of legitimate freedom in the Church of England working in harmony and fellowship. But he had made only a beginning of it by the time he was called to Lambeth. Since then, the years have passed and the tide has ebbed from the controversy, for so long a cause for some and an anxiety for others. Moreover, the Rome which some Anglo-Catholics imitated has itself changed almost beyond recognition, and is in process of doing so further.

On another front altogether, Fisher found that he had to take a leading part in Convocation and in Church Assembly. As to Convocation, one of the great problems was still the marriage discipline which the Church of England ought to adopt. There had been an earlier report on this matter which had led to acute differences. The Anglo-Catholics led by Darwell Stone, of Pusey House, and N. P. Williams, then of Christ

Church, maintained that marriage was indissoluble, by which they meant that nothing on earth could possibly undo a marriage, whether solemnised in Church, or a civil marriage. There were others who argued that the word 'indissoluble' was ambiguous, and could mean either that which cannot be broken, or that which ought not to be broken, but, under due process of law, could be dissolved. There were interminable discussions on this point and on other aspects of it, for Fisher, as always, supported the view that, whatever the doctrinal aspects of the matter might be, it was beyond argument that a marriage legally contracted could, as a matter of plain common sense, be legally ended by the civil process of divorce. It was no kind of use trying to argue that it did not happen, or could not happen. This was the practical problem that the Church had to deal with, first by making it plain that it did not and could not itself divorce anyone, then that it would not itself remarry divorced people, since it held the Christian belief that marriage was for life and, thirdly, that the Church had the immediate duty of caring pastorally for people who had been divorced and had married again. It was no longer possible to distinguish between the guilty party and the innocent party in most divorces. But, more than that, any such person who looked to the Church for help ought to find sympathy and help. There were many proposals for new regulations to govern marriage discipline. But in the northern province before he left it, and in the Canterbury province, Fisher had been given the duty of reducing all the proposals to a single draft, and this draft in almost identical forms, was adopted by the two Houses of the York Convocation. But in Canterbury, while the Upper House adopted it, the Lower House refused to do so, on grounds of doctrine. In consequence, the Church of England was unable to publish any formal statement of its marriage discipline. But in both provinces, bishops and clergy did work to those resolutions and they fully justified themselves in securing a wise and helpful pastoral ministry, under which divorced persons who had married again, were in suitable cases re-admitted to communion, or admitted to Confirmation, by the bishop. It was not until twenty years later that the Lower House of Canterbury could be persuaded to reopen the discussion among themselves, and they then accepted what was in fact the discipline which the other Houses had adopted years before.

Recalling this matter after his retirement, Fisher said: 'I remember now that one of the leading Anglo-Catholic clergy maintained in the Lower House that it would be quite impossible to work a discipline by which these cases should be referred to the bishop, as no bishop would have the time or the interest to give to this kind of thing. He ought never to have made such a suggestion as he was entirely wrong. The bishops have administered this system ever since, with great care and pastoral advantage. As Archbishop, I was administering it, not only in my own diocese, but in the Forces, where I exercised the final episcopal control, and their Chaplains-in-Chief all sent their cases to me. It was most interesting and very rewarding to administer this discipline. It represented many distressing and difficult cases; but in dealing with them, sometimes by personal interview, sometimes through the clergy or chaplain, real conversions to Christian living and to Christ took place. It was a piece of pastoral work to which I gave my best attention, and in it I found great comfort.'[1]

The Convocation of Canterbury Fisher found utterly different from that of York. There was no domestic side to it at all. Every matter was discussed and debated in a full Upper House of twenty-six bishops, with no previous discussion beforehand, so that nobody could know what line any of them was going to take. When he first came to it as Bishop of London, the Upper House was a body rich in individualists with great learning and very pronounced views, such as Bishop Furse of St. Alban's, or Bishop Frere, who believed intensely in the new Canon of the 1928 Prayer Book, or the then Bishop of Norwich, Pollock, of a great legal family, who was a lawyer and a schoolmaster together (he had been headmaster of Wellington), and who opposed the 1928 Prayer Book with untiring resolution. In a rather later generation was Kenneth Kirk, Bishop of Oxford. Fisher's own comment here is perhaps revealing of himself. Of Kirk he said that: 'He was always trying to be as co-operative as he possibly could, but, on the other hand, he had very strong, clear, definite and obstinate Anglo-Catholic views, and those he would not surrender

[1] This whole question, which occupied Fisher progressively at Chester, London and Canterbury, was set forth by him in its various aspects, in an address given to a group of City men in London in 1955, and was published in the same year by S.P.C.K. under the title *Problems of Marriage and Divorce*.

at all. He once said to me, "You know, Bishop, it's a very queer thing: you and I start from opposite points of view but we generally manage somehow to come to the same conclusion." Well, that was true, because by my training and nature, I always sought to be a reconciler, seeking to take a synoptic view of every question, and to find a point where agreement was possible. Kenneth Kirk did it in another way. You could never discover quite how he got from his premises to the conclusion that was wanted, but because he was thus eirenic in principle, somehow or other he managed to do it.'

Of the Upper House, in a remark similarly self-revealing, he said: 'Lang had dominated it too much, and William Temple was a very different kind of person. He was perfectly clear on principles, but he was not really interested in the process of reducing principles to rules or regulations or clear direction. As it happened, I had always had an interest in this kind of process, and a good deal of experience in it. I think William appreciated and valued that fact and it enabled me to take some things off him. As Bishop of London, under him, I made it my duty to keep an eye upon the details of many matters, to see how conflicting details might be brought to order, and irreconcilable views brought together. It was work which exactly suited me; William Temple meanwhile, living on a higher level, spiritually and intellectually, could draw people together in seeking and finding sometimes a statement by a mere verbal alteration in a resolution which could be accepted as the right conclusion in accordance with the will of God.

'There was one time however, when he ran into trouble. The Bishop of Calcutta had asked William Temple what the attitude of the Church of England would be if his Province entered into the scheme for a United Church of South India. William Temple, typically, saw the issue in its grand proportions, and himself drafted a reply which he put before the Upper House, which did not wish to question it much. But then it had to go down to the Lower House, and there objection was made to it, typically, on the grounds that they had not drawn up the letter, nor been consulted upon it, and were being presented with a *fait accompli* as indeed they were. They consequently refused to accept responsibility for it. The situation was overcome. But it was an instance of how the Lower House, by tradition, was very ready to be distrustful of the bishops in general. There had always to be immense care in keeping the Lower House in line with the Upper.'

It is an interesting fact that three of the bishops with whom, in this context, Fisher associated much were three who were to be considered for Canterbury at the same time as himself; all of whom in their different ways were close allies of his, on whom he greatly relied in the conduct of Church affairs in Convocation and Church Assembly. One was Cyril Garbett, sometime of Southwark and Winchester, later Archbishop of York. 'While in the Canterbury Convocation,' Fisher recalled, 'as Bishop of Winchester, he did not take very much part. I don't think he was, by nature, a committee man at all. He would listen to the debate; when he spoke, it was in a fine, magisterial way, giving a view clearly and decisively spoken, and always one carrying great weight. It was equally so in the Church Assembly. But very soon he went up to York, and then the two who stood out in the Canterbury Convocation were George Bell and Mervyn Haigh. George Bell was quite indefatigable.[1] The care that he showed about everything; and his resource in accumulating documentary evidence as to the past of the matter for a long time back; his knowledge of the whole of the inner secrets of Davidson's reign, gave him an immense command of every subject. So equipped, he generally had in his mind the solution to any question before it was debated, and the solution already thought out in great detail. This he would work for, and if he was unsuccessful, he would often "go underground" and still keep it among his active purposes, and, as soon as he saw an opportunity a year, or two, or three years later, up it would come again. This was a characteristic of his that we all knew. One could never be sure that George Bell had dropped an idea for which he had failed to win general approval.

'There were many examples of this. I remember one in which I had great sympathy for him. Trying to bring good order and obedience to lawful authority in his own diocese, as I did in London, he produced, after immense thought and negotiation, what he thought was a reasonable settlement, and put it before a group of leading Anglo-Catholics. They, of whom there were many in Bell's diocese, included some very able and

[1] George Bell, Bishop of Chichester, 1929–1958.

devoted and obstinate men. Those of this group flatly said no; and it almost broke George Bell's heart. I'm told he almost burst into tears when he found that this was so.

'What a devoted man he was; how full of imagination! He had something of the poet in him. He encouraged Masefield and T. S. Eliot and others to produce the Canterbury Festival of Plays when he was Dean there. He was immensely interested in all kinds of things where he thought the Church could take a lead, and develop artistic or literary abilities. In his sympathies, he was always young and idealistic, and with it all he was a most lovable man.'

Less well known to the general public was Mervyn Haigh: 'An absolutely golden person in his own line. He, of course, had worked with George Bell as Chaplain at Lambeth. He had a very acute mind; analytical rather than constructive. But his powers of analytical judgment were quite extraordinary. He was heart and soul with anybody who tried to do something of an evangelistic kind, because in his own heart he was, above all, a pastoral and evangelistic person. But when it came to the politics of the Church, while he could analyse the problem, he found it difficult to back any situation—even his own tentative one—because he could see flaws in it. At Bishops' Meetings, he would get up and tear some proposal under discussion to pieces, and very often it deserved to be so treated. That was one reason why he was so valued by us all. And yet, having got to the end of his destructive speech, he would say: "Well, what we ought to do I really don't know," and would leave us thus, in the air. It was always a joy to listen to him, because he was so brilliant and so competent. We would all wait to see what Mervyn Haigh would say. If his criticism was only mild and gentle, I knew then that the thing was all right and likely to go through. But if it was destructive, it meant a battle of wits and much searching thought. But he was so winning and gracious, so spiritually devoted, that the whole thing was always a joy, a joy of achievement, or the joy of a worthwhile battle.

'It is perhaps a sidelight of his character that latterly he devoted himself almost entirely to the revision of the lectionary, a tedious and detailed thing. He had a precise knowledge of almost every Sunday lesson; why they were what they were, and why they were better than some other alternative. After a time with his committee, he produced a lectionary containing Scheme A and Scheme B, for use in alternate years. Then there were revisions of Scheme A and revisions of Scheme B. When finally he had to retire through extreme ill-health, the task was handed over to the then Bishop of Chelmsford, and his committee in a year and a half produced a result which he wished to recommend to the Church as a final answer. He had brought the committee to a final conclusion after a year and a half, when Mervyn Haigh had become more and more involved in interminable amendments and revisions. It is astonishing that he gave his great abilities so wholeheartedly to such a frustrating and limited task. And since then, the Lower House of Canterbury has, I believe, rejected the scheme finally proposed and sent it back to a new committee.'

In the Church Assembly, while Bishop of London, Fisher became in his own phrase, 'a sort of watchdog for the maintenance of a general common sense view of things, intervening in debates less to make any set speech than to help to keep the debate in the right direction and likely to lead to the right conclusion'. He was, however, involved in one major project. He knew, better than any other diocesan, in view of the experience through which his London parishes had been, how important and difficult reconstruction after the war could be. The Church Assembly appointed a committee, of which Fisher was chairman, to produce a scheme for dealing with all the complications of reconditioning and re-organising areas devastated by war damage. One or two of its main results have had lasting effects upon the Church's organisation. This committee saw that, in some areas, it would be necessary to amalgamate parishes, or rearrange them without regard to the old boundaries. This meant that the money and the incomes would have to be redirected as well. This, in its turn, involved problems of patronage. The proposals, comprehensively worked out, were put before the Church Assembly. They included another proposal which has become a permanent feature of Church administration, and altered altogether the Church Commissioners' dealings with the dioceses in financial matters. In order to take monies away from separate parishes, and redistribute them, each diocese was to hold and manage its own diocesan fund, into which the Church Commissioners would pay monies due to their parishes, to be administered according to the Commissioners' directions. This was to replace a system under which the Commissioners kept complete control of, and made their grants directly to parishes. It created an invaluable relation of co-operation between the Commissioners and the dioceses, and gave the dioceses a responsibility and a prestige such as they had not had before.

It was said, and with some truth, that a few dioceses had not the staff or the diocesan secretary capable of dealing with the considerable financial responsibilities imposed upon them. But the committee pressed on, saying that if this were so, then the diocese must get the competent persons. It fell to Fisher as chairman to produce this new and very complicated measure before the Assembly. It took him an hour and a quarter to expound it and he never forgot that, at the end, William Temple, in the chair, said that they had all listened to this exposition with rapt attention, and that he had never heard a clearer exposition of a complicated business.

On the other hand, one member of the Assembly, Lord Hugh Cecil, did not like it at all. He made a point of securing that it should never apply to any group of parishes unless it was quite obvious that the extent of the war damage had made the old existing system really unworkable. Thus, as far as possible, it became necessary to secure that there was a real war damage case for applying the Reorganisation Areas Measure. But, more than that, he disliked and denounced the morality of what was being proposed because it meant taking property away from the parishes to which it belonged and transferring it, or redistributing it, among others. This was against the first principle of his moral code: so that Fisher heard himself being denounced by Cecil, in the Assembly, for proposing to violate the Ten Commandments. This speech was much enjoyed; but had no further effect. Thus was initiated a completely new chapter in Church organisation.

Another matter which much occupied Fisher in London was his chairmanship of the Churches' Main War Damage Committee, already described by Stanley Eley. The detail of administration involved, as always, was much to Fisher's taste. But the work, on a national scale, had one important and lasting consequence in that, through the War Damage Commission, it brought him into contact with Malcolm Trustram Eve, now Lord Silsoe, who was its chairman. It was out of this contact that

Fisher saw that Trustram Eve, whose family had for long rendered expert services to the Church's administration, might be brought into the service of the Church. He consented to become first Church Estates Commissioner of the Ecclesiastical Commissioners (soon to become the Church Commissioners) in a time when that body was to pass through many changes as regards tailoring of its operations to suit modern conditions.

A further important aspect of this particular labour was that it gave Fisher opportunity for close working with representatives of all the churches of this country including the Roman Catholic. There was the utmost goodwill throughout the whole procedure. On the committee was the Bishop of Pella, a Roman Catholic subsidiary bishop in the diocese of Southwark. Fisher especially remembered the Baptist representative; he was most co-operative and friendly. Even so, when all were agreed that such was the right thing for all the churches to do, this man, Fairbairn, would say, in all meekness, that he was sorry to have to point out that he could not commit any single church of his own denomination on any points, because each church settled it for itself. Even so, this committee under Fisher's chairmanship moved along in harmony, and did an invaluable service to the Churches and indeed to the War Damage Commission also. From time to time they had to go to Malcolm Trustram Eve to get a ruling on some important point. These were occasions which greatly appealed to Fisher. He especially remembered one.

'I cannot recall what the particular point was, but we had studied the War Damage Act with meticulous care and we came to a clear conclusion that, under a certain clause, we could claim for all our churches such and such compensations. We went to the War Damage Commission and stated the case at length, and with scrupulous accuracy and, as we thought, had proved our case to the hilt. But Malcolm Trustram Eve, when I finished, said: "Now, may I say something?" He then would take my case and tear it to pieces, and show that it was quite impossible for us to expect to get any money at all under the clause on which we had built our case. When we were all feeling completely flattened, he would say: "But I think you've failed to notice clause so-and-so, in another part of the Act, and I think, under that clause, you could very well put forward a case.'' He would then, in fact, give us more under the clause we had forgotten, than we could ever have hoped to get under the clause we had chosen for ourselves. I remember saying, after one visit to the War Damage Commission, that it was exactly like being back at school, because, as soon as Trustram Eve began to expound, I would take my notebook out and write down his analysis of the situation, and his argument, with the greatest possible care. We were exactly in the position of schoolboys before a very expert master.'

Meanwhile, the seeds of other developments in the field of Church finance were being planted at this time. Fisher was Archbishop by the time they came to fruition. But they may be mentioned here, if out of chronological order, because they are closely associated with that review and modernisation of the Church's structure which was to be among the notable, if sometimes overlooked, features of his archiepiscopate, and for which his experience in London was so valuable a preparation.

One of these developments was the amalgamation of Queen Anne's Bounty with the Ecclesiastical Commissioners to form the Church Commissioners for England. The actual consummation did not in fact take place until 1948. But the gradual steps taken towards it have their own particular interest, illustrating as they do the fact that almost any excavation beneath an English institution is likely soon to come upon traces of a Dickensian world, bearing marked resemblances to *The Old Curiosity Shop*, with an occasional trace of that mysterious Doctors' Commons in *Bleak House*, whose functions and operations were alike wrapped in mystery. Fisher's account of this amalgamation tends to bear out this observation.

'There were two bodies; the Ecclesiastical Commissioners, vast in their responsibilities and their powers and responsible to Parliament, and Queen Anne's Bounty, a funny little body to which Queen Anne had given the first fruits, for the use of poor livings. This body was as much like Dickens as anything I've ever known. We met and spent a great deal of time giving away sums of about ten pounds, or fifteen pounds, or at the most, twenty pounds, to one parish or another. Each case was scrupulously investigated and reported upon, and there were things called the Gilbert Acts which I never understood, but our officials understood it all and would, with meticulous care, argue why ten pounds was more justified to one parish than another. It was indeed a most extraordinary procedure. But there was an old-fashioned loveliness about it that I much enjoyed. Baker-Wilbraham, with others, conceived the idea of amalgamating the Ecclesiastical Commissioners, as they then were, and Q.A.B. How was the idea received? The Commissioners were under the control, or rather the direction, of Sir James Brown as he now is, then the secretary to the Commissioners, an absolutely superb man, wonderfully clear in mind and rich in spirit. He at once saw that this was essential. Yet, in a way, he was the chief obstacle because he was so good that everybody in Q.A.B. knew that if there was an amalgamation, Q.A.B. would have to pass under his leadership. At that, of course, all the proper self-respect of the Q.A.B. rose in rebellion. The situation was very interesting indeed. The old secretary at Q.A.B., a very wise old man and just retiring, was in favour of the idea: his successor was not. But in the Q.A.B. office, a very brilliant man named Warren, with a genius for financial administration, saw that amalgamation was vital. Baker-Wilbraham, with Sir James Brown and Warren, finally brought the thing to completion. It was a complicated process; but they won through and I backed them in every conceivable way I could. And so the Ecclesiastical Commissioners and Q.A.B. disappeared, and the Church Commissioners took their place. Sir James Brown became the first secretary, and he in due course was succeeded by Warren, both of them magnificent servants of the Church.'

There was also another matter of much importance in this sphere, with no trace of Dickens about it at all, which began to emerge in these years. After the amalgamation, as Fisher put it: 'the general financial policy of the Church Commissioners was under review. The traditional pattern was that all the Commissioners' money was invested in gilt-edged securities. That was all very well for a peaceful world; but it was quite impossible for the world in which we were living. It was, I think Malcolm Trustram Eve who first ventilated the idea that the Commissioners ought to invest some of their money in Equities. Philip Baker-Wilbraham was a splendid man. He was a Fellow of All Souls and a barrister—he never practised—and a country gentleman and one of the salt of the earth. He was very cautious. I remember that he pondered this idea of Equity investment, and then said that perhaps it would be right if not more than twenty per cent of our invested money was put into Equities, and that is where we began the revolution without which the incomes of the clergy would have stayed where they were—pitifully inadequate even then.'

Another concern of Fisher's London days, of an entirely different nature, was his association with the Sword of the Spirit movement, founded in August 1940 by Cardinal Hinsley, Archbishop of Westminster.[1] Bell of Chichester, with characteristic ardour, had from the beginning seen in this not only a matter for admiration, but also for emulation, and had striven to broaden the ecumenical basis of the movement, which began in practice as a purely Roman Catholic enterprise. Interdenominational meetings on 10 and 11 May 1941, the first chaired by the Cardinal, the second by Archbishop Lang, marked the high-water point of this aspect of the affair. Thereafter, however, it became clear that the Roman authorities were not prepared to merge their movement with other churches on a national basis. Bell, however, continued his efforts, seeking support from the Commission of the Churches for International Friendship and Social Responsibility. It was at a meeting of this body that Fisher proposed that 'five members of the Commission—including Bell—be appointed to confer with representatives of the Sword of the Spirit on the possibilities of co-operation; but the form which such co-operation might take was left completely open'.[2]

One result was that a joint committee was established, with Fisher as chairman. There were to be no joint religious services: but co-operation was to be fostered outside those bounds. Before the end of 1942, such co-operative activity had made promising beginnings. But Hinsley's death in 1943 was a sad blow to it, and thereafter the tide of co-operation, for the time being, ebbed. Fisher's account of the matter was succinct:

'I'd worked on a small committee, of which I was chairman, with

---

[1] 'His avowed aim was to unite all men of goodwill—not simply Roman Catholics—in a crusade of prayer, study and action for the restoration of a Christian order of justice and peace. Totalitarian systems, which undermined human society and Christian civilisation were therefore to be opposed, and the Five Peace Points of Pius XII were to be regarded as essential elements in any post-war peace settlement.'—R. C. D. Jasper, *George Bell* (O.U.P.).
[2] *Ibid.*

representatives of the Sword of the Spirit, and we had a grand time. We talked about everything, and we finally produced a document on "Co-operation". Bill Paton was one of the members, and the editor of *The Tablet*, Woodroffe, was another. It was a very high-powered body of the British Council of Churches and the Sword of the Spirit, and the document "Co-operation", was merely putting into words the sort of thing that can happen when two churches try to establish some simple forms of inter-communion. Father Murray, a Roman Catholic priest on the committee, said this must go to Westminster Cathedral to be submitted to the theologians there, and it went. We never heard another word. From time to time, I would enquire what had happened to it, and I was told only that the Roman Catholic theologians had not made any reply. And so the whole thing sank, without any result. That was a great disappointment.'

Then there occurred that event which altered everything. William Temple, under whose vast and beneficent shadow so many promising enterprises had been growing, died, with shattering suddenness and unexpectedness, in the October of 1944. In a moment, among many other things which were altered, Fisher's future was changed utterly. Of that possibility, when the news reached him, he had no thought. How he was in the House of Lords at the time, and how he went to kneel alone in the Bishops' Room there, has already been told. 'I think I was there for an hour,' he said long afterwards, 'not thinking about anything at all, but just trying to assimilate myself to a completely changed world, and a completely changed Church. I wasn't even trying to console myself. I was just numbly waiting for feeling to return. I can say no more about that loss.'

There followed a long, and for Fisher, an unsettled period. Meanwhile, he could not but know that his was one of the names that had been talked about as a possible successor to Temple. The prospect did not alarm him. He had succeeded Temple once before, after all, at Repton. But that was long ago, and this was a very different matter. Even so, he had, as he put it, 'never bothered about being frightened, or not frightened, about any job. If it was mine to do, I had to do it with full courage and reasonable confidence in God.' On the other hand, he certainly was not wanting the primacy. He was very happy in London and would gladly have gone on there for the rest of his episcopate, for there were endless opportunities, endless problems, as well as endlessly lovable people, clergy and laity, in that great diocese. But now he had to wait on what might happen.

Garbett of York used to come and stay at Fulham whenever he came to London, and the two men would talk about the situation, wondering what would happen. 'I said,' Fisher recalled, 'on one occasion, that I had no desire for it at all, that I should hate it, amongst other things because I hate by nature having to make public pronouncements of one kind or another upon any kind of question. I am by nature a pastoral person, a person who likes to find a way to a solution by personal contacts, and personal discussions with people, trying to help them to some commonly acceptable and creative and constructive conclusion. Because of that, I was a good committee man. Nothing has ever pleased me more than the entrancing work of presiding over a committee. I had always had a clear idea, or almost always, of which direction to go in. But my job then was to get everybody else on the committee working and thinking about the matter, and making suggestions, and seeing which of them could live and which couldn't, and so generally proceeding until something like a common conclusion began to emerge. Having got something like a common conclusion, then my interest was always to get it translated onto paper, into words and clauses, into some document, or some draft measure, something which was concrete and could be dealt with concretely, putting an end to discursive discussions about general principles and vague generalities. That was how I liked to work. The one thing I did not like was pronouncements, the sort of thing one has to say on one's own authority, as one's own final judgment or, still worse, on one's own exhortation. I said I couldn't face that, and Cyril said he hated the idea equally; he said that he did not want to be Archbishop; because he was too old for it; and he said that, like me, he hated pronouncements. I don't believe that was quite true. In fact, he rather liked laying down a clear and decisive guidance for the Church on this matter or the other. But there we were; we talked about it quite openly, and each of us decided that we would be well content if the other was appointed as Archbishop.'

Meanwhile, another potential Archbishop of Canterbury was

undoubtedly on the scene, George Bell of Chichester. As to that matter, his biographer has important things to say—important in that, among other things, they go a long way towards dispelling the idea, current at the time, that somehow an injustice had been done by not appointing to Canterbury this notable figure.

'There is no doubt that his speeches on the war had destroyed his chances of succeeding to the Primacy. Dr. A. C. Don, who had been Lang's chaplain at Lambeth, wrote in his diary, "The Prime Minister admires courage and deplores indiscretion; and George has been both courageous and indiscreet in his speeches about the war." The fact remains, however, that his speeches have made a great impression on the Continent, and he was the only bishop except Temple who was really known in Europe. It might be argued that, since Temple's politics had not affected his preferment, why should Bell's? But the men themselves were not easily comparable. Bell had a distinctive position of his own—markedly so among his fellow bishops—and he was well liked. His long experience of Lambeth, his great knowledge of detail and his constant readiness to place them both at the disposal of others, made him a recognised "court of appeal" in many fields. But in those places in England where impressions counted for so much—in the House of Lords, in Convocation and in the Church Assembly—he had not that kind of mastery which was Temple's or, for that matter, Garbett's. He was pertinacious; but his pertinacity could grow to a point at which his influence on others suffered —he could appear to be just obstinate, or harbouring bees in his bonnet. The question would then be asked, "Is it really wise to have such a man at Lambeth?" . . . In some quarters, too, his judgment of people was regarded as suspect. Admittedly, he was constantly on the alert for brilliant and perhaps unusual people, who could make some fresh and distinctive contribution to the life of the Church. But such people were not always well suited for the tasks they were expected to undertake. There was the case of Professor N. P. Williams and his work on Church–State relations: he proved to be a stimulating colleague and his influence on Bell was real. Yet did not Bell take rather too long to discover Williams' propensity for treading on other men's toes? It is doubtful, therefore, whether Canterbury would have proved to be his happiest destination; and the added weight of archiepiscopal burdens might well have reduced his effectiveness in other spheres, particularly in the creation and development of the World Council of Churches.'[1]

And so Bell was left in Chichester; but not Fisher in London. There came a day when he was summoned to No. 10 Downing Street to lunch with the Prime Minister, Winston Churchill. There, in that historic house, where so much had happened in the last five years, and where the war-room far beneath was still in operation, the two of them sat alone. 'It was a funny lunch,' Fisher remembered. 'He was obviously not at all at ease; I was certainly not. But we got on very contentedly and talked about many things, including religion. I remember he said to me at one point something about Renan's *Vie de Jésus*, and I said that I had never read it. He said, "What, you've never read it!" It was for him quite unthinkable that any educated person should not have read a very liberal book which he had read when he was a young man. I'd read other "liberal" books; but not that one. As I say, we had a very happy time, but in fact his experience of life and mine had not much overlapped; and I think probably he said to himself at the end, "Well, presumably he'll have to do!"'

This supposition of Churchill's opinion of him, so characteristic of the unassuming humility never far behind the public face of Fisher, was not, as will be seen, to be borne out by the facts of what will surely come to be regarded as an historic primacy. In any event, the two had cordial relationships with each other always, if little in common. That was perhaps inevitable. At Churchill's death, by which time Fisher himself had retired to a country parsonage, Fisher said, speaking in his little church, that Churchill 'had a very real religion, but it was a religion of the Englishman. He had a very real belief in Providence; but it was God as the God with a special care for the values of the British people. There was nothing obscure about this; it was utterly sincere, but not really at all linked on to the particular beliefs which constitute the Christian faith and the life which rests on it.'

Thus it was done, and the name of the ninety-ninth Archbishop of Canterbury, Primate of All England, Geoffrey Francis Fisher, was

[1] *Op. cit.*

released on 2 January 1945. Shortly afterwards, Henry Montgomery Campbell, later to be himself Bishop of London, welcomed the new archbishop in a B.B.C. broadcast.

'Listeners who heard the Bishop of London's tribute to William Temple on the night of the Archbishop's death will feel that a worthy successor has been found for that great office. It was generally acclaimed as worthy of the great man we had lost, as nearly perfect as maybe both in matter and manner. Not only did that broadcast tell us something of William Temple, it also revealed much of the speaker, too, a mind of deep understanding capable of intimate affection and spiritual appreciation. That is not the side of the Bishop of London that most ordinarily appears; but it would be a great mistake to suppose that in the new Archbishop of Canterbury there is any lack of that important element.

'The ordinary individual who meets the Bishop of London in the House of Lords, at the Mansion House, or at some parochial function in the diocese of London finds at first a most agreeable companion, one who is interested in anything and everything, not in the least anxious to talk about his own business, still less about himself. Next he discovers an extremely acute mind, critical to a degree if the man he is talking to does not know his facts, or draws the wrong conclusions from them. Then if he is fortunate enough to be treading on the Bishop's own ground he will find probably the most lucid exponent he has ever met.

'But these are only his side lines. His business is to be a bishop in the Church of God and his commission is (I quote from the service for the Consecration of Bishops) to be to the flock of Christ a shepherd: "Hold up the weak, heal the sick, bind up the broken, bring again the outcasts, seek the lost". Such are the words addressed to a newly-consecrated bishop, and they will ring in the ears of the newest Archbishop. A shepherd—there is no more beautiful or more accurate word to describe the Christian ministry. Geoffrey Fisher has been a shepherd to boys at Marlborough and Repton, to the diocese of Chester with its villages and its Merseyside, to the diocese of London, the most important diocese in the Anglican communion, and now he is called to be Archbishop of Canterbury, the most important office in that Communion. He will still be a humble shepherd, and London at least can say of his too brief episcopate there what the psalmist said of David: "So he fed them with a faithful and true heart: and ruled them prudently with all his power."'

And so the London years, like those of Repton, like those of Chester, faded into the past. In London, as Roger Lloyd put it much later, 'He had not lost a friend, or made an enemy.' That, all things considered, was in itself no small achievement. And now much greater achievements and much greater events lay ahead.

PART TWO

VI

The Chair of St. Augustine

The stresses within the Church of England, so far as they are due to
tensions between divine truths imperfectly integrated by men, are signs
of truthfulness and of health. They may easily enough be allowed to
cause a confusion of voices. But it is the conviction and the justification
of the Church of England that Christ means us to essay this difficult
comprehension, to hold together, within our communion of the catholic
church what may not be put asunder without grievous injury, and to
present, as far as we may, the wholeness of the Gospel of Christ.

> G.F.F. in his enthronement sermon, Canterbury Cathedral,
> 19 April 1945

．　　．　　．

Much has always depended on the personal qualities and attainments of
the individual Primate. But the course of these last fifty years, more I
think than that of the fifty years preceding, shows that while the
prestige of the institution may have waned, the character and gifts of the
person count for more and more.

> G. K. A. Bell, in the preface to the third edition (1952) of
> *Randall Davidson, Archbishop of Canterbury* (O.U.P.)

．　　．　　．

The job is really impossible for one man, yet only one man can do it.

> J. G. Lockhart, *Cosmo Gordon Lang* (Hodder and Stoughton)

T HE weather of Thursday, 19 April 1945, the feast of St. Alphege,
Archbishop of Canterbury and Martyr, was bright and clear. Press
photographs, taken outside the Cathedral as the various processions
arrived for the enthronement of the ninety-ninth archbishop, show a sun
strong enough to throw shadows, and dapple onto distinguished people
passing between them the outline of trees in spring leaf outside the
Old Palace adjoining the Cathedral. To the West Door came these processions, while the orchestra of the British Broadcasting Corporation played

within, from one fifteen onwards. So, at one thirty, came the Vice-Chancellor of Oxford, the Vice-Chancellor of London, the Warden of All Souls, the Rector of Exeter, the Master of Marlborough, the Headmaster of Repton. Then there was a pause, and then a second procession, representatives of His Majesty's Forces and of the Forces of the United States. A third, wondrously garbed, was made up of the Coronation Barons and Officers of the Cinque Ports, the mayors of boroughs within the Diocese of Canterbury, the Lord Mayor of London and the Mayor of Canterbury. A fourth followed, consisting of representatives of His Majesty's Government, the Lord Chancellor and members of the Cabinet. (One picture of this shows Lord Woolton and a very young-looking Duncan Sandys.) After them came the Lord Lieutenant of Kent with his Company and, last of all, the Canterbury Gospels, very precious, traditionally supposed to have been presented by Gregory the Great to St. Augustine. Carried on a cushion by the Master of Corpus Christi College, Cambridge, to which they belong, they were ready for the new archbishop to take his oath upon them. After that, at one forty-five precisely, the Members of the Foundation went out to the Old Palace to conduct Geoffrey Francis Fisher to the West Door. He was ready for them, splendidly vested in cope and mitre, with his chaplain, the Rev. Ian White-Thomson, now Dean of Canterbury.

And then, when the new archbishop reached the West Door, they opened, the trumpets sounded, all the people stood and, in a procession of great magnificence, the Lord Archbishop went up through nave and choir to the high altar, while the trumpets sounded a second time, and the choir sang the forty-sixth Psalm, 'God Is Our Hope And Strength'. Before the high altar Fisher knelt and, after the singing of a prayer for grace, he rose, and the Dean, having taken the pastoral staff therefrom, placed it in his left hand. It was a moment of great significance, especially, perhaps, for those who had seen the same staff, on that sombre day of Temple's funeral, taken from his coffin and placed on the altar. Now there was another archbishop, and the service went forward through its time-honoured ritual of enthronement, culminating in the actual moment of his being placed, by the Dean, in the Chair of St. Augustine, outside the screen regally overlooking the people in Canterbury's splendid nave. And so it was done, the trumpets sounded again, and the whole congregation sang:

> Now thank we all our God,
> With hearts and hands and voices.

It was a happy day. If Fisher felt any of the strain of it, he certainly did not show any, and this impression of complete ease and dignity, with cheerfulness as usual breaking in, is borne out by the press pictures of the occasion, which show the central figure, as regards manner and bearing, quite devoid of what a former age might have called prelatical pomp. The family pictures taken at the time are understandably cheerful, too. It was the first occasion for a number of years when all the six Fisher sons were together. Four of them were in uniform, home from the wars, and the press clearly found a matter of interest in an archbishop who was so obviously a family man. It was a long time indeed since there had been one.

And so, that happy day passed. It remained for the new archbishop to get down to the tasks facing him. They were many and complex, as was to be expected.

It is surely doubtful if any of his predecessors had ever faced anything quite like the situation, at home and abroad, which Fisher had before him. The war in Europe was less than a month from its end by the day of his enthronement; but it left a Europe in ruins. Japan surrendered the following August, leaving much of Asia shattered, and the whole world knowing for the first time that it had henceforth and for ever to live with the Bomb. Between these two events, there had been in Britain the return of a Labour government in July, destined to bring about profound social changes. Everywhere foundations were shaken, and continued to shake as, indeed, they still do. Fisher's primacy was also to be co-terminous with sunset upon an empire upon which, at one time, it had been said that the sun never did set. Everywhere, throughout his time, there was to be change, if not necessarily decay. Thus it is exactly true that 'he had to operate for long years in a jaded, frightened and uneasy world in which the years of terrible suffering had spent all passions but one, the desperate search for some unity of man to establish real peace, and in which each person might at last find some answer to the perplexing riddles of his own identity'.[1]

As to the nature and work of an Archbishop of Canterbury, two approaches to some description of it seem possible; the one from the outside, touching upon the subject with the gravity and formality of those portraits of archbishops which look down from the walls of Lambeth. The second, from the inside, counterbalances these tendencies, helping to humanise the subject and to show the man as he was in the circumstances as they were. The one difficulty in the way of this inside view has hitherto been that, by the time the tale came to be told, the man himself was no longer present to convey this personal aspect of it. Fortunately, this has not been the case with this narrative.

Even so, the outside, impersonal view of an archbishop's work and position in the modern world is of much importance. Over the years, they have altered much. Few have written more succinctly of these changes than George Bell of Chichester, in the preface to the third edition of his classic biography of Randall Davidson. And though he does not mention Fisher by name, the matters to which he refers have as direct a bearing on his tenure of the office as they have to those of whom Bell does speak; Davidson, Lang and Temple. Bell begins, in his preface, by contrasting the pomps of the past with the realities of the present, as he knew it. Thus, of Archbishop Howley, who died in 1848, he wrote that 'He was the last Prince Archbishop of Canterbury. When he dined out, no one left the room till he rose to go. At the public banquets at Lambeth, "the domestics of the Prelate stood, with swords and bag-wigs, round pig and turkey and venison". He drove abroad in a coach-and-four, and when he crossed the courtyard of Lambeth Palace from the chapel to "Mrs. Howley's Lodgings" he was preceded by men bearing flambeaux. How different from the picture of William Temple, touring the parishes of Croydon on a summer evening with Mrs. Temple, in his chaplain's little car, as the bombs exploded, or sleeping on a sofa in a ground-floor passage at Lambeth during the air-raids of 1944!' The same could certainly be said of Fisher, who succeeded to a Lambeth Palace which, by 1945, was virtually a bomb-shattered wreck.

[1] Roger Lloyd, *The Church of England, 1900–1965.*

There had also been marked changes, by the Fisher's time, in domestic staff and income to maintain them. Lady Fisher, writing of the restoration of Lambeth Palace, a gigantic task, recalled that: 'We had two resident domestics who came with us to Lambeth from Fulham Palace, and we were fortunate to be able to have the help of the gardener's wife, Mrs. Wright, and a Mrs. Berry who, with her husband, had for many years been housekeeper and caretaker of the Lollards' Tower rooms. They had now moved out, owing to the bomb damage and were living at Streatham. When we came to Lambeth, the gate-keeper was still Mr. Woodward, who had been appointed in Archbishop Davidson's time. It should be remembered that, up to Archbishop Fisher's time, each succeeding arch-bishop was himself the landlord of the Palace, and out of his income bore all the expenses of its upkeep. In former times, when taxation was negli-gible and wages low, it was possible to maintain a very large staff and live on a grand scale. We were told that the Davidsons employed over forty people; butler and three footmen, valet, lady's maid, housekeeper, cook and four kitchen and scullery-maids, two still-room maids, eight house-maids, five laundry-maids, a night-watchman, carpenter, coachman, grooms and gardeners. Mrs. Davidson rode in the park on most days. By the time we came to Lambeth, taxation was reducing the income to barely a quarter, and wages and all other expenses had increased in proportion as the net income decreased.'

Thus had the outward splendours of the primacy diminished. Perhaps it had ebbed to its lowest point, as regards Lambeth Palace itself, the scene of so many splendours in days past, by the time of a visit paid to Lang by Bell on a July evening of 1941. 'I arrived at Lambeth at 6.45 on a hot July evening. Walking in, and looking about, I found the Archbishop, a solitary old figure, moving about in Miss Fuller's room, only the chaplain's room (my old room) and her room were available now. He explained that this was all he had, and he slept in the basement. Out for meals, dinner at the Atheneum, except that he had tea brought to him in the morning. Obviously, no settled place, Ichabod! Later, he took me round the Palace to show the chief bomb damage. Desolation and disorder hardly conceiv-able.'[1]

[1] Quoted in R. C. D. Jasper's *George Bell*.

Meanwhile, the sheer volume of the work required of an Archbishop of Canterbury had been increasing as the pomps of his position decreased. To quote Bell again: 'The contrast between the last Prince Archbishop and his modern successors may also be seen by a comparison of their correspondence; though something must be allowed for the personal characteristics of an archbishop, as well as for the introduction of the typewriter. "In Archbishop Howley's days" (writes Mr. George Lipscoomb, a porter at Lambeth for forty-two years) "the General Postman, dressed in bright scarlet, brought the country letters every morning, and came round again at five o'clock in the evening to collect the letters. He went to the front door, ringing in his hands a heavy bell to give notice of his coming. He had a guinea a quarter from the Palace. The general-post letters in the morning for the Archbishop and Mrs. Howley were put into a china bowl in the hall. There were scarcely enough to cover the bottom of it. When the Archbishop was at Addington, and I had to forward the letters there I could put, as a rule, all the letters of the day, servants' included, in a medium-size envelope." In 1912, excluding the immense number of official and legal letters, that part of Archbishop Davidson's personal correspondence which was carefully filed at the close of each year consisted usually of about six hundred and fifty or seven hundred sets of subjects, any one of which might comprise perhaps ten or twenty, or even fifty, letters. And by 1928, anything from seventy to a hundred letters were posted from Lambeth each day, in addition to the private correspondence.'

What these seventy or a hundred letters of 1928 had become by 1945 and subsequent years is anybody's guess. The only one which may be made with confidence is that the number had increased, while to the pressures of correspondence had been added, and in Fisher's time continued to develop, the demands of radio, television, and long-distance travel. It was as well that Fisher was a prodigious worker, with a convenient expertise in the use of tape. It was not unknown for him to begin dictation to a tape on a Saturday afternoon in his study at Lambeth, and continue solidly at it throughout any Sunday that might be comparatively disengaged. Secretaries arriving on Monday morning would find tapes awaiting them which required perhaps a full week to clear. In this connection, there is a true story to be told. At a time when there was a number of bishops staying in the Hostel at Lambeth Palace for the Church Assembly, they were assembled one morning for Matins in the small temporary chapel which served till the historic chapel was restored. The Archbishop was reading the Old Testament lesson which ended: '. . . Rachael weeping for her children, and would not be comforted'. 'Yours sincerely', said the Archbishop, lapsing into letter-dictation. Somehow they restrained themselves until the service was over, and then dissolved in helpless laughter, and it was said that for the rest of the day inside the Church Assembly and outside, these bishops, singly or in groups, were observed, for no apparent reason, to burst into fresh paroxysms, muttering through their gasps: '. . . and would not be comforted. Yours sincerely.'

However, to return to the matter of changes in the functions and position of the Primate in modern times, it may be noted that Bell, in his preface, stresses the importance of the relationships of twentieth century archbishops with the Crown and with the State, notably with successive Prime Ministers, variable though these relationships were as circumstances and personalities changed. The point he is making is that the Primate of All England has to have contacts with, and be active in both these fields, quite apart from having 'the care of all the churches'. He continues:

'I have said nothing of relationships with foreign countries or their rulers or statesmen. But one of the most striking features in these forty-one years is the growing significance of the Archbishop of Canterbury in the international field. All three archbishops counted increasingly here, not only at home but abroad. Archbishop Davidson took an active part in the international developments which followed the First World War. Archbishop Lang was sharply attacked in Germany and Japan for his public pronouncements between the wars. President Roosevelt testified to King George VI of Archbishop Temple that "as an ardent advocate of international co-operation based on Christian principles, he exercised profound influence throughout the world".'

Bell then makes the point that the Church Assembly, under the chairmanship of successive archbishops, has made them 'familiar to the people of the Church of England in a way impossible before'.

That was most certainly true of Fisher, who relished the Assembly and rarely missed a meeting. Bell also makes the point that the 'moral authority of the Archbishop over the bench of bishops has greatly increased'. Few would deny this of Lang, at least, even if the manner in which the authority was exercised might sometimes have been rather formidable. There was an occasion, as Fisher recalled, when he and William Temple, no less, appeared, under a misapprehension as to the time, at half-past ten for a meeting which had been called for ten. When Temple apologised, saying: 'We are sorry, Your Grace; but we thought the meeting was at ten thirty', Lang's reply was: 'You have no right to think!' Such imperiousness did not always find acceptance, and Lang's effect on the American bishops at the Lambeth Conference of 1930 was not, in fact, of a nature to justify Bell's remark, also in this same preface, that 'the tact and wisdom which Archbishops Davidson and Lang displayed while on the throne of St. Augustine, especially at successive Lambeth Conferences and in various ways . . . have materially increased the influence and prestige of the Archbishop of Canterbury with the whole Anglican episcopate'.

Next, Bell draws attention to the manner in which 'the three Archbishops of Canterbury have rendered outstanding service to their Church in the realm of Christian unity. Relations between the leaders of the Church of England and the leaders of the Free Church in England were transformed in this period, most of all as a result of the *Appeal to all Christian People,* issued by the Lambeth Conference of 1920. All three archbishops were active in this work, although less has actually followed from the prolonged conferences on church relations than many hoped. Archbishop Temple did a notable service in connection with the inauguration of the British Council of Churches in 1942. Again, many new contacts have been made with foreign churches.'

Fisher was certainly to carry this process further. And the same may be said of the Ecumenical Movement, 'the great new fact of our time' as Temple described it.

Fisher was to inherit this responsibility also, and to make much of it. The tasks before him, then, even as outlined in these generalisations, were enormous. Well may Bell have added: 'It is a far cry back from 1944 to 1848, the year in which Archbishop Howley died and Archbishop Davidson was born. There is no comparison between the burden of the Primacy now and the burden then.'

So much, then, for the outer picture of the situation, and the duties confronting the new archbishop enthroned in 1945. What in fact was its inner reality? How did he live; how plan his work, and with what tools and resources? Two discrepancies become apparent as soon as something is known about the last aspect of this matter. Thus Roger Lloyd, in his book, when speaking of Fisher's earliest years at Lambeth, has this to say, arising out of the fact that the country at that time was preoccupied with the end of the war and its aftermath. 'One consequence would be that the normal pressure of daily work on Lambeth (which Lang had called incredible, indefensible and inevitable) must be lessened. Other archbishops had been flung into the frenzy immediately after enthronement, and without so much as a single day's breathing space. Fisher was luckier. His first year in Lambeth Palace was probably the easiest of all, and he had time to think and pray.'

Pray no doubt he did. But the impression given, that Fisher experienced a kind of Sabbath calm in which to think out his policies, while an adequate and smooth organisation in Lambeth stood ready to help him carry them out, is simply not true. The opposite was, in fact, the case.

It is true that archbishops have always been served by a succession of faithful and able chaplains, as Fisher was throughout his Lambeth years. But an organisation designed to relieve the Primate of some of the huge burden of administrative work had never existed, though Fisher himself provided, in his time, for much to be taken on by central bodies. What Fisher had by way of help in this respect at the beginning of his time was sparse, even by these extraordinary standards. 'In Lambeth', he recalled, 'from the past I inherited to carry me through the first stages, one chaplain, my beloved friend Ian White-Thomson, now Dean of Canterbury, and one old male stenographer, Clements, who had started with Archbishop Davidson at Winchester as a bootboy, and had been trained by the Archbishop's own personal secretary to understudy him and in the end succeed him. He had no particular education, but he had learned simply by practice. At the same time, he was a very shrewd old man, and had learned a lot simply in the course of events. But that was the total staff that I inherited. I brought my own woman secretary with me from Fulham, who had been with me also at Chester, and knew my ways. But with no more than that, I had to find my own way forward.'

As to the matter of a leisurely thinking-out of policy, this was entirely against the grain of Fisher's nature and inclination. Rather was it his instinct to seize upon the tasks he found immediately at hand, and to get on with them. In his own words: 'I've never tried to think out a considered plan of what I ought to do through the years; I've never tried to formulate a general policy that I ought to follow; I've just gone forward and taken up each task or group of tasks as they appeared to demand attention, and no doubt there came to me some kind of pattern forming in my mind into which they all fitted. Roger Lloyd speaks as though in those war evenings I spent my time thinking out general policies. I never did anything of that sort. I've always been content to do the next thing, or to do a number of things, taking them as they presented themselves to me in a convenient order. I remember a Cheshire clergyman saying that I seemed to be like a juggler, with always six or seven balls in the air, and keeping them all going. This leads me to say one other things about myself. A juggler fixes, momentarily, his whole attention on the one ball that he is next wanting to put into the air. I never had the slightest difficulty in concentrating wholly on the matter which was immediately before me, and I could switch from it to the next thing without any difficulty. I think this was really due to the fact that I had a fairly clear, precise mind, which kept everything in good order, so that I could deal with one thing without confusing it with another thing, and could move from one to the next with a fresh and unpreoccupied mind.'

There were several 'balls in the air' when Fisher arrived at Lambeth, and it was in keeping with the situation as it was in fact, rather than in theory, to examine the first one which came to his hand at the time, knowing that others, some of them of greater import, would be bound, as by a law of gravity, to do the same thing in due course.

Thus the first 'ball' or issue which descended upon him in these early Lambeth days, happened to deal with a somewhat esoteric issue of diocesan constitutions. The matter came from the Bishop of Mombasa, as he then was, in the form of a draft new constitution for his diocese. Fisher took it away with him on his first summer holidays and dealt with it, thinking that was his task, quite unaware that anybody else ought to be doing it. It was, in any event, the kind of work he liked doing, he having been interested in regulations of that kind applied to schools then, in a wider context, to Church affairs. 'If I had had another career,' he once remarked, 'I might have become a perfectly competent Parliamentary draughtsman.' So he completed this Mombasa Constitution, showing it to his Registrar, Dashwood, and so it went back. The Archbishop did not know then, or for some time, that there was a special committee which dealt with constitutions of overseas dioceses and provinces. The chairman of it was Bishop Palmer, once of Bombay, who had seen through the whole of the constitution of the Independent Church of India, Pakistan, Burma and Ceylon, and who had a committee concerned with such matters. Perhaps this lack of knowledge on Fisher's part was fortunate because, when he did find that the committee existed, and asked advice, the replies were so full of complicated considerations and precedents that the Archbishop found it more effective to stick to the kind of solutions that had already occurred to him. If he had come upon this circumstance earlier, the drawing up of constitutions for new provinces in Africa—Uganda, West Africa, Central Africa and East Africa—might have been rendered considerably more complicated and prolonged. This proved, as time went by, to be both important and timely as regards that development and consolidation of the Anglican communion, which was to be an important part of Fisher's archiepiscopate. Yet here again an element of chance, together with the instinct of his to seize upon whatever came to hand by way of a problem, and to endeavour to solve it, was far more of a causative factor than deliberate planning. It was administrative experience which showed him that it was vitally important to establish these separate provinces. As it was, everything had to come to him from the extra provincial dioceses in African and other distant places. Each diocese had a bishop; each bishop had only one superior officer, and that was the Archbishop of Canterbury. It followed that the Archbishop of Canterbury was the court of appeal on every kind of question. What finally showed Fisher the oddity of this arrangement was when an appeal was addressed to him by an African priest in West Africa, who had been found guilty, by ecclesiastical authorities, of selling rice from his back door, a thing against the law. The man appealed to Lambeth against his sentence. Fisher did his duty, received all the evidence and read it through conscientiously, and came to the not unnatural conclusion that, all things being considered, the judges of the case had made the right decision. But it was a curious employment for an Archbishop of Canterbury, and the oddity of it remained in his mind.

The larger fact emerged that the Archbishop of Canterbury ought not to be responsible for these distant dioceses, and that the dioceses ought not to be responsible to him. Thus, as and when the bishops concerned were prepared for advance, these new provinces were established. It was fortunate indeed for the Church that, as one African nation after another achieved independence as the years went by, there was already a self-governing Anglican Church, and that Uganda, West Africa and parts of East Africa dioceses had already developed a vigorous native episcopate with bishops and assistant bishops used to authority and used to leadership.

Central Africa, when it came to the making of the province there, presented problems of its own. There were three dioceses, and there had to be four to make a province: and it was simple to divide one diocese into what are now the dioceses of Mashonaland and Matabeleland. But they were both in the province of South Africa, under the jurisdiction of the Archbishop of Capetown. So in Salisbury, at the inauguration of that province, the beloved and very able Archbishop Clayton of Capetown, and Fisher from Canterbury, collaborated in surrending their rights, and so setting up the new Province of Central Africa. Then later the Province of East Africa was founded, and Fisher was present at a splendid service at Dar-es-Salaam for its inauguration.

'Constitution making,' Fisher once commented in a remark revealing one aspect of his character, 'was very simple, and much more simple than it might have been because the dioceses were so sensible, and I was not cluttered up with too many advisers.'

But this constitution making, and African province creating—the latter extending far beyond the early years of Lambeth—were, as has been said, but some of the many 'balls' or concerns which the Archbishop had to keep in the air at once. There were other, and certainly more domestic ones to be dealt with as time passed. There was, for instance, a happy, gaily-coloured one, a royal wedding in the offing. There was a sombre one, which might be labelled 'Bishop Barnes and *The Rise of Christianity*'; there was a complex one, which might be marked 'South India'. There was a weighty one which might be indicated by the words 'The Cambridge Sermon, or a Step Forward in Church Relations'. There was yet another, not at all easy to control, marked 'Preparations for the Lambeth Conference of 1948'. All these will come to hand in time. Meanwhile, what of the juggler himself? How did he and his multifarious concerns appear in these years to some of those close to him?

Stanley Eley, his first senior chaplain, and one who had worked with Fisher throughout his London days, was certainly one of them. 'In the October, towards the end of 1946,' he recalled, 'the Archbishop asked if I would go as his senior chaplain. We had worked together, and he felt that we could go on working together. Consequently, on the first day of December that year, I moved my work to Lambeth, although in those days Lambeth was such a wreck that there was not any room for a single chaplain, let alone a married one, to live there. The result was I lived in my own house, and went down to Lambeth daily.

'One of the first things that struck me when I went there was the immense damage that had been done to Lambeth, and the extremely uncomfortable and inconvenient circumstances in which the Archbishop and his family were living in the basement. He had a study upstairs, and a chapel, and two chaplains' rooms and a sort of general office. The rest of the Palace was practically unusable. But here one saw Fisher's quite amazing resilience. For the new Archbishop of Canterbury, in addition to the burden which would have fallen on a reigning archbishop when the war ended, had none of the normal facilities available to an archbishop in those circumstances. This meant, of course, that he had to do a good deal of improvising from time to time, but nothing daunted him and he just carried on with the task.

'However, it was part of his nature to initiate, and he preached the famous Cambridge sermon in the autumn of 1946, in which he suggested that the time had come to open the whole question of reunion with the

Free Churches here in England. It was a sermon which aroused immediate interest and attention, and the Free Churches came forward at once and said "Can we come and discuss this with you?"

'The meeting was held at Lambeth in the December of 1946, I think, and representatives of the Free Churches came, and there was a general measure of agreement that there must be set up, at once, a series of conversations between the theologians of the Free Churches, and the theologians appointed not by the Church of England, but by the Archbishop himself, as he had been responsible for the sermon and the initiative.

'For the next four or five years, these conversations went on. The Archbishop took immense interest in all that was done, and I was able to give him verbatim reports of the sort of things that were happening. John Rawlinson, then Bishop of Derby, was in very close touch with him, too, and so indeed was Bishop Stephen Neill at that time, who was one of the foremost thinkers and writers on the whole subject of ecumenical relationships.

'That was the great achievement, I think, of the winter of 1946–1947. But there were other matters of outstanding importance to the Church, that welled up after the war. The first, of course, was the preparation for the Lambeth Conference of 1948. Then there was the wedding of Prince Philip and Princess Elizabeth, as she was then. The Archbishop not only took a personal interest in, but supervised the details which were necessary. The wedding was, I suppose, one of the greatest events after the war, and the natural dignity, homeliness and yet the deep pastoral care which the Archbishop exercised on that, and other, similar occasions, were quite obvious to anyone who happened to be near him during that time.

'Then there was the dedication of the Battle of Britain windows in Westminster Abbey. There again, not only his great dignity but his homeliness and friendliness with all those concerned were obvious to anyone. There was the silver wedding of King George VI and Queen Elizabeth in St. Paul's. We had a great service for that and, as an example of his thoughtfulness, I may say that I saw him suddenly take his manuscript and add a tribute to Queen Mary for her part in the success of the marriage, by the example she had set of her own faithfulness as a wife and a mother. This gave immense pleasure and satisfaction to everybody, not least the then King and Queen.

'The last occasion I remember distinctly was the dedication of the Roosevelt Memorial in Grosvenor Square, which was another memorable moment, when everyone who valued the work that Roosevelt had done in the war, and for the war, and for us, joined in that great tribute to him, when the Americans took over the piece of land on which the memorial stands to Roosevelt.

'Notwithstanding all these activities, he was never blind to the importance of ecumenical relationships on the continent, and his Council for Foreign Relations opened up many new fields of co-operation with churches on the continent, and of mutual understanding . . .

'So far as working with him was concerned, one admired his immense industry above all things. It was quite incredible the amount he did get through. He did not find it easy to delegate to other people; he had such infinite capacity for work himself that he was inclined, I think, at times to do a good deal of the drudgery that others could have done for him; but that was part of his nature. His geniality and ability quickly to get on easy terms with the most varied type of people was another notable feature. He thought of little ways of doing nice things for ordinary people. For example, when the Palace was restored in 1948—the main part of it was finished before the Lambeth Conference—one Sunday afternoon, just as it was on the point of being ready, the whole of the building workers, who were engaged on it, were invited to a tea-party in the Great Hall which they had restored. And also, during their work-days, after lunch, whenever he had not a particularly important appointment, he would wander round and chat to the workmen; I think he knew more about their families by the time the work was finished than certainly their employers did. In that kind of way, in which he made himself readily accessible to people, and didn't put them off, he had a kindly generous attitude always, with no air of superiority, although no one could have upheld his great position with more dignity than he did when it was required.'

This restoration of Lambeth Palace was a massive undertaking, extending over a decade—1945-1955. Its importance in this narrative is considerable. Firstly, it contributes to the picture of the Archbishop in his place of work. It was the Old Palace at Canterbury which the Fishers tended to regard more as 'home'. Then again, it sets the scene for the notable Lambeth Conferences of 1948 and 1958, since it was there that they took place. It takes the reader, too, through the doors of that enigmatic, withdrawn-looking pile on the south bank of the Thames, just over Lambeth Bridge, and shows what really was in there at this time. The fact that what was chiefly in there, on the Fishers' arrival, was wreckage, and that what was there when they left was an expertly restored great house in a part of which the Archbishop lived modestly, speaks much of the vigour with which he and his wife and staff approached the task, which at one time appeared so hopeless as to lead some experts to the opinion that the Palace should be abandoned as beyond repair. And certainly the manner of its restoration, with Fisher, immersed in a mass of other concerns, giving meticulous attention to the details, has something to add to a portrait of him. So also has this, from his own account of the matter:

'I remember being told that Archbishop Lang, in his vast study, used to say: "When people come to see me in this study, they realise that the Church of England is a great institution!" Well, that's not the kind of way I feel about anything, to tell you the truth. I don't feel that a palatial room adds anything to the dignity of the Church, and I should have been miserable working in that vast room.'

The palace itself was curious enough. Built about 1830, it had replaced by a simpler design a muddle of old rooms and passages and corridors which had come down from early time. The visitor, having passed through the front door, went up a flight of steps onto the main floor. Beneath, on ground level, were the kitchens and offices of all kinds, suitable for a grand house of the Victorian period, with many servants' and still-rooms, and housekeepers' rooms, and butlers' rooms and so forth. The main floor was really a gigantic flat, where the Archbishop lived. At the extreme right was a huge study for the Archbishop. Next was a little sitting-room. Next, with a bathroom tucked away, was the Archbishop's bedroom. Next to that was what was called a parlour, a room into which visitors were shown. Beyond that, there was a gigantic and lovely drawing-room, with a large bow window over-looking the garden, and through that a kind of ante-room leading to the chapel. It was possible to pass through this immense series of rooms without going into the main passage at all. Across the passage on the south-east side were the secretaries' rooms, three of them, and on the south front a single chamber, which was a little dining-room. The great dining-room was the guard-room, which was off at right-angles at the north-west side, with the great library beyond it forming the one side of the courtyard stretching towards Morton's Tower and the Gateway in it. Both the small dining-room and this guard-room were an immense distance from the kitchens, which were not only on the ground floor, but along and under the guard-room, in almost a separate house.

Above the main floor was the first floor, all bedrooms, which had not been redecorated or changed, in some cases, since the house was built. These were very lofty rooms, narrow and long, looking out on the north side. At the west end of the house there were other rooms, approached by what was called Crooked Lane, and beyond which lay Cranmer's Tower and the chapel.

Such was Lambeth for many years, the nineteenth century successor of an antique Lambeth stretching back into time and history. 'I had not known it,' Fisher recalled, 'in Davidson's time, but came to know it in Lang's, when it was a forbidding place. Everything was overwhelmingly Victorian. The bachelor Archbishop was the sole resident, so to speak. People came to him as to a great person in a great institution. There was the heaviness of a grand architectural style, and everything was handled after that manner. I remember a bishop from overseas once coming to stay with us. My wife asked whether he liked a bath in the evening or the morning. He said with some embarrassment that he would not want a bath. He was with us for a day or two, and the next day he said, "Perhaps you wondered why I said I wouldn't have a bath. Well, I didn't know whether things had changed since I stayed here in Archbishop Davidson's time. Then I was asked the same question and I said I would like a bath in the morning. So, in the morning, there was a great beat on the door, in walked a butler followed by two footmen. The butler was carrying a round tin bath, the two footmen cans of hot water. I said 'no' to your invitation because I was afraid that the same conditions might still obtain".'

They did not. Under the Fishers, the place was not only restored, but changed in character. Lady Fisher has an interesting account, both of the process of restoration and of some of the events which took place during the course of it.

'In the spring of 1945, when we arrived at Lambeth, the Palace had been severely damaged by bombs of different kinds. In 1941, fire bombs had gutted the chapel and damaged the library roof, burning about a third of it. A direct hit had destroyed the drawing-room, and rooms above and below. And in 1944, the blast of a flying-bomb, which fell on Lambeth Bridge Road, had wrecked all but one of the cottages and left a huge gap in the boundary wall, broken practically every window in the Palace and brought down many ceilings.

'Archbishop and Mrs. Temple had already made a flat on the ground floor, but its passage was still stone-flagged and bitterly cold in winter; the central-heating stove was right away in what is now the Cloister by the Library, and had been out of action since the bombing had destroyed most of the circuit. Upstairs, on the main floor, the Temples made the former bedroom of the Archbishop into a drawing-room, and the room next to it into a parlour for Mrs. Temple. The Archbishop used the room at the end of the passage as his study, and the two rooms next to it for secretaries. As our family needs required more space in the downstairs flat, we moved the chaplain (Mr. White-Thomson) up into what had been Mrs. Temple's parlour and made it into a bed sitting-room. The original parlour was a temporary chapel, equipped by the Temples. It held about sixteen people and was to serve as our chapel until 1955. During those years, it was to be the scene of some very moving services. In 1946 when the first delegation from the Russian Church came over to visit us and stayed with us at Lambeth, this was where they joined the Archbishop at prayer. It was led by Metropolitan Nicolai Vinutitsky who became a great personal friend of the Archbishop and kept in touch with him under great difficulties until he disappeared from the Russian ecclesiastical scene.

'In 1947 Prince Philip, accompanied by the present Queen, then

Princess Elizabeth, came for a little ceremony in which he was received as a member of the Church of England from the Greek Orthodox Church, with the full understanding of the representative of the Oecumenical Patriarch in London, Archbishop Germanos. This ceremony also took place in the temporary chapel. It was shortly before their marriage, and they were all involved in the many and complicated arrangements for that event. This made the Prince say, jokingly, at tea; "Why not be married now? Here we both are; and there's the Archbishop!"

'The Great Library was partly roofless, and stacks of books, sodden and burned, were piled on every table and on the floor. Dr. Irene Churchill and one assistant were struggling against impossible odds to rescue some of the books, or at least to discover which ought to be rescued and restored. Using penknives, they tried to part the fragile leaves, stuck together as a result of being drenched by the water which had been used in putting out the fire.

'The footmen of former days actually slept in the tower over the front entrance, and had seventy-two steps to climb up a circular staircase every time they went to their rooms. There had been no footmen since the war began. The tower was completely derelict. Morton's Tower had suffered from blast but was partially habitable. The gatekeeper and his wife, Mr. and Mrs. Woodward, lived in rooms on the ground floor, on each side of the entrance gates, and on the first floor in Eastern Tower. The rooms on the second floor, once a flat occupied by Dr. and Mrs. Bell when he was chaplain to Archbishop Davidson, were capable of being made habitable, so some of them in the western and eastern towers on that floor were made into a flat for one of the secretaries.

'We moved into these conditions, thankful to the Temples for producing as much order as they had, and for making it possible for us to live there at all. In view of the conditions still prevailing at Lambeth, we decided to take most of our "home" things to Canterbury and make it our family centre, and Lambeth our official residence. It didn't work out quite like that; the fact of Lambeth being so central made it a splendid centre for the family; but we did always gather at the Old Palace (which we loved dearly) for the great festivals, and of course were there as much as possible at other times. Faced by the immense amount of destruction to be made good, the Archbishop realised that he must speedily have schemes prepared for the Church Commissioners to take over both the Palace and the Old Palace at Canterbury. In view of the great expense to be involved in restoring the crippled Lambeth Palace, there were some who felt it should be abandoned, but the Archbishop and many others realised that its long and important contribution to the life and development of the Church must not be broken, and that it must be restored at all costs, and so the long period of restoration began.

'The date of the Lambeth Conference was fixed for 1948, and the most urgent repairs were those to the Library, which is traditionally the meeting place of the bishops in conference.'

The architects, who clearly delighted both the Archbishop and Mrs. Fisher, by their keenness, vision and immense skill and ingenuity, were Seeley and Paget. Richard Costain and Co. were the builders and Green and Vardy, who later on were appointed to undertake the woodwork of the new House of Commons, were responsible for the restoration of the Library roof.

The domestic disorder which was an inevitable accompaniment to all this work naturally exercised Mrs. Fisher considerably. 'The work on the bombed drawing-room,' she remembered, 'involved first pulling it down entirely, and this was followed by a period when a pile-driver worked all day long to provide foundations for the new building. Anyone who complains of noisy workmen, or of their length of stay in a house, might be checked in their complaining by being told that the Archbishop and his staff worked for weeks with pile-drivers and drills actually within the house, and that as the work progressed furniture was constantly having to be shifted from one part to another of the palace. Work on the Great Hall and the drawing-room section was not complete by 1948, but was sufficiently advanced for the rooms to be used for the Lambeth Conference. The Great Hall walls were covered, temporarily, with hessian and the Archbishop managed to secure the loan of some very fine tapestries to cover some part of them. The new drawing-room walls were rough brick and the ceiling was unfinished, but the Byam Shaw School of Art painted a large canvas of classical figures, which was hung from the ceiling and provided material for much comment during the Lambeth Conference meals.

There still remained to be altered and remade the whole section of the Palace which was to become bedrooms, in what was to be a hostel section of the Palace, but this had to wait until the first important sections were completed. As regards this, the Archbishop said: 'For the upper floors, we had developed a completely new idea. There were to be fifteen bedrooms or so, and a sitting-room, and there people could come to stay in the hostel; bishops coming up for meetings, and others, by arrangement. But more than that, visitors, bishops or laity, from overseas, recommended to us, could come and we were delighted when we had established a lively connection by which, from all parts of the Anglican Communion overseas, people came and stayed at Lambeth when they were visiting England. Equally, we could put up in the hostel smaller groups, of fifteen or twenty. Thus Lambeth completely changed its character, and came to belong in a new sense to the Church at home and overseas.'

Among many other extensive works which were a part of this restoration was the creation of rooms adjoining the inner courtyard to make offices for the Church of England Council on Foreign Relations, which was thus brought close to the Archbishop for the first time. Finally, and after many vicissitudes, the chapel was beautifully restored by Seeley and Paget. Fortunately, the walls were in good enough condition to take the weight of the roof, and so, except for the roof and, of course, the actual glass in the windows, it is still the original chapel of 1260. Thus it came about that, in the tenth year of his archiepiscopate, Archbishop Fisher had the satisfaction and joy of using the thirteenth century chapel of his predecessors. This restoration of the chapel was, indeed, for the Fishers the most important and deeply moving part of all the work. Lady Fisher recalled: 'On the occasion of its re-dedication, a series of services was planned, and early in the year, the Archbishop approached the Queen to ask her if she would be willing to attend the service of re-dedication itself, and to accept an invitation to dine afterwards with all the Diocesan Bishops. The Queen graciously accepted, with Prince Philip, as did also the Queen Mother and Princess Margaret, and the whole event was one of great beauty and much happiness. The Royal ladies wore evening dress and tiaras and looked lovely. Apart from the Ladies-in-Waiting, there were only four other women at the dinner which followed, myself and

Miss Forman, Mrs. Temple and Mrs. Wand. For the service, the bishops were all robed in their scarlet Convocation robes, only the Archbishops wearing copes and mitres. The Chaplains wore the Coronation cloaks of blue and gold, lined with red silk. The East Window was floodlit from outside so that its colours and pictures could be seen by all in the chapel.'

Thus, on this splendid note, the vast work was completed, and the historic centre of the Anglican Communion brought back to life. Essentially, however, it always belonged, as it had done for Lang, to the primatial part of the Archbishop's life. 'Home' was always for them at Canterbury itself where, as Archbishop Fisher always believed, by a providential fact of history, an Archbishop of Canterbury has to act as the particular bishop of a particular diocese with its particular parishes, clergy and laity, in addition to his other duties. It is an important part of a picture of Fisher to see him in his diocese as well as on the greater stage of the archbishopric.

Before, however, leaving this London end of the matter for a look at the Canterbury end, there is a glimpse of him as he was at this time which is certainly a part of the overall picture of him. It comes from the Very Reverend O. H. Gibbs-Smith, now Dean of Winchester, formerly Archdeacon of London.

'I found that once I had established a relationship with him, I maintained it without any difficulty, and I still do. I felt that, with him, so long as you kept (not that I particularly tried) on the right side, you were quite certain of a constant and good relationship for life.

'A small incident I remember at St. Paul's one day was when, with the rest of the Chapter, I was waiting at the West Door for Royalty, with the Archbishop. He was holding his sermon, when he dropped it and moved off to speak to someone. I observed this incident, retrieved the sermon, and handed it back. But he thanked me just as though it didn't really matter, and I don't think it did matter, because he would no doubt have done just as well without the manuscript.

'I have seen him in action on State occasions frequently, mostly in St. Paul's. He was quite natural; his voice went through the microphone beautifully, it was always completely audible. He knew exactly the pace at which to talk, the volume to use; he would get flexibility into his

utterances, and he did it as if he did it every day. I have heard him preach
to the Queen and the Royal family on all sorts of occasions, and I have
seen him at receptions afterwards in the City. I have heard him at City
dinners and receptions. In fact, I briefed him at least once for a speech
at a City dinner, and listened to my own briefing coming out in his much
better phraseology! I have heard him pulling the Lord Mayor's leg year
after year, at the Annual Banquet, when the Lord Mayor entertains the
Bishops at the Mansion House. I have heard him propose the health of
successive retiring Lord Mayors, give a little character sketch of them, with
plenty of amusing bits, and bring down the Guildhall in roars of laughter,
while maintaining just the dignity that he should maintain as Archbishop
toward the Lord Mayor. He is very, very good indeed at thus playing with
people, in the sense of speaking lightheartedly about them in a way that
is not in any way offensive; but it shows that he has a remarkable understanding of people, and can pick out their weaknesses and strong points,
with a sure and kindly hand.

'I have often been near enough to him at table to know that he didn't
bring any notes; but at a certain stage in the dinner, he would start
scribbling on the back of his menu, and often pick up points from earlier
speeches and then produce a masterpiece of a speech of his own.

'My chief recollection of him at these functions is as the representative
man who is friendly, understanding, human, humorous; never missing
anyone out.

'In the course of my work as Archdeacon, I had occasion to go to Lambeth Palace on several occasions. I remember when I went with the draft
of the City of London Guild Churches Bill, a thing I had drafted myself.
I received wise advice and searching questions. I found that, in a flash,
he could focus on some completely new subject and sometimes quite an
obscure one, like the Parliamentary Bill, and could master its details in
incredibly quick time. I remember eventually beginning to explain clauses
to him, and then realising that he knew perfectly well what I was trying
to say.

'There was another occasion when I had to organise a rally in Hyde
Park. I can't remember the occasion; but I rather think it was the
Festival of Britain. Anyhow, I had a huge crowd there, and when it was

all over I had to get him back to his car. I thought it right to go in front myself to help clear a way. I looked round every now and again, but after a while found that he had disappeared. The fact is that he had spotted an old face in the crowd, and had left the procession and was warmly shaking hands with someone perhaps who was at Repton with him. So I had to wait, and we got him back again to the procession. Then the same thing happened once more. He dived off in another direction. Eventually as we were getting him to the car, a man approached him. I don't know what he meant to do; but I didn't like his manner, and I more or less guarded the Archbishop and said we must get him back. But Fisher would not have this, and went up and put his hand on the man's shoulder. The Archbishop had that engaging way of a short man, of putting his hands on your shoulders and looking up at you, which was very characteristic of him and very disarming, especially if you were slightly in awe of him. Eventually, I got him back into his car and away.'

To take a glimpse of the Canterbury setting for the Archbishop's life and work is to enter a distinctly different world. Here, as has been said, he was a diocesan bishop, as all his predecessors had been. Curiously enough, none is on record as having lamented the fact: and some have found refreshment in the opportunities which the arrangement gave of exercising pastoral oversight on a more intimate plane than the office of an archbishop by itself, occupied with large-scale concerns, could possibly do. Fisher loved Canterbury, as his family did, and especially the Old Palace, a house contiguous to the Cathedral, which had been restored and enlarged by Archbishop Frederick Temple in the days when the Primate had no home whatever in Canterbury. This love for the place, and care for the diocese which Fisher showed, as one who was under him there for much of the time can testify, was warmly reciprocated, and he was a very highly-regarded Father in God of the diocese, clearly giving it, and its extension in Croydon, the closest attention, ably assisted by his suffragans and diocesan staff. At village confirmations and institutions he was at his happiest and best, and no suggestion of the many other cares which lay upon him ever seemed to dim his enthusiasm and obvious pleasure in being where he was.

One of his diocesan staff was the Venerable J. A. M. Clayson, for most of Fisher's time secretary of the Canterbury Diocesan Board of Finance and later Archdeacon of Croydon. Of Fisher, he wrote: 'I once saw a parson come out from an interview with him in tears, having been called, as it were, to the headmaster's study. On the other hand, I know clergy—and there must be many more whom I do not know— who thank God for his compassion and understanding. The image of Geoffrey Fisher in the minds of most people who knew him intimately is of a lovable, fatherly person who was intensely interested in those with whom he had to deal, and had a deep sympathetic understanding of their problems.

'One picture of the feeling for him on the part of the diocesan clergy will always remain in my mind. At the end of the first residential conference for the clergy, held at a holiday camp at Dymchurch, there was an air of expectancy as we waited at our breakfast tables for the Archbishop to appear. He stood in the doorway, a humble man, with a hot-water bottle in one hand and a tin alarm clock in the other (no doubt borrowed from someone). There was a spontaneous burst of applause, which rose to a crescendo and seemed to go on interminably. There was no doubting the affection and admiration all felt for him, and he was visibly moved.

'His memory for facts was phenomenal. When the Church Commissioners brought out a new scheme for grant aid for parsonage houses, he asked me what I thought of it. When I said I had not yet received the information he said, "Well, you wouldn't expect me to remember the details; we had a wad of paper several inches thick." But he then proceeded to outline the scheme, and tell me all the figures involved, both nationally and for the Canterbury diocese.

'He was very observant, even in a crowd. Once in the Mayor's Parlour at Croydon Town Hall, with a large number of people present, I found myself standing alone. No doubt I was tired and I relaxed for a moment. I heard the Archbishop's voice calling me: "Clayson, moments when we think we are unobserved are most illuminating. Don't stand there looking so old!" Only once did he give me a dressing down. I can't remember what it was about; but the next time I saw him about a week later I said to him, "The last time I was in this room, you gave me a rocket." He looked most apologetic. "No, did I really? I'm so sorry!"

'He always liked to see bishops and archdeacons what he called "properly dressed", that is, in their gaiters. He once sent for me on an Easter Monday, and I entered his study dressed in a lounge suit. He said at once: "Why aren't you properly dressed?" I said, "This is Easter Monday, and I didn't expect the Archbishop of Canterbury to send for me." He merely replied, brushing the matter aside, "I won't be a moment." He was writing in a large ledger, and after a minute or two, he closed it and said, "There. That is my income-tax return done for another year." I said, "Surely you don't deal with your own income-tax?" "Oh, yes," he said, "I love it. It's my Easter Monday recreation. If I hadn't been a schoolmaster, I might have been an accountant."

'It seldom occurs to those who are in lower positions that an archbishop is appreciative of praise. But I remember that, at a Diocesan conference, at a time when the conflict between the Roman Catholic Church and eastern European Communist states was in full flow, the Archbishop made a statement to the Conference which was, of course, intended for the national press. As we left the conference hall at lunch-time, I said to Mrs. Fisher, "I thought the Archbishop did that brilliantly." She said, "Do tell him, do tell him!" And so I did, and the Archbishop looked as pleased as a schoolboy being commended by his headmaster. He was most attentive to advice offered to him. At staff meetings, he would listen carefully to all that was said for and against the candidates put forward for a benefice, and could always see quite clearly which man was the right one for the job, and sometimes, with a twinkle, he obviously recognised that someone present had his own reason for pressing his particular candidate.

'He took great delight in discussions with people whom he thought needed educating on a particular point. A boy's club in the Lambeth district had apparently said hard things about the Archbishop of Canterbury. So he visited the club and spent an evening with the boys and they had a very different picture of the Archbishop as a result. On another occasion, having received a resolution from a very low church parochial church council, about the Canon dealing with the Vesture of the Minister, he spent four hours one evening with the council, trying to get them to alter their views. He confessed afterwards, however, that he had not moved them one iota.

'It was his habit to wander about Canterbury at times in an ancient suit, wearing a collar and tie. On one occasion, he went to see the ruins of St. Augustine's Abbey and climbed a low railing to take a short cut. The guide called to him: "What the hell do you think you're doing? This is the way in. Sixpence please!" The Archbishop was much abashed. "I'm so sorry," he said. "I was only going to see if I could find the tombs of some of my predecessors." The guide replied, "You'll be telling me next you're the Archbishop of Canterbury."

'Despite his public image, I knew him to be a humble man. My lasting impression is of a man full of affection, who loved his fellow men, and to whom all came alike and all were treated with the same respect and friendliness.'

On the other hand, there were problems in Canterbury. One was the Dean of Canterbury, Hewlett-Johnson, 'The Red Dean'. The tale which this extraordinary man, in many ways so gifted, in other ways so bizarre, told of himself in his autobiography, scarcely explains his oddities.[1] And in view of what has since come to light about Stalin's Russia, his eulogies of that State have been revealed as strange, to say the least of it, just as his appearances in the Kremlin sometimes, dressed in the full rig of an Anglican dignitary, topped by a tonsure of white hair, might possibly have appeared to some of his hosts as a little odd also.[2]

For Fisher, whose description of him was: 'a charming, gracious, friendly, pastoral man, once he was off his main subject of socialism and Russia', the problem lay in the fact that he himself was, and especially

[1] Hewlett-Johnson, *Searching for Light* (Michael Joseph, 1968).

[2] In this connection, a footnote from Harold Nicolson's biography of King George V is not without interest: 'It is only fair to say that successive Prime Ministers . . . were extremely scrupulous in advising the Crown on candidates eligible for Church preferment. As an example of the great care taken, may be cited the appointment in 1924 of the Vicar of St. Margaret's, Altrincham, as Dean of Manchester. On the death of Dr. McCormick, Lord Stanfordham wrote both to the Prime Minister and to the Archbishop of Canterbury giving a list of possible successors. The Archbishop then consulted Dr. Temple, Bishop of Manchester, asking whether he had any special candidate to propose. The Prime Minister's private secretary then visited the Archbishop at Lambeth and informed him that the Prime Minister, if there were no other special candidates in the field, would like to suggest the name of the Vicar of St. Margaret's, Altrincham. Both the Archbishop and Dr. Temple thought the Prime Minister's candidate wholly suitable. "He always," wrote the Archbishop, "carries weight with thoughtful people."' Harold Nicolson, *King George V* (Constable).

overseas, where the eccentricities of some English institutions were not always fully understood, either confused with the Dean or else regarded as responsible for his actions and opinions. Such misapprehensions had at times to be corrected with vigour, and were. Thus Henry Sherrill, Presiding Bishop of the Protestant Episcopal Church of the United States, and a close friend of the Fishers, came upon a remarkable scene when he met the Fishers at the dockside in New York, on the occasion of the Archbishop's visit in the autumn of 1952 to the General Convention of that Church. The arrival took place in the midst both of a natural thunderstorm, and of a man-made tempest generated by the Dean's statement about alleged American use of bacteriological warfare during the conflict in Korea. 'On landing,' Sherrill remembered, 'the Archbishop, who in the United States press was often confused with the Dean of Canterbury, was taken to the microphone and began by shouting over the storm: "I am not the Red Dean!" Thunder and lightning. "I repeat," said the Archbishop again, "I am not the Red Dean!" Thunder and lightning!'

The American magazine *Newsweek* of 5 June 1952, had another comment on this matter. In the course of an article on Fisher, it ran a paragraph headed 'The Two Canterburys': 'The biggest burden Dr. Fisher has to bear is his Dean of Canterbury. An open champion of communism, Dr. Johnson is considered more of a joke than a danger by the British public and his fellow clergymen. But the seventy-six-year-old 'Red' dean's mixing of politics and religion has caused a good deal of harm abroad, as many uninformed people, hearing the name Canterbury, take him for the head of the Church and ascribe his views to the Primate. Dr. Johnson doesn't try too hard to correct their views. The 1947 Czech edition of his book *Soviet Power* said on the cover that the author was "Arcibishup Canterbursky". Dr. Fisher has had to repudiate publicly his dean's views three times in the past five years. The third reproof came last week in a letter to the Mayor of Auckland, N.Z., for Dr. Johnson is now on a Down Under tour (the United States refused him a transit visa to get there). "My advice to overseas Anglican churches is completely to ignore the dean's visit," wrote Dr. Fisher. "He cannot be removed from his office until he breaks some law, ecclesiastical or civil, and has perfect liberty to say what he does since there is no law against it."'

At other times, the Archbishop's disassociation of himself from the Dean's doings were more magisterial. Arthur Bryant, chairman of the publishing firm of A. R. Mowbray, and for many years a member of the Canterbury Diocesan Conference, remembered such an occasion.

'At one of the early Conferences I attended, the opening statement of the Archbishop concerned the doings of the Dean of Canterbury. The Dean appeared in the doorway of the Chapter House as the statement began, and disappeared immediately it was finished. This was the only occasion I saw the Dean attend a Diocesan Conference, although he was rarely absent from the service beforehand. The gist of the statement was that, while the press had reported that the Archbishop had visited Soviet Russia, and perhaps China as well, and had made various speeches about the virtues of the Communist system, it was in fact the Dean who had made the trip, and certainly *not* the Archbishop. The Dean was, of course, entitled to his views but the Archbishop, on behalf of the Church of England, disagreed with all the Dean had said. As soon as the Archbishop sat down, the majority of the press left the Conference, walking ever faster in order to get first to the door. Some even left by a window. Outside, they could be seen running round the cloisters, no doubt to reach the nearest telephone.'

The same observer noted other aspects of Fisher in this diocesan setting: 'I first saw Archbishop Fisher sometime in 1947. I had travelled for a Diocesan Conference from Croydon, and on arrival at the Cathedral had found a place opposite the Archbishop's throne. At the end of the procession, at the commencement of the service before the Conference itself, the dean entered, preceded by a verger. Another procession then entered, a much shorter one. The Archbishop's chaplain carried the Cross of Canterbury; next came two suffragan bishops, then the Archbishop himself. I noted particularly his massive head, making him appear shorter than he really was. In his hand he carried the gilded pastoral staff of Canterbury, which he was swinging like a walking-stick, taking long strides, his shiny black toe-caps protruding in front of his robe as he walked. For the first time, I heard the Archbishop's voice. It was one I shall never forget; mellow, and somehow by its very tone expressing mature judgment. The prayers, too, were unusual. They were brief, yet wide in scope, directing our thoughts first to the diocese, and then to the

Church at large and to the troubles and problems of the world scene. Afterwards, in the Chapter House, the Archbishop made his way to the platform, with the press table on his left. The proceedings then followed a pattern I came to know well over the years. Immediately upon arriving at the platform, the Archbishop motioned to the Conference to be seated, and then read a prepared statement, which was directed at the national press rather than at the Conference itself. This national business being disposed of, the Conference turned to more domestic matters, probably finance, and after the adjournment for lunch, there was a set speaker. I think that at my first Conference, the subject was a report of the Board of Women's Work, and here I remember an interesting incident.

'Two or three potential speakers stood, from the floor of the hall, including a woman in a brown hat, some way back on the Archbishop's right. The Archbishop looked to his left and pointed to a speaker, calling her by name. The speaker came to the platform and addressed the assembly through a microphone. As soon as she finished, more speakers stood, and the Archbishop again looked to his left. The lady in the brown hat also stood, and said: "Your Grace!" The Archbishop continued to look to his left and called another speaker to the platform. When he had finished, the lady in the brown hat again stood up and again said: "Your Grace!" The Archbishop this time looked to his right and said, "Mrs. Fisher."

'During the summer months, the crowds of visitors to the Cathedral increased year by year. Frequently, the Diocesan Conference emerged from the Chapter House to a throng of holiday makers. On one occasion, I remember coming out to see four girls, who proved to be from Germany, who were wearing very brief sun-tops, short panties and gay sandals. The attendant at the bookstall looked as though she was about to ask them to go away and get properly dressed, but at this moment the Archbishop came out. He greeted them with a smile, and asked them where they came from. They told him, and then one of them asked: "Are you the Archbishop?" With a nod and a smile, he chatted gaily with all four before passing on.

'This ability to get on in this way with anybody was one of the Archbishop's great assets. It came out especially at institutions of new incumbents. For instance, there were thirty-four parishes in the Rural

Deanery of Croydon, and during the ten years or so after the war, the majority of them acquired new vicars. Whenever he could, the Archbishop came and presided himself, and after the formal part of the service, would preach. The sermons were remarkable for their simplicity and the manner in which they held the attention of everyone. I remember an institution at Selsdon, near Croydon, where there must have been four or five hundred people crowded into the hall after the service. The Archbishop went here and there trying to shake hands with them all. He had at this time an extremely good-looking secretary (she later married one of his chaplains). She was standing with the chaplain and one or two others at the door of the hall, and this chaplain plunged into the crowd to remind the Archbishop that it was time he was on his way. The Archbishop drifted near the door, and then drifted away again. His secretary drew herself up to her full height, and with an expressive gesture of despair said: "Your Grace of Canterbury; do you know that you are due at Lambeth in forty-five minutes?" His Grace of Canterbury apparently could not care less. But five minutes later, no doubt knowing full well that the journey was likely to take precisely forty minutes, he drew to the door again, and with farewell handshakes and waves from everyone, he got into his car and drove away.

'His extraordinary close attention to financial matters was brought home to me by the affair of what were known as the Ralph Snow Trustees. As with so many other ecclesiastical trusts, it was administered by a body of trustees who tended to become self-perpetuating, although appointments had to be approved by the Archbishop of Canterbury. In this instance, the trustees had not done so badly, but some had become elderly and had died, with the exception of one gentleman who wished to retire, and my own father. He was a chartered accountant, and had been a member of the Canterbury Diocesan Board of Finance and of the Church Assembly, under Archbishop Lang, was extremely conscientious in such matters. He sounded a number of prominent church people in Croydon. Having gained their consent, he submitted their names to Archbishop Fisher with a request that he would approve their appointment as new trustees. The Archbishop thought otherwise. The Church had lost too much money by the maladministration of local bodies of trustees, and he decided to find new ones himself. So he wrote to my father and indicated that he was not prepared to accept the names submitted, and moreover was not at all satisfied that the fund had been administered efficiently.

'I never saw my father more indignant. Not only was he acutely embarrassed at having to inform the nominees, whom he had taken such pains to secure, that their services were not required; he felt that his integrity had been impugned. Had the writer of the letter been any other than the Archbishop of Canterbury, I am quite sure he would have issued a writ for libel. This, however, was not the end of the matter. The following day, a colleague of mine in Croydon who was doing much work for the Laymen's Fund for Clergy Stipends there, Harry Wheeler, a general manager of Barclay's Bank, and myself, received extremely cordial letters from the Archbishop, asking us if we would be willing to serve as trustees of the Ralph Snow Charity. My father eventually saw the funny side of the affair; but I never saw the reply he sent to the Archbishop. Shortly afterwards, there was a Diocesan Conference, and as I entered the Archbishop grasped me by the arm, and with a tremendous laugh said that he had no idea that I was a son of the chairman of the Ralph Snow trustees, He withdrew unreservedly any adverse comments he had made regarding the administration of the trust!'

For the rest, in this Canterbury scene, there were, as the Archbishop put it long afterwards, 'endless things—I never knew how many—which would just crop up from time to time. The only thing was just to look into them, see whether they were doing anything worth doing, and get them somehow or other straightened out, and note what work needed to be done.' Among these 'endless things' may be mentioned the transference of the Royal School of Church Music, which had had its headquarters in Canterbury but which, when for various reasons its position there became untenable, moved to Addington Palace, near Croydon, where it continued its admirable and important work. The Archbishop's own part in this complex rescue operation was decisive and important. Nor would Canterbury have been in character as an ancient foundation if it had not had, quite apart from its remarkable Dean, some clashes of temperament among its Chapter, and some oddities, like the canon who used to puzzle Fisher by referring, at staff meetings and elsewhere, to some clergyman as 'Mr.'

and to others as 'Father', although why, as the Archbishop observed, 'he should differentiate in that way was not obvious'.

Also, and equally inevitably, there were situations of quite Trollopian peculiarity which arose from time to time, such as the burning issue of the status of the Bishop of Dover (one of Canterbury's suffragans) in the Cathedral on great occasions. The Archbishop recounted the matter thus: 'On the Saturday before Easter, the Bishop of Dover came down to me. He had just had a note from the Dean to say that on Easter Day he would not come into the Cathedral with me, in my procession, but would be assigned to a stall as an honorary canon, which he was, by the Dean and Chapter, since as a canon he was one of the Corporate Body of the Cathedral. The Bishop said that, of course, in this case, he would not come to the Cathedral at all on Easter Day. I naturally said, "When we are in the Cathedral together, you come in with me behind the primatial cross, carrying your pastoral staff in front of me with mine; we are the corporate episcopate, acting together and entering together." The Bishop had come in with me like that on Christmas Day; but the Chapter did not approve and told the Dean to tell him that he must never do this again. The Dean typically forgot all about it until just before Easter, and then sent a note up to the Bishop in this disastrous way. The whole thing was perfectly absurd. What happened I can't remember; but after some wrangling, I made a proposal which the Dean and Chapter were good enough to accept; I said that the suffragan bishops attached to me should always be seated in the three stalls immediately to the left of the Archbishop's throne. To this I was told: "The one next to the Archbishop, by tradition, is the stall of the Archdeacon of Canterbury. It is true that he never sits in it ordinarily, except on an ordination. But it is his stall." So I said: "Very well; if and when the Archdeacon wants to use his stall, any suffragans present must move down one, so as to make room for him. But normally they will occupy the three stalls next to the throne." And this was done.'

But such extraordinary preoccupations could be found elsewhere as well (as no doubt they can be in other spheres, where dignity, precedence and precedent have their places). Fisher recalled one: 'There was a queer tradition at Westminster Abbey. There, the Archbishop had no place at all, and there was a ceremony by which, now and again, the Dean in the vestry read to the Archbishop a traditional form, declaring that the Archbishop had no rights whatsoever in the Cathedral; but was there only by courtesy of the Dean and Chapter. William Temple used to laugh about that. As Canon of Westminster in his time, he had heard this read. Then as Archbishop, he had had it read back at him. It was normal that if I went to preach at the Abbey as a guest, the Dean accompanied me in and out, walking by my side. But I did not think this was suitable when I was attending a service as Archbishop in full state. If the Dean and Chapter let me in at all, so to speak, I must take my precedence as Archbishop. On another special occasion, a division of opinion arose, and I said that when I went as Archbishop, I processed in with my primatial cross in front, and my chaplain behind, and without the Dean by my side. In the end we came to a reasonable conclusion, that when the Archbishop went as a friendly visitor, he would be escorted up the Cathedral by the Dean; but when he went as the Primate of All England, then he would proceed in his own group. It is strange how often it is over such little points of protocol that argument arises.'

The Abbey takes this tale away from Canterbury, and back again to the Lambeth part of the Archbishop's work, where great issues indeed are to be found, and it will not return to Canterbury again. Let it but be remembered that there it was, all through his archiepiscopate, a place greatly loved by him and Lady Fisher, as it had been by so many of his predecessors; the Cathedral especially a thing of beauty and a joy for ever. And if this present writer may permit himself one brief personal reminiscence, it would be of a summer afternoon's Evensong in the Cathedral, when the singing was as of heaven itself. The service passed through its accustomed form. And then, at the end, a short, stocky man, in a lounge suit, with a large, impressive head, who had been kneeling by himself in the back row of the choir stalls, rose, and slipped out. It was the Archbishop of Canterbury.

VII

A Sermon at Cambridge

It has been the great achievement of the past two generations, of the Ecumenical Movement, of Lambeth Conferences, and countless faithful souls, to focus attention upon that which all denominations hold in common and receive from Christ, their one shepherd.

G.F.F., in a sermon preached before the University of Cambridge, 3 November 1946

. . .

The Church, as it has come down to us through history, has to face not only its triumphs; but its failures, too. Its unity has been impaired, battered, broken by inevitable diversities of idea and thought . . . But a great change has been in progress, and is becoming daily more marked. There is an increasing and happy recognition that all the churches are a real part of the Catholic Church of Christ if they sincerely and devoutly retain and use, according to the measure of their faith, those gifts which Christ has given to His Church, loyal faith in His Person, reliance upon the Holy Spirit, Creeds, Sacraments, Ministry and Scripture.

G.F.F., in a B.B.C. broadcast, Whit Sunday 1957

. . .

I might say as a general principle, that by nature I was always interested in starting new ventures to meet new situations and new needs.

G.F.F.

'I HAVE never tried,' the Archbishop said of himself, in a passage already quoted, 'to think out a considered plan of what I ought to do through the years; I have never tried to formulate a policy that I ought to follow; I have just gone forward and taken up each task, or group of tasks, as they appeared to demand attention, and no doubt there came to be some kind of pattern forming in my mind into which they all fitted.' The passage may, with advantage, be placed alongside a comment made by Stanley Eley, Fisher's first senior chaplain at Lambeth: 'It was part of his nature to initiate, and he preached the famous Cambridge sermon in the autumn of 1946 in which he suggested the time had come to reopen the whole question of union with the Free Churches here in England. It was a sermon which aroused immediate interest and attention . . . That was a great achievement, I think, of the winter of 1946–1947.'

'Reopen' is the significant word here. The significance of the Cambridge sermon cannot be understood unless the background to it be noted. The matter is well summarised in a pamphlet published by S.P.C.K. in 1950, under the title of *Church Relations in England, Being a report of conversations between representatives of the Archbishop of Canterbury and representatives of the Evangelical Free Churches in England.*

'As long ago as 1920, as the outcome of the Lambeth Conference held in that year, the bishops of the Anglican Communion issued an appeal to all Christian people, acknowledging all who believe in our lord Jesus Christ, and have been baptised into the name of the Holy Trinity as sharing with them membership of the universal Church of Christ, which is His Body. They confessed frankly their own share in the guilt of the divisions, whereby the Body of Christ is crippled, and the activity of His Spirit is hindered, and called for new efforts aimed at the restoration of unity.'

This appeal was transmitted by the Archbishop of Canterbury in the August of 1920 to the different Christian churches at home and abroad. One result in England was a statement, *The Free Churches and the Lambeth Appeal*, issued in April, 1921 on behalf of the Federal Council of the Evangelical Free Churches of England. Subsequently, these appointed delegates to confer with representatives of the Church of England, and a series of joint conferences at Lambeth, beginning in 1921 and continuing at intervals until 1925, took place. They were then suspended for a time; but resumed after the Lambeth Conference of 1930. 'A number of documents were published from time to time, the process culminating with the issue in 1938 of three such documents: *Outline of a Reunion Scheme, The Practice of Intercommunion,* and *1662 and Today.* 'Of these documents, the most important was the *Outline of a Reunion Scheme,* submitted to the "careful consideration of the churches represented in the joint conference" and giving a general outline of the kind of church in which the churches represented in the conference might find themselves united without loss

of what is specially valuable in their distinctive traditions.' It is noteworthy, in view of what the Archbishop was to say in the Cambridge
sermon of so many years later, that the kind of church envisaged in an
Outline of a Reunion Scheme, 'would have a ministry fully unified for its own
internal life, on the basis of episcopal ordination'.

The process of discussion of these reports, both by the Church of England and by the Free Churches, continued until in 1941 *A Reply of the
Free Church Federal Council* was issued. It was at once friendly in tone and
critical in nature, and at the same time indicative of the fact that it was
unlikely that union on the basis of the *Outline of a Reunion Scheme* would
find general acceptance.

Further discussions were suspended during the war period and then, in
1946, Fisher reopened the matter by enquiring of the Congress of the
Free Church Federal Council and of the Conference of the Methodist
Church, whether they wished to reopen the matter. Before either had
replied, he had reopened it himself with his sermon at Cambridge.

Such, then, was the background to one of the weightiest tasks which
Fisher found demanding attention at his first going to Lambeth. But that
there was a pattern forming in his mind is clear from the fact that he
acted, when he did, at a time of his own choosing, and in a manner
clearly indicative of his own thinking. The Cambridge sermon, seminal,
of lasting importance and, as if indicative of the fact, included in the
fourth series of Bell's *Documents on Christian Unity*[1] was preached not only
before either of the Free Church bodies to whom he had addressed his
question had replied; but also before either of two other groups whom he
had asked to look into the matter had reported.

These two groups were, on the one hand, a number of Catholic-minded
theologians and, on the other, a group representative of the Evangelical
school of thought within the Church of England, each of which was asked
to present a report indicative of its own particular viewpoint. The purpose
of the exercise was clearly set forth in a passage from the preface to the
report eventually produced by the first of these groups.[2] 'In November
1945, your Grace invited Dom Gregory Dix to convene a group of

[1] G. K. A. Bell, *Documents on Christian Unity, Fourth Series, 1948–1957* (O.U.P.).
[2] *Catholicity. A Study in the Conflict of Christian Traditions in the West* (Dacre Press, 1947).

Anglicans of the "Catholic" school of thought to examine the deadlock which occurred in discussion between Catholics and Protestants, and to consider whether any synthesis between Catholic and Protestant is possible.'

The group, which clearly went about its task with deliberation, did not report until some months after the Archbishop's sermon. Its members included the present Archbishop of Canterbury; the present Dean of Westminster, E. S. Abbott, at that time Dean of King's College, London; T. S. Eliot; Dom Gregory Dix, Monk of Nashdom Abbey; Canon Charles Smyth, Canon of Westminster, Rector of St. Margaret's and Fellow of Corpus, Cambridge; the present Bishop of Exeter, R. C. Mortimer, and other persons of distinction. How far their collective thought was able, in the event, emerging as it did after he had made his own utterance, to affect Fisher's thinking, is impossible to say. But a passage from his own foreword to the report is interesting, especially in the light of much later developments, and even controversies, in this field.

'The larger part of the report consists of analysis. When it comes to syntheses it shows perhaps more of anxiety to avoid wrong methods, than of ability to elaborate a right method. But the general description which it gives of the right method will command general consent. "That unity," it says, "which must be reborn, will include something of all the patterns, not in their falsities and negations, but in those elements of devotion and conviction, of dogma and discipline which they contain. As the strength of these traditions, in their isolation, has lain in their convictions, so the only motive that could truly unite them is a common conviction about the truth of the Gospel and the Church." In that sentence the report expresses what has been the real strength and motive force of the Ecumenical Movement in recent years. As "tensions" created the disastrous divisions, we must expect "tensions" no less in overcoming the divisions. Our aim must indeed be to recover the "wholeness of the Body of Christ", recognising gladly that it will always include "many variations of function, practice and theological emphasis, if the Church is to present to the world all the riches of Christ, the whole treasure in its earthen vessels".'

The Evangelical group entitled its report *The Fullness of Christ, the Churches' Growth into Catholicity*.[1] This group included F. D. Coggan, at that

[1] S.P.C.K. 1960.

time principal of the London College of Divinity, now Archbishop of York; S. F. Allison, then principal of Ridley Hall, Cambridge, now Bishop of Winchester; Henry Chadwick, Fellow and Dean of Queens' College, Cambridge and subsequently Regius Professor of Divinity at Oxford; G. W. H. Lampe, Fellow and Chaplain of St. John's College, Oxford, now Ely Professor of Divinity at Cambridge; S. L. Greenslade, Van Mildert Professor of Divinity at Durham; Canon Herklots of Sheffield, now of Peterborough; the Rev. C. F. D. Moule, Dean of Clare College, Cambridge, now Lady Margaret Professor of Divinity in that university; M. A. C. Warren, at that time general secretary of the Church Missionary Society, now Canon and Sub-Dean of Westminster Abbey and R. R. Williams, principal then of St. John's College, Durham, now Bishop of Leicester. The group also included the principals of St. Aidan's College, Birkenhead and of Wycliffe Hall, Oxford. Bishop Stephen Neill, Associate General Secretary of the World Council of Churches, was also a member. The Archdeacon of Sheffield, D. E. W. Harrison, subsequently Dean of Bristol, was chairman.

The terms of reference provided by the Archbishop were the same for both groups.

1. What is the underlying cause—philosophical and theological—of the contrast or conflict between the Catholic and Protestant traditions?
2. What are the fundamental points of doctrine at which the contrast or conflict crystallises?
3. Is a synthesis at these points possible?
4. If a synthesis is not possible, can they co-exist within one ecclesiastical body, and under what conditions?

Inevitably, there were considerable divergencies in the answers. But the relevance of the whole exercise, with its painstaking gathering together of representatives of very differing traditions, to this narrative, is the evidence it offers of a quality in Fisher not always recognised in this area of concern—a desire to be scrupulously fair. Here he was obviously concerned, and deeply so, to see that each side should have its say, and that under the most distinguished auspices. It was also characteristic of him that his own sermon was preached, and his own policy expressed, before either of these bodies had reported. Subsequently, the Free Churches issued a report of their own, *The Catholicity of Protestantism*, so that Fisher's Cambridge sermon was productive, besides much else of wider import, of three documents of some theological importance. But he was not at that time under any illusions as to the difficulties which lay around the path of ecumenicism; difficulties which were liable to increase rather than diminish the further the path was followed. But that steady advance was possible he steadfastly believed. A passage from his foreword to *The Fullness of Christ* makes both these points clear:

'Great themes are discussed in these reports—soteriology, scripture, sacraments, ministry, creed and the nature of authority in the Church. There is not complete agreement upon these great themes; if there were, one could be certain that it would be short-lived. No age of the Church, no school of theologians, no single church has ever comprehended the "wholeness" of the Christian Faith without any falsity of emphasis or insights. As in the past, so in the future, in the whole church and in its several parts, one age will need to correct another and one truth will rise to preserve another from the corruption of itself . . . As we consider advance towards intercommunion, it is well to keep in mind the admirable clause in the agreement between the Church of England and the Old Catholic Churches which says: "Intercommunion does not require, from either communion, the acceptance of all doctrinal opinion, sacramental devotion or liturgical practice characteristic of the other, but implies that each believes the other to hold the essentials of the Christian faith." I believe that these words indicate the right line of advance.'

What, then, was this highly influential sermon, preached before the University of Cambridge in Great St. Mary's Church on 3 November 1946? To reproduce it in full would clearly be impossible in this place. To give the gist of it is essential.

Taking as his text John x. 9–10, 'I am the Door: by me, if any man enter in, he shall be saved and shall go in and out and find pasture. The thief cometh not but for to steal and to kill and to destroy: I am come that they might have life, and that they might have it more abundantly', the Archbishop passed, after due exegesis, to the heart of the matter. 'It is of the unity of the Church, or rather of some matters relating to it, that I wish to speak; and therefore I have put first the unity which already exists before speaking of that which does not. In every main Christian denomination are found in abundance those who have entered by the one door, have found the one Saviour, and draw from him their life. Of all such, Christ is the shepherd, and all such belong to his flock; but they are in different folds, fenced off from one another by barriers, some trivial enough, some reaching up (as it would seem) to heaven itself, which the long course of the Church's history has erected.'

Turning next to the 'scandal and rock of offence' which these barriers created, the Archbishop noted that the 'minds of Christians are turning earnestly towards recognising in one another the manifest signs of the faith and life of Christ, and towards praying that the many may again become visibly one in the Holy Catholic Church of Christ'. He then went on to refer to the background of conversations between the Church of England, the Church of Scotland, and the Free Churches which had, in the years before the war, been taking place. The question now was how was a new beginning to be made. 'I sense,' he then said, 'a certain reluctance to begin at all. A distinguished theologian has recently expressed the opinion that all schemes of reunion should be postponed until further study, theological thinking and prayer in all Christian communions have led them to a recovered apprehension of the integrity and balance of Christian truth, alike in the sphere of Faith and in that of Order, based on a renewed understanding of the Scriptures of the Old and New Testaments, and of the witness of Christian antiquity. That is to suggest that nothing should be done until the theologians have begun all over again and reached agreed conclusions; the past does not suggest that such theological unanimity will come in any foreseeable future . . . I believe the difficulty of beginning again', the Archbishop continued, 'lies elsewhere. Schemes of reunion have generally been what I would call constitutional. They posit between two or more denominations an agreed constitution, by acceptance of which they become one. Its articles must be such as to satisfy and to bind the negotiating parties. They must contain all that each negotiating party especially values and omit anything which it stubbornly resists; they must be non-committal where there is unresolved difference of opinion; they must set out an organisation and a method of government; with this new constitution in their hands, the negotiating denominations are to lose their formerly separate identities and become a "new Province of the Universal Church", unsure at its birth what will be its relations to other Christian Communions, and whether former affiliations of the united bodies will be impaired or not'.

Going on to suggest further reasons why, especially in England, the constitutional method of reunion would be fraught with particular difficulties, the Archbishop came to the heart of the matter. 'There is a suggestion which I should like, in all humility, to make to my brethren of other denominations. We do not desire a federation; that does not restore the circulation. As I have suggested, the road is not yet open, we are not yet ready for organic or constitutional union. But there can be a process of assimilation, of growing alike. What we need is that while the folds remain distinct, there should be a movement towards a free and unfettered exchange of life in worship and sacrament between them, as there is already of prayer and thought and Christian fellowship—in short, that they should grow towards that full communion with one another, which already in their separation they have with Christ . . .

'My longing is not yet that we should be *united* with other churches in this country; but that we should grow to *full communion* with them. As I have said, and as negotiations have shown, no insuperable barrier to that remains, until we come to questions of the ministry and government of the Church. Full communion between Churches means not that they are identical in all ways, but that there is no barrier to exchange of their ministers and ministries. Every Church's ministry is effective as a means by which the life of Christ reaches his people. Every Church's ministry is ineffective because it is prevented from operating in all the folds of his flock. For full communion between Churches, there is needed a ministry mutually acknowledged by all as possessing not only the inward call of the spirit but also the authority which each Church in conscience requires.

'At the Lausanne Conference of Churches in 1927, it was said that in view of the place which the Episcopate, the Council of Presbyters and the Congregation of the Faithful respectively had in the constitution of the early Church, in view of the fact that these three elements are each today, and have been for centuries, accepted by great Communions in Christendom, and that they are each believed by many to be essential to the good order of the Church, "We recognise that these several elements must all . . . have an appropriate place in the order and life of a re-united Church." The non-episcopal Churches have accepted the principle that episcopacy must exist along with the other elements in a re-united Church. For reasons obvious enough in Church History, they fear what may be made of episcopacy. But they accept the fact of it. If they do so for a re-united Church, why not also and earlier for the process of assimilation, as a step towards full communion? It may be said that in a re-united Church they could guard themselves, in the constitution, against abuses of episcopacy. But they could do so far more effectively by taking it into their own system.'

The phrase, like the suggestion, has, in the years since, become celebrated. It formed the heart and centre of what the Archbishop was proposing in his Cambridge sermon. And then, in a notable passage towards the end, he gave his reasons for making it, and his own ardent desire for a growth towards full communion before ever the stage of constitution-making, as between hitherto separated Churches, could be reached. 'It is because I fear a stalemate, that I venture to put this suggestion forward for examination. I love the Church of England as the Presbyterian and the Methodist love their Churches. It is, I think, not possible yet nor desirable that any Church should merge its identity in a newly-constituted union. What I desire is that I should freely be able to enter their churches, and they mine, in the sacraments of the Lord and in the full fellowship of worship, that his life may freely circulate between us. Cannot we grow to full communion with each other before we start to write a constitution? Have we the wisdom, the humility, the love and the spirit of Christ sufficient for such a venture as I have suggested? If there were agreement on it, I would thankfully receive, at the hands of others, their commission in their accustomed form, and in the same way confer our own; that is the mutual exchange of love and enrichment to which Lambeth, 1920, called us.'

The sermon led to an immediate response from the General Purposes Committee of the Free Church Federal Council in the same month of its delivery, November 1946. The General Purposes Committee then 'invited its constituent Churches to appoint representatives charged with the duty of seeking from the Archbishop an elucidation of his University sermon and of exploring its implications. The appointed representatives were received on Thursday, 16 January 1947 at Lambeth Palace by the Archbishop, who was accompanied by the Bishop of Derby. The Archbishop replied to a number of questions put to him, and it was agreed that, if formal discussions were to take place, they would not be between the Church of England and the Free Church Federal Council, but between the Church of England and the various individual Free Churches. The Council, however, might well be concerned, from the Free Church side, in the organisation of the discussions, and might itself be represented at them. He concluded by asking the representatives of the Free Churches who were present to convey to the Free Churches of England a definite and official invitation to resume conversations with the Cambridge sermon as a starting point, and with a view to the securing of full intercommunion.'[1]

These conversations, thus inaugurated, continued for the next five years and, as Stanley Eley has already said, 'the Archbishop took immense interest in all that was done', keeping in close touch throughout with John Rawlinson, then Bishop of Derby, and Bishop Stephen Neill. Eventually there emerged, as a very important consequence of the Cambridge sermon, the inauguration of the Anglican-Methodist Conversations. Those who had taken part in the general conversations which had led, in 1950, to the publication of *Church Relations in England* had left it to individual churches 'to decide whether, as a result of our work, they shall enter upon the stage of definite negotiations'.[2] The Methodist Church decided to do so, and Conference, in 1953 'approved a proposal of its Faith and Order Committee "that the Methodist Church would be prepared to proceed to a further stage in the promotion of intercommunion with the Church of England", subject to the Church of England giving certain assurances which that Committee described as follows: "It would need to be satisfied (a) that the Church of England acknowledges that our divisions are within the Christian body, which is throughout in a state of schism; (b) that the same liberty of interpretation of the nature of

[1] *Church Relations in England*, p. 17 (S.P.C.K., 1950). [2] *Ibid.*, p. 43.

158

episcopacy and of priesthood would be accorded to the Methodist Church as prevails in the Church of England; (c) that the Methodist Church would be free to preserve the relations of intercommunion and fellowship with other non-episcopal Churches which it now enjoys."'[1] The convocations of Canterbury and York in 1955, after consideration of these proposals of the Methodist Faith and Order Committee, accepted with certain reservations the points raised, and the Methodist Conference of 1955 resolved to enter into consultations. In 1958 an *Interim Statement*, representing the joint thinking of committees appointed by the Church of England and the Methodist Church, which had begun in the July of 1956, made its appearance. The next stage was the report on *Conversations between the Church of England and the Methodist Church* which, appearing in 1963, contained the subsequently well-known proposals 'for the coming together of our two Churches in two stages. The second stage is the final goal of union in one Church. For various reasons, administrative, legal and other, we believe that this must be preceded by a stage lasting for some years at which our two Churches enter upon full communion with one another, while retaining their distinct life and identity . . . During this period of full communion, we should expect that our Churches should grow together and learn how to achieve the final goal of unity'.

A comment of Fisher's a long time afterwards upon these protracted negotiations was: 'The first Anglican-Methodist discussions, under George Bell, produced the *Interim Statement*, which was really carrying out my Cambridge sermon in 1946, and making a way by which the two Churches could come into full communion. Then, after that came the second joint group with Methodists and Anglicans meeting together, the Methodists under Roberts [the Rev. Dr. Harold Roberts, principal of Richmond College, Surrey, president of the Conference, 1957], the Anglicans under the Bishop of Oxford [the Right Reverend H. J. Carpenter] who were to carry on from where the *Interim Statement* had ended. I remember a time when, quite separately, first Harold Roberts came to me and said: "We are stuck—we can't move," and the Bishop of Oxford came to me and said: "We're stuck— we can't move." The thing was

---

[1] *Conversations Between the Church of England and the Methodist Church: A Report* (Church Information Office and the Epworth Press, 1963).

on the point of falling to pieces. I said, "We must get going." I sat down and wrote a scheme for progress and sent it to the two of them. It was a thought-out plan by which each Church could sign something which ought to satisfy the other, and was meant to be a means of getting over the barrier and into full communion. It did start the Commission going again, and from that point on they continued and produced what was called *Conversations*. But they then altered course completely, for whereas the *Interim Statement* was aiming at full communion, the *Conversations* were aiming not at full communion, except as an intermediate step, but to full integration or amalgamation, or organic union, by which the two Churches should become one single Church. Having taken that step, and having determined that the reconciliation should take place before the Methodists had become episcopal, they spent all their energies trying to make it possible to reconcile two unreconciled Churches. They thought they could do it by reconciling the ministries, but, as I said ultimately in a pamphlet,[1] it was impossible to reconcile ministries, since ministries are dependent upon Churches. They were wrong in trying to put over to the two Churches amalgamation, without stopping to consider what effect that would have, in all kinds of ways, upon the Establishment and what it would require in the way of detailed arrangement of a binding kind, upon the two Churches.'

Such was the Cambridge sermon, and such have been to date some of its consequences. Obviously the matter is not yet concluded or settled. But that the sermon opened the way towards far-reaching discussions and explorations there can be no doubt.

[1] *Covenant and Reconciliation: A Critical Examination* (Mowbray, 1967). This pamphlet of Lord Fisher's emanated from his retirement, and, therefore, may properly be regarded as beyond the scope of this book.

VIII

A Controversy and a Wedding

In the early Church there were great struggles, heresies and schisms:
but out of them came certain agreed declarations and definitions of
scriptural truth, most of which have been accepted by faithful people,
by the Church, ever since.

G.F.F., in a B.B.C. broadcast, Whit Sunday 1957

.   .   .

Are you ready, with all faithful diligence, to banish and drive away all
erroneous and strange doctrine contrary to God's Word; and both
privately and openly to call upon and encourage others to the same?
Answer: I am ready, the Lord being my helper.

The Book of Common Prayer: the Form of Ordaining or
Consecrating an Archbishop or Bishop

.   .   .

Although, as the Primate of All England said in his address, the rite
was, 'in all essentials exactly the same as it would be for any cottager
who might be married this afternoon in some small country church in a
remote village in the dales', although its surrounding circumstance was
not in the least more elaborate than the dignity of a king's daughter,
who may be Queen regnant hereafter, imperatively required, none of the
millions who followed its progress could escape the sense that here, in
this simple union of hearts and lives, was history moving upon its way.

The Times, 21 November 1947, in a leading
article on the wedding of H.R.H. Princess Elizabeth to
the Duke of Edinburgh

Two events which took place within successive months of the
autumn of 1947 brought the Archbishop much into the public
eye. Both stirred him; the one to considerable indignation; the
other to that deep satisfaction which he always found in the exercise of a
pastoral ministry. Each, moreover, exhibited a different aspect of his

character: the one showing him, when the occasion seemed to demand it, as a formidable disciplinarian: the second as one who could invest even the most stately occasion with genuine naturalness and sincerity.

The first was the publication, by Bishop Barnes of Birmingham, of his book *The Rise of Christianity*.[1] Nearly a quarter of a century later, when theological speculation has gone so much further in the questioning of what, for generations, had been regarded as immutable truth, the furore raised by this book is not easy to understand. Nor is understanding made any easier by the fact that it was a poor book 'which by its wild negations of so much of the Gospel narrative, and its unscholarly procedures and unscientific assumptions made many wonder how he could conscientiously remain a bishop', as Roger Lloyd put it. Fisher wondered, too, how its writer could conscientiously remain a bishop, and said so in Convocation.

Ernest William Barnes, King Edward's School, Birmingham, and Trinity College, Cambridge, F.R.S., Sc.D., Hon. D.D. of Aberdeen and Edinburgh, Hon. LL.D. of Glasgow, in his Cambridge days President of the Union and, after taking a first in Mathematics, a Fellow of his college, was clearly a person of high intellectual distinction. He was Master of the Temple from 1915 to 1919, a Canon of Westminster for six years. In 1924 he was appointed, on the recommendation of Prime Minister Ramsay MacDonald, to the bishopric of Birmingham, remaining there for twenty-nine years. Some people had a high regard for him. Thus, Norman Tiptaft in his book *My Contemporaries*: 'One could hardly expect a man armed with such intellectual qualifications, and a value for truth above all things, to remain silent in face of current problems; or to express views universally acceptable on religion, science or politics. The Bishop does not go looking for trouble, but he never hesitates to say what he believes, because it might provoke it. He wants to harmonise science and religion, and miracles, he says, do not harmonise. The alternative to disbelieving in miracles is to repudiate the growth of modern knowledge. He will never do that. At a British Association meeting in Birmingham, he preached on *Science, Religion and Moral Judgment*. The Great Hall of the University was packed. His audiences may disagree, but they listen. His recent utterances on genetics, asking that we breed humanity at least as

[1] E. W. Barnes, *The Rise of Christianity* (Longmans, Green & Co., 1947).

carefully as we breed cattle, have again disturbed the orthodox . . . Where-ever he preaches, people crowd to hear him and the Press reports him well. But he is not encouraged to express his views by high ecclesiastical authority. Indeed, high authority has "ticked him off" on various occasions.'

That was perfectly true. There had been a considerable clash between Barnes and Archbishop Davidson twenty years before the Bishop's dispute with Fisher. 'On Thursday morning, October 20, 1927,' wrote Bell in his biography of Davidson, 'the public was startled by reading in the press an open letter from the Bishop of Birmingham to the Archbishop of Canterbury. The purpose of the letter (so the Bishop told the Primate) was to give vent to certain reflections upon an interruption to the service in St. Paul's Cathedral on the previous Sunday, when the Bishop was preaching . . . The Bishop of Birmingham had long been known as a militant liberal Churchman. He was a mathematician and a scientist, and an outspoken champion of the evolutionary view of the origin of man; and he claimed a freedom to remodel Christian theology on that basis. He was also a decided opponent of distinctively Anglo-Catholic teaching.[1]

This matter of the Real Presence was a *bête noire* with Barnes. 'They pretend,' he had said, 'that a priest, using the right words and acts, can change a piece of bread so that within it there is the real presence of Christ. The idea is absurd and can be disproved by experiment.' He added that he would believe in the doctrine of transubstantiation 'when I can find a person who will come to the Chapel of my house and tell me correctly whether a piece of bread which I present to him has undergone the change for which believers in transubstantiation contend.'[2]

It was an address on sacramental teaching, delivered to a lunch-hour service in Birmingham, which had led to the interruption in St. Paul's, made by a leading Anglo-Catholic, Canon Bullock-Webster, who had appeared with a body of laymen in support. Barnes's letter to Archbishop Davidson was the result. The whole affair was unedifying, to say the least of it, especially as regards the press publicity which the Bishop chose to give it. But of his sincerity, then or at any other time, there was no doubt. He was passionately concerned to reconcile what he regarded as the new truths which science, as he believed, had discovered, with the

[1] George Bell, *Randall Davidson.*   [2] *Ibid.*

essential truths of Christianity which had been overlaid, as he saw the matter, by much extraneous material which would not stand up to scientific investigation. A further difficulty was that the Church would not acknowledge the fact, and as a consequence was alienating many modern minds who would otherwise be prepared to give it a hearing. 'One cause of weakness,' he had said in a sermon preached to the British Association in Cardiff in 1920, 'has arisen from the apparent determination of religious teachers to ignore scientific discovery, though all competent biologists accept man's evolution from an ape-like stock.'

The statement places him immediately in historical context, as one involved — albeit in the role of reconciler — in that war between religion and science which might be said to have begun with the Darwins and Huxleys of the nineteenth century. It is a warfare which seems now to have died away, except for sporadic outbursts, now that science and religion, both having travelled far from their old, opposed certitudes, are often to be found jointly exploring mysteries common to both. But in Barnes's day it was not so, certainly not in 1927, the same year in which he published an earlier controversial book, *Should Such a Faith Offend?*

The reply he received from Archbishop Davidson after the St. Paul's incident was, according to Bell, lengthy, courteous and frigid. After having made plain that, for him at any rate and, as he believed for many others, the matter of the Bishop's criticisms was by no means new, Davidson went on to draw attention to their manner. 'I have an intense dislike for the use of the daily press for the discussion of such subjects. I purposely refrain from trying, in a letter such as this, to discuss the profound and life-giving doctrines involved, but, of course, I am more than ready to go into the matter with yourself at any time, should you so desire. But your open letter forces me, however reluctantly, to some reply. Formally and publicly you invite me "to consider what steps can be taken to help those of us who are giving of our best to fit the Church to be in the future the spiritual guide of an educated nation". That is a large and difficult matter, needing time and care, but I can say at once that in my judgment one of the first steps is to secure the scrupulous use of the most careful language possible in dealing with doctrinal matters of deep solemnity, which affect devotional thoughts and prayers of Christian people.'

Barnes, however, was unrepentant, and the matter rested until twenty years later with the appearance of *The Rise of Christianity*. The affair, according to Stanley Eley, 'caused Fisher deep distress. We were bombarded at Lambeth with letters about it, and Fisher had to resist the pressure to take decisive action against Barnes'. Decisive action meant that Bishop Selwyn of Winchester wanted Fisher to bring Barnes before an ecclesiastical court. What, then, was this book which gave rise to such a disturbance?

To condense it is virtually impossible and certainly, at this distance of time, unprofitable. Barnes's well-known admiration for 'modern science' was, naturally, much in evidence, and the 'orderly universe of modern science' was contrasted sharply with the, by inference, disorderly and therefore unacceptable miraculous elements in the Gospels. 'During the last three centuries of our modern era, a wholly new understanding has gradually, and of late rapidly, grown strong. Science has been built upon "the uniform repetition of likenesses". Observed sequences are formulated as invariable laws of nature. The triumphant discoveries which have resulted from scientific research based upon these principles, bid fair to transform human life . . . Modern man, with his thoughts shaped by scientific activities, is certain that miracles, in the sense of finite-scale activities contrary to the normal ordering of nature, do not happen.'[1]

The Virgin Birth was another matter which caused Barnes concern. One passage in the book in this context is so characteristic of his approach to such matters as to be worthy of quotation. It also accounts for some of the offence which such presentation of his views was bound to give. Having produced parallels from mythology and ancient history of similar alleged phenomena, he went on to say: 'Biological research seems to indicate that a human virgin birth may be proved to be possible. Among the insects, reproduction from unfertilised egg-cells is common. The artificial growth of a frog from an unfertilised frog's egg has been achieved: and a frog is relatively high in the evolutionary scale. If, however, biological research should show that in humanity a virgin birth could take place, and that therefore the "miracle" of the virgin birth of Jesus was not impossible, those who now regard the miracle as essential to the Christian faith would feel disquieted. It would be asked why the son of God should be born in a

[1] E. W. Barnes, *The Rise of Christianity*.

manner common among the insects, rather than by a normal human process.'

And so it goes on. The Gospel accounts of Jesus are examined in a manner which many found disturbing and which many now might well find naïve. Nor were fundamental doctrines left unscathed. Thus: 'The story of the resurrection is so intimately bound up with Christian feeling, and so strongly entrenched in Christian tradition, that the need to abandon belief in it as a physical fact causes much distress. Yet . . . we cannot, out of deference to religious sentiment, reject the principle of the uniformity of nature which is fundamental in the outlook created by modern science . . . We might possibly claim that the physical resurrection — the resuscitation of the dead body — of Jesus provided the single and momentous exception to the general law, if critical analysis of the New Testament records yielded overwhelming testimony in its favour. But the outcome of prolonged and many-sided enquiry is, as we shall see, to cast grave doubts on the story of the physical resurrection.'[1]

So there it was, and the impact of it all on the popular mind was made all the sharper by the fact that the *Sunday Pictorial* ran a series of articles by Barnes. In these circumstances, the Archbishop felt he had to take action. This he did on two levels. The first is indicated by a passage which appeared in the *Sunday Pictorial* in the November of 1947.

BISHOP BARNES AND THE CHURCH
The Primate's Request To The Pictorial

The Sunday Pictorial is able to announce today that the Archbishop of Canterbury has chosen Dr. Alfred Blunt, Bishop of Bradford, to reply on behalf of the Church to the widely discussed articles from the pen of Dr. Barnes which are now appearing in this newspaper. Dr. Blunt is world-famous for the outspoken speech in 1936, in which he publicly criticised King Edward VIII.

A few days ago, in an astonishingly frank speech at a diocesan conference, he compared Bishop Barnes with 'Jerry Cruncher' — a body-snatcher character in Dickens. 'Dr. Barnes believes himself to be a

[1] *Ibid.*

preacher of the new truths. But he is only a resurrection man of dead theories.'

Dr. Blunt's outspoken articles, beginning in our next issue, will be published at the personal request of the Primate, who is anxious that the public should hear both sides of this important religious controversy.

Bishop Blunt was a good choice, a scholarly and able writer whose articles dealt faithfully with those of Barnes. But before that, in the October of 1947, in his Presidential Address to the Convocation of Canterbury, Fisher himself had acted on a higher level and with great force, in a brilliant speech which, after opening with a tribute to Barnes' sincerity of purpose, passed on to a hard-hitting attack on the book, and ended with the blunt statement that, in the Archbishop's view, Barnes was disqualifying himself from continuing to hold episcopal office in the Church.

'A bishop,' Fisher said, 'from the nature of his office, by reason of his responsibilities to the Church and to its members, is, I think, called upon to judge himself by, and to be judged by, stricter standards than may be allowed to others. So long as he retains that office, he must satisfy himself, and seek to satisfy others, that he is adequately and faithfully expressing in his teaching the general doctrines of the Church and their scriptural basis which he is placed by his office to defend and promote. The Bishop of Birmingham may be satisfied that his teaching in this book conforms to those requirements. I would have no trial in this matter: but I must say, for my part, that I am not so satisfied. If his views were mine, I should not feel that I could still hold episcopal office in the Church.'

It was a strong blow—strong enough to lead some to complain that Fisher had been too hard. Others welcomed it, finding true the words with which the Archbishop closed the matter: 'I trust that what I have said, with the full sense of the responsibility of my office, may serve to minimise the harm and give to members of the Church such reassurance as they may need.'

Recalling these events, years later, from his retirement the Archbishop said: 'I did see Barnes myself, to discuss his book, and he defended it against me and against my criticisms, and upheld that it was a perfectly proper book and a great book for him to have written for the Church. I remember I put one question to him. I said: "According to your book, the resurrection was no more than an impression, a spiritual searching, a spiritual awareness in the minds of the disciples, and it came to them without any visual aid; it came to them that Our Lord was risen and alive." He said: "Yes, something like that." I said: "Then how do you account for the fact that while this went on and evolved into a belief in the resurrection, they established Sunday, the first day of the week, as the day on which Christ rose? That is a precise date—why did they fix it?" He had no answer of any kind at all; I don't think he had ever thought of the question. It was, in fact, a question that pricked him, and his theory, very deeply.'

Thus ended the affair of Bishop Barnes, although he himself went upon his way convinced of the rightness of his cause and unrepentant of any criticisms which he might, and in fact did, frequently arouse, until on 29 November 1953 he passed to that bourne from which no traveller returns, and where it may be presumed he found the answers to most of his questions. He also left behind him a curiously mixed memory compounded, so far as his own diocese was concerned, of on the one hand admiration and even affection, and on the other of what may mildly be described as considerable disapproval. He also left behind him a number of legends or stories, some no doubt apocryphal, of incidents during his episcopate. Thus it was alleged how, on a Sunday after he had preached a sermon in which he had denounced much current eucharistic theology as neither more nor less than magic, he encountered in the street three of his clergy and approached them to ask them their names. They replied somewhat coldly that they were three of his local magicians. The nature of some of his confirmation addresses were, it was alleged, liable at times to be a little peculiar, so that startled candidates might find themselves the recipients of a discourse on the virtues of passive resistance as practised by Gandhi.

But these are trivia—the kind of gossip which often sticks to the personality of a notable character like weed on the hull of a ship. Over the matter of *The Rise of Christianity* it was perhaps his misfortune to meet in Archbishop Fisher a bigger and a stronger man who dealt with him in a manner which he had not experienced before and did not experience again. It remains the case that there is something pathetic about Barnes in all his undoubted sincerity, and in spite of his great intellectual gifts. He was an eccentric, in his way, in the grand style. Maybe there is a good epitaph to him in something which Norman Tiptaft wrote: 'One Bishop Barnes is urgently needed. Probably the Church couldn't stand more.'

. . .

The most notable event of 1947 which brought, by contrast with the Barnes affair, much joy to the Archbishop, was the royal wedding which took place on 20 November of that year. The event had been presaged, on the 10th of the previous July, by a portentous leader in *The Times*.

'An event of the most auspicious interest to every subject of the Crown is announced today in the betrothal of Her Royal Highness Princess Elizabeth, heiress-presumptive to the Throne, to Lieutenant Philip Mountbatten of the Royal Navy, and until his recent naturalisation a prince of the kingdom of Greece. The King will give his consent to the marriage, as is required by the Royal Marriages Act, in Council. The sovereign Governments of his Dominions overseas have been informed, according to the courtesies of the Commonwealth, in advance and have responded with warm approval and good wishes . . . The pleasure of the people will be the greater because it is apparent that there can have been no motive but the impulse of their own hearts to bring this young couple together . . . Mr. Mountbatten left Greece in early childhood, and since then has known no home but England. English is his mother tongue; he has been educated in British schools; and he has embarked on a characteristically British career in that navy in which his grandfather, Prince Louis of Battenburg, and his uncle, the present Lord Mountbatten, have served with such outstanding distinction. His naturalisation came to him by right—the same right by which it is accorded to other members of the fighting services who have proved their title by their deeds.' This naturalisation, in fact, took place on 28 February. It was followed by another occasion preparatory to their marriage; 'a little episode', as Fisher later recalled it. 'The Duke of Edinburgh, of course, grew up as a member of the Greek Orthodox Church. When the time came for him to be married to Princess Elizabeth, it occurred to me that he must be a full member of the Church of England. I talked to my beloved old Archbishop Germanos, the representative of the Oecumenical Patriarch in England, a grand man. He saw the point, and he did not raise any objection. And one day the Duke of Edinburgh and Princess Elizabeth came to Lambeth, and I took them into the temporary chapel and in a very simple little service of only a few minutes, I received him into the Church of England.' The way was thus opened for the marriage to take place, preceded by the immense and detailed preparations which greatly occupied the Archbishop, and the many associated with him, both as regards the temporalities and the spiritualities of the occasion, for months beforehand. As Stanley Eley, his Senior Chaplain, has already recorded, the Archbishop took immense pains over all the details of the occasion. His personal joy in it all was also intensified by a genuine regard for the bride and groom, amounting on his part, at least, to a personal affection quite additional to the natural demands of royalty. The young couple clearly got on well with the Archbishop from the start, and they were thoroughly prepared by him for their marriage. Of Prince Philip, as Fisher found him then and always afterwards, the Archbishop had this to say: 'Freedom and openness were exactly characteristic of all my dealings with him. As everybody knows, he is that kind of person. He enjoys an argument: he lightens it with laughter, and learns from it even though it may not change his point of view. That suits me, because it is what in my own way I think I am myself.'

This rapport, thus established between the Queen, her Consort and the Archbishop, was lasting and important. They formed a part, though obviously a very important part, of the relationships of Fisher with the Royal Family in general, which were many and intimate.

Now there was this bright and joyous occasion, all the more welcome because it brought back, for a moment, youth and gaiety, colour and pageantry into a grey time of austerity after so many years of war and its aftermath. It came at the very moment when so many were wanting exactly what such an occasion had to offer: something of pomp and circumstance and, at the same time, something to warm the heart and bring promise for the future. Thousands of words were written about it, millions of people all over the world listened to the broadcast direct from Westminster Abbey, and the combined homeliness and dignity with which the Archbishop conducted the service was the subject of much favourable comment.

'The ministrations of the broadcasting service,' said *The Times* of 21 November in a splendidly pontifical sentence, 'have never been more helpful.' It added, as though the miracle had been wrought by some early form of sound-radio, 'The actual voices of the bride and bridegroom, as they made their vows, were heard thousands of miles away, and enabled millions to share in the happiness of the great occasion.' In fact, the sound-radio coverage of the ceremony was generally agreed to be a triumph of expertise, good taste and success. The event also marked something of a debut for B.B.C. Television, which had cameras outside the Abbey and for the first time brought a great royal event into the homes of some people, although the numbers were comparatively small because television was still in its infancy. Clearly, this was something which had come to stay, and henceforth every royal personage, not to speak of every Archbishop, would have to expect, on great occasions, the exacting scrutiny of that electronic eye. Fisher was the first Archbishop of Canterbury to be put through this particular test. That he passed it so well may have owed not a little to the fact that his habitual total absorption in what he was doing made him quite oblivious to anything else. Television has had few more relaxed performers than Fisher, who, now and always, gave the impression of being quite unbothered by it in any way. The whole wedding was admirable. *The Times* leader of the period, couched in the high imperial style still affected by that journal even as late as 1947, has embalmed forever something of the flavour of it. Thus, on 20 November, under the headline: 'The Human Hope', the first leader had this: 'His Majesty has marked the joyful day of the royal wedding by raising his daughter's betrothed to the style and precedence of His Royal Highness, to knighthood in the first order of chivalry, and to the rank of Duke of Edinburgh. Thus is signalised, with due state and ceremony, his adoption into that Royal Family, which is the representative family of all the British peoples. The Poet Laureate, on the day of national rejoicing, set as it is against the chill background of the world's present fortune, hails the Crown as "a gleam, a star, to point men from despair".'

And, on the following day, there was this: 'Colour came back, for a little while, into the life of a people starved of visual inspiration. There can be no doubt at all that the decision to restore the escort of Household Cavalry to the full splendour of their full-dress uniform was right. The brilliant picture had a tonic effect upon the eyes and hearts of all who saw it—and it was seen by many who were not physically present beside the processional way. The lifting of spirits that came with it will be a refreshing memory when they return to the daily task.'

And turn to the daily task they did, as the glass coach drew away, and the bells of the Abbey pealed, and the Household Cavalry jingled off, and the television faded sound and vision, and the Archbishop of Canterbury, well satisfied, returned across the river to Lambeth Palace to face many, many tasks awaiting him.

IX

Conferences and Councils

Meeting again in conference after a long interval of eighteen years, after the grievous separation of war, we declare our thankfulness to Almighty God for a profound and joyful experience, in this meeting, of our unity in the faith of Christ and in the fellowship of the Holy Spirit.

Encyclical Letter from the Lambeth Conference, 1948

The Anglican Communion is faced, in this mid-twentieth century, with problems of great complexity, both in its witness to the world and in the strengthening of its inner life. The very recognition of these problems might cause despair, save for the faith that in Almighty God the Church can learn the will of God and receive power to do it.

Encyclical Letter from the Lambeth Conference, 1958

The World Council of Churches is composed of churches which acknowledge Jesus Christ as God and Saviour. They find their unity in Him. They have not to create their unity; it is the gift of God. But they know that it is their duty to make common cause in the search for the expression of that unity in work and in life.

Report on policy adopted by the First Assembly of the World
Council of Churches, Amsterdam, 1948

ONE of the most formidable undertakings awaiting the new Archbishop was concerned with the Lambeth Conference of 1948. 'When I became Archbishop,' he said later, 'I was perfectly aware that one of the major tasks awaiting me was to take up again the postponed Lambeth Conference of 1940. The last one had been held in 1930. Archbishop Lang had been getting everything in train for the 1940 one, for they were usually held at ten year intervals. Then came the war, and now it was already 1945. When was the next Lambeth Conference to be held? This weighed on my mind a very great deal. There was not only the matter of bringing the bishops from all over the world, but what to do with them when they came. The Lambeth Conference had always been held in Lambeth Palace itself, and this was, in a real sense an essential part of the event. The Lambeth Conference had started as a little domestic affair, the Archbishop of Canterbury calling the comparatively few bishops from overseas; and it had remained essentially domestic in character. The main thing now was to revive the whole idea of the Lambeth Conference as the great family gathering of the Anglican Communion. When could it be? We finally decided that 1948 was the earliest that we could manage, and the earliest point at which we could expect to make the bishops from overseas reasonably comfortable. And after a discussion with them, we decided that it should be in 1948.'

The first Lambeth Conference had been held under the presidency of Archbishop Longley in 1867. On that occasion, 144 were invited; seventy-six attended. This time the number involved was vastly greater, and there was the further difficulty that eighteen years had elapsed since the last, so that interest in the nature and origin of the Lambeth Conference itself, together with its place in the life of the Anglican Communion as a whole, needed to be revived.

One problem loomed at the outset. The question was whether the bishops would come, because travel was expensive, and it was a great business to leave their dioceses, often shattered by war experience. And yet it was vital, in Fisher's mind, for the Anglican Communion, that after this long interval all the bishops should come together to rediscover themselves and to renew the broken fellowship. Particularly he thought of the American bishops. 'During the war, I had formed a great personal friendship with Henry Sherrill, later to become the Presiding Bishop of the Episcopal Church in the United States. He had been in England and in Europe in charge of the chaplains looking after the U.S. Forces. I remember that we first met in the south aisle of St. Paul's Cathedral, and fell into each other's arms at sight. From then onwards we were completely devoted to each other, with no barriers of any kind, able to talk freely, to laugh freely, to think together along the same lines of sanctified common sense and eager to promote the common welfare of the Anglican Communion in every possible way. And we each possessed a certain amount of drive, to get things moving. So we were poised for this great enterprise.'

The Right Reverend Henry K. Sherrill recalled this encounter himself. 'My first meeting with Archbishop Fisher occurred in April of 1945. Bishop G. Bromley Oxnam of the Methodist Church, and I had flown to England for the service of enthronement, he representing the Federal Council of Churches in the U.S.A. and I representing the Protestant Episcopal Church. Shortly after our arrival in London, we had been asked to walk in a procession at the service in memory of President Roosevelt at St. Paul's Cathedral. After the service, Archbishop Fisher came along in his informal way, arm in arm with chaplain John Weaver of the U.S. Army, who was to be one of the Archbishop's attendants at the Enthronement. The Archbishop invited us to lunch at Lambeth Palace the next day. At the luncheon I said, "Your Grace, you have paid a great compliment to the United States by having your Enthronement on the 19th April." He replied: "I don't know what you mean." "Well," I said, "tomorrow in Boston is Patriot's Day. Paul Revere will be riding to Lexington, crying 'The British are coming!'" The Archbishop, in a characteristic gesture, threw his glasses to the top of his head. "Well, it came out all right," he said. "We wouldn't want to be bothered with you now."

'The next day, Oxnam and I went with the other foreign guests to Canterbury. The service, with the admirable address of the Archbishop, was most inspiring. Afterwards, he took particular pains to greet us all personally, and to point out items of interest in the Cathedral. Later on in the week it was my privilege to present at Lambeth Palace a private communion set to the Archbishop, and a handbag to Mrs. Fisher as gifts from our American chaplains in England, in appreciation of the Fishers' hospitality and kindness to them. My next contact with the Fishers was at our General Convention in 1946 in Philadelphia, and he and Mrs. Fisher were honoured guests and made a deep initial impression. He gave several fine addresses. But at that time I was very busy with Convention affairs and saw very little of him. It was at that Convention I was elected Presiding Bishop.

'Immediately after my assuming office on 1 January 1947, the Archbishop and I began considerable correspondence about the various affairs of the Anglican Communion, especially in regard to the Lambeth Conference in 1948. It was no secret that many of the bishops of the Church in the United States, as well as others in the Anglican Communion outside England, had not felt too happy about their place in the Lambeth Conference of 1930. They had felt in essence that they were onlookers rather than participants. In fact, some of our bishops said that they would not attend another Conference. Archbishop Fisher must have been aware of this feeling, for he exerted throughout every effort to make all bishops, from any part of the world, feel at home. As a help to this end, at his request, I prepared and sent to him a thumb-nail sketch of our bishops in the United States, to assist him in the appointment of the various committees of the Conference. This was an indication of his concern and care in preparing for the Conference. Various committees as to housing and welcome were appointed by him, Mrs. William Temple taking an important role.'

But before this stage had been reached, and before even the first of Fisher's several visits to the United States, of which that to the General Convention of 1946 was the first, he had himself begun to see the needs of the situation. 'I quickly sensed that, in fact, American bishops as a whole would have been not particularly interested in the idea of a Lambeth Conference. After all, the whole of the Atlantic separates us. Of course, the American Church had all kinds of ties with us; but they were in their world, and we were in our world, and they did not quite feel that we belonged intensely to each other, and I asked myself what could be done. When I remembered that Archbishop Davidson had, I think in the first or second year of his archiepiscopate, gone on board Pierpont Morgan's yacht, on a cruise, which had taken him across the Atlantic, and that he had set foot briefly both in Canada and in the United States, I saw clearly the one thing that I must do at all costs.'

Bishop Sherrill, on this matter, filled in the details: 'Archbishop and Mrs. Davidson had come to the General Convention of 1904 as guests of Bishop and Mrs. William Lawrence for the General Convention in Boston. From all accounts it was a dignified and friendly occasion in keeping with the temper of the times. But it took World War One to bring about the closest relationship between Great Britain and the United

At Lindley Lodge Preparatory School, Nuneaton. G.F.F. fourth from left, top.

Lindley Lodge School, Nuneaton. G.F.F. second from right, second row from front.

Speech day at Repton, 1928.

Entering Chester Cathedral for enthronement as Bishop of Chester, Michaelmas Day, 1932.

Entering St. Paul's for enthronement as Bishop of London, November 1939.

As Bishop of London at a meeting with Cardinal Hinsley and Archbishop William Temple, Waldorf Hotel, London 1941.

The Archbishop with members of the Russian Patriarchal Mission, 1945.

With H.R.H. Princess Elizabeth at the rededication of St. John's, Waterloo Road, the festival of Britain Church, 1951.

With H.R.H. Princess Margaret, President of the Church of England Youth Council.

Doing homage at the Coronation Service, 1953.

Family reunion in the Old Palace, Canterbury, April, 1945

Enthronement in the Chair of St. Augustine, Canterbury Cathedral, 19 April, 1945.

Greeting African and Indian ladies, Mbale, Uganda, 1955.

Consecration of four African Bishops, Namirembe Cathedral, 1955.

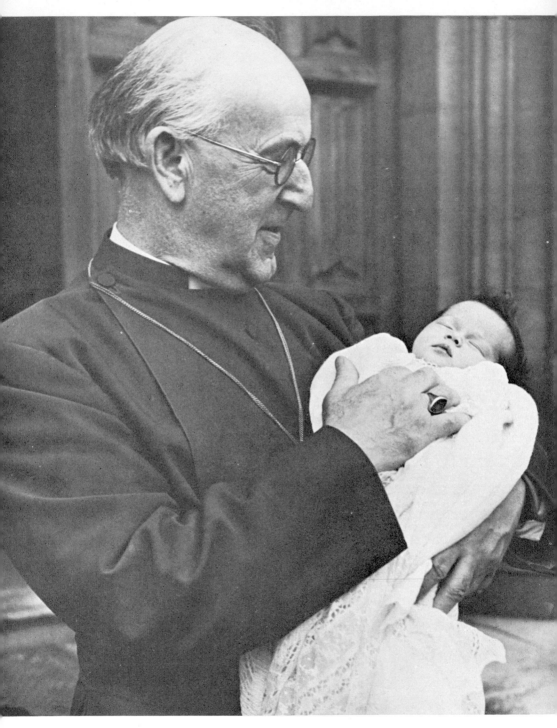

Christening of a granddaughter at Lambeth Palace, 1954.

With President Truman at the White House, 1946.

Wedding of H.R.H. Princess Elizabeth to Lieutenant Philip Mountbatten, November 1947.

Holy Land visit, 1960, in the Church of the Holy Sepulchre, Jerusalem.

In the Holy Land, 1960, at the Place of the Baptism in the Jordan.

With the Oecumenical Patriarch, 1960.

At Lambeth Palace, 1960.

In retirement, at Hound Street, Sherborne 1961.

With Lady Fisher at Trent village party on his 80th birthday.

States. Even in my own youth, in many Fourth of July celebrations in small towns, local orators fought again the battles of the American Revolution. With the great immigration of the Irish, this feeling was intensified. The Church of England and the Protestant Episcopal Church had close and friendly relations, due principally to the various Lambeth Conferences. But England seemed a long distance away and to most Episcopalians the Archbishop of Canterbury seemed a formal and shadowy figure . . . With the end of World War Two the situation had changed with the rise of new nations and the deepened brotherhood between the United States and Great Britain. The time was ripe for a new approach within the Anglican Communion. Archbishop Temple would have realised this beyond question. He was greatly admired in the United States, and he and Mrs. Temple had made a triumphant tour when he was Archbishop of York. But his untimely death brought Archbishop Fisher to Canterbury. His leadership laid strong foundations for the future.'

Thus it came about that, as one of the first essential preliminaries to the Lambeth of 1948, the Fishers crossed the Atlantic in 1946 to put, as Fisher expressed it, 'the Lambeth Conference on the map'. The journey began with an amusing incident. They travelled across to Canada first, by the *Mauretania*. On the same ship was Field-Marshal Montgomery, who proved to be an entertaining companion. Once, on deck, he said to Fisher: 'Archbishop, I want to hear how you run the Church of England. Will you come with Mrs. Fisher to tea one day in my cabin?' So there they went, and had tea with Montgomery and his A.D.C.s, one of them being the son of the Bishop of Rochester, Chavasse. Tea being ended, the Field-Marshal pushed back his chair and said: 'Now, Archbishop, I will tell you how to run the Church of England. You need more discipline!'

At Winnipeg, Fisher addressed, in St. John's Church, all the bishops and the whole synod of the Church of Canada, and began a close and affectionate interest in its affairs. From there he and Mrs. Fisher went down to Philadelphia for the United States Episcopal Church General Convention.

This was the first of numerous visits to the United States where Fisher, always highly acceptable to the Americans, made a strong impression. The marked social geniality which others had noted in England greatly appealed to the Americans also, among whom such a quality has always been highly appreciated. In all, before his retirement (there were other visits afterwards) Fisher made four visits to the United States: to the General Conventions of 1946 in Philadelphia and of 1952 in Boston, to the first Anglican Congress in Minneapolis and the General Assembly of the World Council of Churches in Evanston in 1954, and to the meeting of the Central Committee of the World Council of Churches in 1957. Summing up the effect of all these, Bishop Sherrill said: 'On all these visits he made a great impression not only upon our own church people, but upon the entire public. He was very popular with the press. They enjoyed his clarity, his repartee. He was also extremely photogenic. I can see him now, seated in a chair on our lawn at Boxford, surrounded by reporters and photographers reclining on the grass. The session was marked by keen questions and answers, with enjoyment on the part of all. The Archbishop showed a genuine interest in all kinds and conditions of people. Today, in our little town of Boxford, the local postmaster and our storekeeper often ask after him. The Archbishop had an unusual quality of seriousness and of humour, of dignity and of informality. This gift won the hearts of all. During their visits to the United States, the Fishers shook hands with thousands of people at various receptions, no small physical task in itself, especially on some occasions in great heat. The Archbishop understood our people. It was often said that, except for Mr. Churchill, Great Britain could not have sent a better ambassador of goodwill and understanding.'

To return, however, to the Episcopal Church General Convention at Philadelphia in 1946; the Archbishop's address—what his hosts might have called his 'keynote speech'—has a lasting importance as indicative of some of his own convictions as to the fundamental nature of Anglicanism. Having mentioned some of the problems which had arisen over the years in England, both from differences of emphases within the Church and from the complexity of its relations with the State, and having indicated some of the means by which these faults were being corrected, he went on to state, in a notable passage, some of his feelings regarding the Anglican tradition in a wider context.

'The Anglican tradition has its strong Catholic element, which emphasises the historic continuity and organised life of the Church as the appointed channel of divine grace through Creed, Ministry and Sacraments. It has its strong evangelical element, which emphasises Gospel before Church, personal conversion before corporate expression of it, spiritual immediacy, the direct response to the Holy Spirit, wherever He may breathe. It has its third strong element, not easy to give a name to, which acts as a watchdog of both the other elements, and brings into our tradition a special element of intellectual integrity, of sobriety and moderation of judgment, of moral earnestness: an element which is as aware of what we do not know as of what we do, which does not wish to go beyond the evidence, but to judge all things with a large and reasonable charity.'

It was well received, and succeeded admirably also in emphasising the world-wide extent of the Anglican Communion. 'The Anglican Communion embraces many national churches, provincial in name or character, and a large number of dioceses not yet organised as separate provinces or national churches. They are spread all over the world. The name Anglican is already a misnomer; it indicates their remote origin, but it does not at all describe their present condition. They are indigenous churches, not only here and in England and in the British dominions, but in India, China, Japan, Ceylon, and Africa, East and West. Wherever they are, they stand for a particular tradition within the Holy Catholic Church of Christ, and until that tradition is taken up into a wider fellowship, they must cohere.' That such a far-flung communion should give attention to 'securing a frequent and effective interchange of thought and understanding' was, he maintained, self-evident. The point was taken as regards the Lambeth Conference. He had, again as his hosts might have said, 'sold them on it'. He recalled, 'Bishops said to me afterwards: "This sounds something we ought to come to. Is that so?" And I told them that indeed it was!'

Without any doubt, this first American visit was a great success and had lasting results. Stanley Eley said, as regards both these points, that 'this lengthy tour really broke the ice with the Americans. They had always had a great love and affection for the Mother Church, but somehow or other, I don't think they thought that they really belonged, that they were an integral part of it. From that moment onwards, however, they knew they were, and his speeches and sermons out there were of first-rate importance in preparing for the spirit of the Lambeth Conference of 1948. From then onwards, he began to visit other parts of the Anglican Communion and he was indeed an ambassador and, building upon the foundations of the Lambeth Conference and his visit to America in 1946, he established similar relationships with Australia and New Zealand, and various parts of Africa.'

It remained next to return home and face the formidable task of arranging, in all its aspects, from agenda to hospitality, this Lambeth Conference. As regards the agenda, this was largely based on that which had been prepared for the 1940 Conference, and those who care to consult the records of Lambeth 1948 will find set forth the matters with which it principally concerned itself: the Christian Doctrine of Man; the Church in the Modern World; the Christian Way of Life; the Unity of the Church the Anglican Communion; the Church's Discipline in Marriage. Events have long overtaken some of the conclusions reached, and time has proved the inaccuracy of one forecast in the Encyclical Letter which, according to custom, emanated from the Conference at its conclusion. 'For those who have eyes to see, there are signs that the tide of faith is beginning to come in.'

Even so, the Conference was to be of great importance, in the history of the Anglican Communion in particular, as a landmark in the process by which that body became more conscious of itself; in the history of the Church in general, insofar as it touched upon issues of universal import, such as its attitude to the Church of South India; and in the archiepiscopate of Fisher, in that it represented one of the most challenging of all the tasks he was to face, and also one of his greatest triumphs. Of Fisher's personal part, Stanley Eley who, as senior chaplain at the time was in a unique position to observe it, had this to say: 'His leadership was magnificent. At times, possibly, there was just a little over-anxiety to get the thing cut and dried fairly quickly, which wasn't exactly impatience, it was something rather different. It was an unwillingness to go on wasting time, frankly, with a lot of repetitive talk; an eagerness to get the team really together, and as a result I think that the goodwill that was engendered by that Conference amongst the Anglican Communion was something quite extraordinary. It was at this time that the Anglican Communion realised that it was a communion. The Conference was big and came from all over the world. When you have over a hundred United States bishops meeting half a dozen Japanese bishops only three years after the war actually ended, the emotional currents were bound to be there. Yet, sinking all that in their common Anglican heritage, the fellowship—in the best sense of that word—and the love that grew out of that Conference between the various parts of the Anglican Communion welled up again in the Minneapolis Congress of 1954. Within a very few days, there was a spirit of informality and yet discipline which is typical, I think, of Fisher.'

The great opening service of the Conference took place at St. Paul's on 4 July 1948, at which the Archbishop, by a happy thought, that being American Independence Day, had asked Bishop Sherrill to preach. For Fisher personally this was a memorable occasion, and one particular circumstance added to the fact. One of the three Japanese who attended the Conference was the Right Reverend M. H. Yasiro, Presiding Bishop of the Church in Japan and Bishop of Kobe. He had brought with him a lovely cope heavily embroidered, which had been worked by the women of the Church of Japan, and the money provided by the men of the Church of Japan. This gift Yasiro brought, as a peace offering, to obliterate the memories of all that had happened during the war. The Archbishop discovered, however, that this gift, the nature and occasion of which moved him much, was at the docks and that there would be a two hundred pound import fee on it. He accordingly went to the Chancellor of the Exchequer who arranged for the fee to be cancelled so that Fisher was able to wear the cope at the opening service of the Lambeth Conference of 1948. Furthermore, when in due course the Coronation came, he chose it for that occasion, and it was in a Japanese cope that he crowned Queen Elizabeth.

And so the Conference of 1948 got down to its work, meeting in the hastily restored Great Library at Lambeth. The results of its toils are embalmed in the Resolutions and Reports of the Conference. They are indicative not only of much labour; but also, when studied twenty years later, of the fact that in a world of such rapid change as this present one, the conclusions, however carefully considered, of one day, soon become outdated by time and circumstance. Thus, to take one example, while it remains true, as the Report on the Christian Doctrine of Man pointed out, that the major threats to the human spirit lay on one side in political despotism and, on the other, in economic materialism indifferent to human factors, subsequent developments such as the modern tendency for the machine to take over more and more sections of work, with the resultant problems of redundancy and increased leisure, both unheard of in 1948, would be important elements to be considered in any discussion of the theme now. And then again, subsequent developments have made the formal character of the Church's marriage discipline, as reflected in the 1948 Conference report on that subject, increasingly a matter for questioning. It is also noteworthy that the Lambeth of 1948 said nothing on the question of contraception, although the Lambeth of ten years later did. The impression given, on the whole, by the reports and resolutions of this Lambeth of 1948 is of a Church thinking aloud before the era of that theological 'shaking of the foundations', which has happened since, had begun. Problems enough, indeed, there were. But, for the most part, attempts to deal with them seem to have been approached from positions of certitudes not now as easy to assume as then. On the Anglican Communion, however, the Conference had much that was constructive to say and considerable fruitful action did result.

As the testing weeks of the Conference passed, it was natural that moments of tension should arise, all of them bearing heavily upon the Archbishop as president of the Conference and stretching his capacities to the full, both as reconciler and as leader. One point of difficulty arose over the question of the Church of South India. In his own words: 'As was to be expected, the most important committee was that which dealt with the unity of the Church. The Church of South India had just been created.[1] It had been looked forward to by the 1930 Conference, but now,

---

[1] Inaugurated on 27 September 1947 by the union of the Anglican Church of India, Burma and Ceylon in respect to four of its dioceses, the South India Province of the Methodist Church, and the South India United Church, which included Presbyterian, Congregational and Dutch Reformed bodies, C.S.I. represented the outcome of negotiations which had begun as far back as the May of 1919, when a group of thirty-three men, ministers of varying denominations, had met together to consider methods by which the

in 1948, it was a fact. We had to come to some kind of agreement as to how we were to be in touch with it. Feelings ran high. Was the Church of South India a respectable Church at all? Into it had come members of Methodist, Presbyterian and Congregational churches, entirely innocent of any episcopal ordination, and they were to take their places, with nothing said, in the Church of South India on equal footing. This offended a number of bishops; all were unhappy about it. The question was, whether it made the Church of South India so unsound doctrinally that the Church of England could not touch it at all? That was the great debate. The question was raised at one point as to whether bishops or clergy ordained in and by this new Church would be validly ordained. The majority thought that they would: a minority differed. However, the Conference as a whole took it quite quietly, and came to the conclusion that the Church of South India deserved blessing, and encouragement, and friendship as far as it could be given, and the hope was expressed that, in due course, the Churches of the Anglican Communion could all come to be in full communion with the Church of South India, though it was recognised that, at the moment, any idea of full communion was ruled out.'

Here was a perilous passage indeed for the Archbishop, as president of the Conference, to negotiate. He recalled: 'There was one very unhappy moment. The debate was drawing towards its close on a hot summer evening. At four o'clock a good number of bishops slipped off on ploys of their own. The next, and the final speech, was made by Bishop Stephen Neill, an ardent advocate of the Church of South India. There were no further speakers. There was nothing left for me to do but to put the matter to the vote. It was said by some of the disgruntled that I had arranged this so that the vote should be taken while quite a number of possibly anti-South India people were absent. Nothing was further from

divisions among themselves might be overcome in order that their collective Christian witness and work might be rendered thereby more effective. The birth and development of the Church of South India represent important elements in the Ecumenical Movement as a whole, and led to complexities, chiefly based upon the feeling, deeply held by some, that the proposed arrangement represented a grave threat to Church order. The matter was complex, and full treatment of it would need to be lengthy. It may be sufficient to state here that the 1930 Lambeth Conference had given guarded approval to the general proposal, and that the scheme in the meantime had been considerably revised.

my thoughts. As a good chairman conducting the business I let the debate continue until the list of speakers came to an end, and then I put the vote. Anyhow, the conclusion was reached and we were content with it, and it left plenty of room for growth.'

Another matter of an entirely different nature that came out of this Conference added a new element to the Anglican Communion. It was felt that the Lambeth Conference itself, once every ten years, with bishops only, did not provide a sufficient means of keeping the Communion in touch between its various particular Churches. Accordingly, it was proposed that at every mid-interval, between conferences, there should be an Anglican Congress—bishops and clergy and laity from all over the world, coming together in one place to discuss, hear papers, worship together, and above all get to know each other and the fellowship to which they belonged. There was great enthusiasm for this. It was adopted, and in due course the first Anglican Congress was held in Minneapolis in the year 1954.

The Anglican Advisory Committee for Missionary Strategy also emerged from the Lambeth of 1948, not indeed as something altogether new—it had existed since the Lambeth Conference of 1878, if rather as an idea than an actuality—but as something of value given a new skeleton organisation. For many years the idea was kept alive only by the devoted labours of Canon McCleod Campbell, one of those dedicated men who find themselves with a task laid upon them by the Church without at the same time being given the means to carry it out. Fisher, always appreciative of this kind of service, recognised the value of all that Campbell had done. 'He was one of the heroes of the development of the Anglican Communion,' he said. 'His books about the history of the Communion played a very great part in this work. He was Secretary of the Church of England Missionary Council, and as such had the duty of co-ordinating the two main societies, S.P.G. and C.M.S. and all the other little societies, and bringing them into a common sense of fellowship and united effort. He invented united statements, which once a year were presented to the Church Assembly, giving a picture of the whole work of the Anglican Communion year by year, through the eyes of the Missionary Council. He became the Secretary of the Advisory Council, but it was really a hopeless task. There was no separate secretariat for it. There was no money for it. There were merely members in each part of the Communion appointed to it, who had no means and no money, no opportunity of ever meeting together. But there they were, and Campbell kept the thing in being. Yet it was destined to play a great part in years to come.' What that part was emerged at the Lambeth of 1958 with the appointment of an Anglican Executive Officer. Meanwhile, this Advisory Committee for Missionary Strategy was entrusted with one piece of work by the 1948 Conference—to establish a central college for the Communion, at St. Augustine's, Canterbury, a promising venture which fully justified itself but has now been discontinued.

One of the many other things which came out of this Conference of 1948 was the suggestion, in a sub-section of the Report on the Christian Doctrine of Man, that there should be a simple list of Rules of Church-manship, which all ordinary people ought to know and obey. Fisher, and Garbett of York were asked to draft something. They did so, and the draft, after debate in Convocation, was duly adopted. In view of its clarity and value, it seems surprising that more has not been made of it. To this day people are still enquiring about it in bookshops.[1]

So ended, with a great concluding service at Westminster Abbey, the first of the two Lambeth Conferences over which Fisher was to preside. All through, it had been very much his affair, and his the main burden. One very important part of the whole Conference had, however, been the responsibility of Mrs. Fisher and her helpers, responsible for the immense hospitality which greatly impressed, among others, the Americans. A comment of Bishop Sherrill's, which may be taken as a final word on this Conference of 1948, makes this very clear:

[1] These Rules, originally seven in number, were as follows:
  1. To follow the example of Christ in home and daily life, and to bear personal witness to him.
  2. To be regular in private prayer day by day.
  3. To read the Bible carefully.
  4. To come to church every Sunday.
  5. To receive the Holy Communion faithfully and regularly.
  6. To give personal service to church, neighbours, and community.
  7. To give money for the work of the parish and diocese: and for the work of the Church at home and overseas.

'The arrangements were perfect. Both the Archbishop and Mrs. Fisher were so hospitable. They entertained scores of bishops and their wives, both at Lambeth and at the Old Palace in Canterbury. This was especially difficult in 1948, when there were such great shortages both of food and of help. They showed a great concern for the comfort of all. All this resulted in the happiest atmosphere throughout the Conference and had a great effect upon the discussions. The Archbishop was an admirable presiding officer. There was no question who was in charge. His ready wit enlivened many sessions. He was incisive as to length of speeches, but gave every bishop an equal opportunity to be heard. He seldom interfered from the Chair, but he followed the discussions and the reports of the various committees with meticulous care, which must have meant long hours of study after the day's work was apparently over. I cannot recall hearing an unhappy or critical remark by any of our bishops or their wives—no small achievement in itself . . . It was the Archbishop's own personality which made the new spirit within the Anglican Communion. At a critical period of change and re-adjustment he made a contribution which has made possible future growth and development. Mrs. Fisher was a tower of strength in every way with her dignity, hospitality and friendliness. She shared to the full his visions and his course of action.'

.   .   .

The Fishers were next in the United States for the General Convention of the Episcopal Church in 1952: a very happy visit further strengthening the links which the Archbishop had already made with the Americans. On the Sunday before the Convention, Fisher preached at Christ Church (the Old North Church) in Boston, in a service which was broadcast in sound and vision across the States. Two passages from his address deserve quotation: the first because it is an example of the oratory of which Fisher, when he cared to speak in that way, was a master; and the second because it stated a truth still very much with us.

Thus, having referred to the links with America's past which the Old North Church represented, he went on: 'Centuries of immigration have also brought to you, and made a part of you, the rich and glowing spiritual heritage of England, of Europe, and of European Christendom. I dare not attempt to describe that heritage. At its heart are such things as these: belief that each man has a personal worth which every other man must honour and respect; belief that man is responsible for his brother's good, at least as much as he is for his own; belief that society must be directed first by order and then by freedom, first by duties and then by rights, first by just laws and then by the liberties they secure; belief that society and each member of it, is responsible to a truth which is above man and which judges him, is responsible to God.'

The second was this: 'If our civilisation fails, it will fail because of an atheism no less real because it has not been deliberately chosen, but is the casual result of ordinary people letting their absorption with the cares and riches and bustle of this world shut their eyes to God, and atrophy their powers of reverence and worship, their powers of moral discipline and self-dedication, their ability to be silent before the majesty of God and the mystery of his love.'

The Rev. James W. Kennedy of the Church of the Ascension, New York, who was at that time responsible for the broadcasting aspects of the Convention, recalled another address by Fisher—this one from an ecumenical mass-meeting in a Baptist church, in connection with the same Convention. 'There was great excitement, mainly because His Grace was the speaker. Our timing had to be exactly right, and I was a little nervous because I had never dealt with him in such a responsible way before. He was most co-operative, and in a few preliminary remarks had all the audience in the palm of his hand, so that by the time he began his formal address on the air, everyone was in a festive mood, ready to laugh at anything he said. I don't remember the details of his address, except that it really gave the World Council its most solid, authentic, and persuasive presentation to Episcopalians. It was interspersed with so many anecdotes that I am sure everyone who heard it carried away not only a sense of the magnificence and importance of the Ecumenical Movement, but that it was really fun to do things together.'

The same writer recorded a memory of a different order, revealing something of Fisher's prowess as a humorous after-dinner speaker: 'One more thing from that Convention was the dialogue between Geoffrey

Fisher and Henry Sherrill which reached its climax at one of the large dinner meetings of the Convention held in the gymnasium of the Massachusetts Institute of Technology. The two of them bantered back and forth at the dinner, concentrating heavily on the visit the Fishers had made to Boxford, the Sherrill home, prior to the Convention, with anecdote after anecdote involving cows and pigs and chickens and almost everything else you can imagine on a farm. I have never forgotten the image created in my mind at that time of the Presiding Bishop of the Episcopal Church and the Archbishop of Canterbury having in common the glorious experience of scratching pigs' backs.'

In a more serious vein, *Time* magazine carried a long piece on Fisher at this season, in its issue of 1 September 1952, which was very percipient.

'Dr. Geoffrey Francis Fisher is a deeply pious Christian. He is also a gentleman of rational disposition, settled habits and scholarly inclination. This blending, perhaps more frequently found in the British Isles than elsewhere, has made him just about the ideal man for his job: ninety-ninth Archbishop of Canterbury, Primate of All England and the active spiritual head of the Anglican Communion . . . As spiritual leader of the world-wide Anglican Communion, Dr. Fisher is one of the six presidents of the World Council of Churches. He also favours church unity as an ideal. But, practically speaking, he has his reservations. "The World Council of Churches" he sums up, "is not a church. It is none of its business to negotiate a re-union between the churches. The World Council and the Council on Faith and Order can go on forever discussing the question of doctrinal change. If the Council tried to force any changes in our church's creed," said the Archbishop, "we should clear out."

'In this ultimate stubbornness, the Archbishop is supported by most Anglican churchmen. In his quiet way, Anglican Fisher has intensified the predilection of his flock for their middle way in Christendom, and has added to their confidence that it is a true way, a good compromise between Geneva and Rome.'

This reference to the World Council of Churches brings into focus an event which had occurred on 23 October 1948, immediately following the Lambeth Conference of that year. This was the first assembly of the World Council of Churches, formally brought into being in the Concertgebouw at Amsterdam. The Council, composed of Churches which 'acknowledge Jesus Christ as God and Saviour' was, while being far from representative at that time of world Christianity in its totality, since it included neither representatives of Roman Catholicism nor of Orthodox Churches within the Russian orbit, as well as having numerous other absentees, marked an important development in the advance towards ecumenicity. Formed from the fusion of two earlier ecumenical movements—'Life and Work' and 'Faith and Order'—it was the first truly interdenominational international Christian consultative body to come into existence. As such, the occasion of its inauguration in Amsterdam was of historic importance, and Fisher 'happened', as he put it, to be in the chair. His account of the event has a special interest as illustrative of an unemotionalism only very rarely disturbed. He said: 'It was a great moment. Some chairmen would at that time have become emotional in their prayers, their thanksgivings, their loud *Te Deums*. Being myself a very restrained person, I had to say something, and said a few words of unpremeditated prayer: but it was all on a very quiet and deep, and unostentatious, note.'

But behind this moment lay years of association with the British Council of Churches and in front of it further years of involvement with the World Council also. To both of them Fisher attached great importance, and his own account of how he was drawn into this field has particular interest, and may be conveniently looked at in this place inasmuch as a great deal of his work in and for the Councils took place in the decade between the two Lambeth Conferences of his archiepiscopate, while two of his American visits in the same span of time were concerned with the World Council. 'When I went to London as bishop,' he recalled, 'I first came into touch with the Ecumenical Movement. The form it took when I first got there was the creation of a British Council of Churches. William Temple introduced me to this work, and in it to William Paton and the great leaders of the other Churches: John Bailey of the Church of Scotland; Archie Craig, who afterwards became the first secretary of the British Council of Churches; and Payne of the Baptists, a superb man, and Newton Flew of the Methodists, who had been up at Oxford at my time, and was a dear friend and a good scholar. In my last year at Oxford,

I had been told to go in for a college prize which was also a university prize, for an essay. I won the college prize; but the university prize went to Newton Flew so that I became *proxime accessit*, and this was a standing link between us. At appropriate moments, Newton Flew would just remind me that, in fact, I was only *proxime accessit* to him.

'So I was introduced to all these people, the two best-known men being William Temple, of course, and William Paton. Bill Paton was a heavy man, heavily intellectual, a true Scot, testing every yard carefully, but full of zeal and full of determination to increase the unity and the power of the Church, and with a vast knowledge of all kinds of churches and their affairs. It was through these men that I found myself coming in to the British Council of Churches as soon as it was formed under William Temple, and finding myself, as Bishop of London, as chairman of the Executive. That was a grand experience. The British Council of Churches has done its job, I think, extremely finely, with a reticence which is right, and a sobriety which is necessary.

'I became its chairman when I became Archbishop, and I never had anything but happiness and joy when I was conducting their sessions. I remember two things in particular over which difficulty was liable to arise. First, when anything came up about gambling, the Free Churchmen were quite adamant against it, and very aware of its dangers. The Anglican speakers on the subject were almost always arguing that on the one hand, of course, there was nothing essentially evil about gambling in itself, while on the other hand, it was a very serious social evil. On this and other social problems, Anglicans would speak with this double voice, while Free Churchmen were not ashamed of the Puritan spirit, and we used to have to reckon with that. The other thing was of a much larger kind. The best example of it I can give was over Central Africa and Nyasaland, when political problems were entangled with missionary policy. The Church of Scotland was very deeply committed to Nyasaland and other parts in Central Africa, terribly sensitive to the spiritual issues, and ready at many points to tell the British Government precisely what they must do to give the African a fair deal, and advance him in power and prestige. Now they were perfectly right in all they were seeking after, and we agreed with them. It was merely a matter for discretion. It was so easy for Churchmen to speak dogmatically, even violently, to the secular authority, knowing indeed very often more about the real situation than the secular authority, and thinking that their special knowledge and insight gave them a special power and right judgment. But in fact, it was very often unwise and even dangerous, because other Christians, even other members of their own Church, might not agree with them. Various views were possible among Christians, and in any case we on the British Council of Churches did not bear the responsibility for political action. It was not for us to say "This shall be" or "That shall be". Only those with the full range of responsibilities and knowledge could do that in the political sphere. And therefore all we ever ought to do was to provide for a report by those who were specially knowledgeable, discuss the report, and then to commend it to the Churches, and possibly direct that it be brought to the notice of the responsible Government department. All that was within our province: but it was very easy to become dictatorial, and I always fought hard against that. I remember one particular time when Pitt-Watson, a dear man who had acted with me in the Coronation service, and shared with me the Presentation of the Bible, was urgent that the Government should be denounced for its treatment of an African problem, I think in Nyasaland. And I was deliberately trying to restrain him, and saying we could not properly go that far. The Council was unhappy; but the resolutions that we passed on such subjects were always, I think, wise and tempered.

'The whole of the work of the British Council was absorbingly interesting, and I did not fear, every now and then, to try to prevent something rash being done out of a laudable enthusiasm. Especially when Church unity was under discussion, and idealism began to outrun discretion, I would rely on John Bailey and Archie Craig and others to stop the Council committing itself to some unwise resolution. It often took a very great deal of trouble to save the Council from being carried away into sentimental and enthusiastic utterances which, because they were out of touch with practical possibilities, would damage the cause we were all serving.

'As to the World Council of Churches, here again there were grand people. Dibelius, Bishop of Berlin, was one of the most notable and remarkable of them for what he achieved, just by quiet fearless faithfulness for the Church, in contrast with the more ebullient and unrestrained Niemoller, who was no less a remarkable person. Fry, of the United States was another; a remarkable stateman, with a pawky sense of humour who did a very great deal for the Council. George Bell was always at the very heart of it, and at the very front of it as well, and there were many others whom I remember now with respect and affection. It was always interesting; one always had to be watching; one had to be careful against some who were a little too single-minded in one way or another. But we did some grand work. We carried on the Ecumenical Movement from step to step, with a sense of purpose and development and high enterprise and sound thinking. That was a thing very well worth doing, and I am thankful to have had my part in it.'

So characteristically cool an assessment should not be allowed to obscure, however, that with the first assembly of the World Council of Churches a significant new chapter in the history of the Churches had begun. The services to it, and the long connections with it along the road to formal inauguration of George Bell, with his great network of international contacts, should also not be overlooked. There seems little doubt also, that the existence of the World Council had considerable effects upon the thinking of the Roman Catholic Church, which has since 1948 become much more associated with it. Nor should Fisher's characteristically cool account of the moment when, under his chairmanship, 'the thoughts and hopes of all the years' came into being at Amsterdam, in the August of 1948, conceal the fact that, as George Bell later wrote: 'It was a thrilling moment, for here at last the hopes and prayers of years were to be fulfilled. Some of the oldest Churches in the world were represented—the Church of Ethiopia and the Orthodox Syrian Church of Malabar, for example; and some of the youngest, like the Presbyterian Church in Korea . . . almost every grade and denomination was to be found: and more striking still, laymen and women and ministers of every colour and race. It was a truly international and inter-racial gathering, ecumenical in the largest sense.'[1] Nor, once again, should Fisher's cool account be allowed to obscure the fact of his own great

[1] George Bell, *The Kingship of Christ.*

personal contribution to the work of the Council, with which he was to be clearly associated throughout his archiepiscopate.

• • •

To return to the purely Anglican scene, the Congress, a new thing in the history of the Anglican Communion, resolved upon at the Lambeth Conference of 1948, was duly held at Minneapolis, Minnesota, and proved an immense success. Indeed, there was only one possible place to hold it in 1953, and that was America. There alone were the resources to make the thing workable at that stage. The Americans undertook it with, in Fisher's words, 'miraculous energy, insight and hospitality. There we were for the first time, representatives of the Anglican Communion; bishops, clergy, laity; living and working together, worshipping together and finding ourselves a family. There were no divisions. We were there to express ourselves as a united family in Christ, and the hospitality was the secret of the whole thing. For instance, the Americans, who aren't used to afternoon tea as we are, had a huge tent put up in the proper place and there tea was available, and all came to it, and all the chat and friendship which was born there was vast and bore fruit abundantly.'

There was, too, in addition to the reading of various papers, of which those by Bishop Wand and another by the American Massey Sheppard, were outstanding, the devotional side, deep and lasting in its effects. 'Every morning,' to quote Fisher again, 'we met at the Communion service according to a different Anglican liturgy, and that taught all of us a good deal, too. And always there was this atmosphere of loving trust holding us altogether in the united spirit of the Anglican Communion.'

So cool and modest a comment might give the impression that Fisher's personal contribution to Minneapolis was minimal. But two other comments, one from an American and the other from an English layman, somewhat alter this impression. Thus Bishop Henry Sherrill: 'According to the plans made by the Lambeth Conference, I was chairman, as the Presiding Bishop in the United States. But the Archbishop sat beside me. In many ways this was an advantage, for, not being Presiding Officer, he was able to intervene with his judgment as to the right wording of several important resolutions. He preached at a service in the Cathedral, at Faribault, Minnesota, and gave a charming address at a dinner for the church people of Minnesota. Perhaps the happiest contribution the Fishers made was at the afternoon teas held in a tent outside the Cathedral in Minneapolis. There they mingled and talked with delegates from all over the world.'

An English delegate, that same Arthur Bryant who first encountered Fisher at the Canterbury Diocesan Conference after the war, had this to say: 'The Archbishop's handling of the Congress was superb. At the end of the many colourful processions, behind a long line of three hundred bishops who brought up the rear, the Archbishop and Bishop Sherrill walked side by side. The Americans loved it. I cannot remember that Geoffrey Fisher ever took the chair himself. He sat in black coat and gaiters towards the back of the platform, and one sensed that he was the presiding genius.' He added: 'It was generally felt that another Congress ought to be held in about ten years' time, to fall between successive Lambeth Conferences, the only problem being whether any other Church in the Anglican Communion was wealthy enough to put on such a tremendous show of warmth and hospitality as had been shown by the Diocese of Minnesota.' This further Congress was in fact held at Toronto in 1963. But that was after Fisher's retirement. The relevance here of the matter was that the consideration of it, and of the labours involved, was one of the factors in his mind when he came to consider retirement.

. . .

The second Lambeth Conference of Fisher's archiepiscopate, that of 1958, while equally important in results, was in one sense less testing upon him personally than the previous one, because such excellent foundations had been laid in 1948. That Conference had been largely pioneering. This time, many of the bishops knew each other and trusted each other and there was a feeling of fellowship from the very beginning. As in 1948, the hospitality arrangements were meticulously organised by Mrs. Fisher and Mrs. Frances Temple, the widow of William Temple, and all her admirable body of helpers. During the Conference, as one aspect of this hospitality, the Fishers had a group of people every week-end, and all through every week, the week-end at Canterbury, the week at Lambeth entertaining bishops. It made a great impression.

To list the main subjects considered by this Lambeth Conference of 1958 is merely to repeat what is already on record in the customary resolutions and reports, together with the Encyclical Letter issued at the Conference's end. The main subjects were, in fact, the Holy Bible: Its Authority and Message; Church Unity and the Church Universal; Progress in the Anglican Communion; the Reconciling of Conflicts Between and Within Nations; and The Family in Contemporary Society. But to pinpoint some of the conclusions reached and resolutions made by the Conference is to be made conscious of how much the world had changed, even in the decade since 1948, and how keenly aware the bishops of 1958 were aware of the fact. Thus on nuclear warfare—enlarged enormously in potential since 1948 with the invention of the hydrogen bomb—the Encyclical Letter had this to say, under the heading of 'Reconciliation in Society':

'The evil of war has become more vile through the hideous weapons of destruction which man's ingenuity has placed in his hands. Successive Lambeth Conferences have asserted their belief that war as a method of settling international disputes is incompatible with the teaching and example of our Lord Jesus Christ, and we are united in both hating war and pressing for its abolition. The use of nuclear weapons is repugnant to the Christian conscience. Some of us would go further and regard such use in any circumstances as morally indefensible, while others of us, with equal conviction, would hold that so long as such weapons exist, there are circumstances in which to use them might be preferable to political enslavement. We believe that the abolition of nuclear weapons of indiscriminate effect and destructive power, by international agreement, is an essential step towards the abolition of war itself. So we appeal to all Christians to press through their governments for the banning of such weapons, accepting such limitation of their own sovereignty as may be required to ensure inspection and control, so that no government may make them.'

The Conference, indeed, talked much of reconciliation in other fields also, both between nations and in nations. This had become, partly by Fisher's own action, the keynote to the whole Conference. It formed a theme of the Encyclical Letter, and he preached in Canterbury Cathedral at the beginning of the Conference on it. A comment of his, made years later in private conversation, reveals another and more personal reflection on a matter in general: 'The more the world goes into its difficulties, the more I feel that you can only talk about, deal with, and pray for *persons*, rather than abstract things like peace or settlement or justice or any other generality. It all depends upon the leaders and their personality, and the kind of people they get to follow them. It's a question of personal morality, if you like to use that word, personal wisdom, which in the end settles it: how people handle other people, and bring to their common task good or bad ideas. Responsibility is personal, just as I believe that sin is entirely personal; and once you get out of touch with persons, sin doesn't mean anything at all. All this, I believe, is too little realised in the world in which we live.'

This 1958 Lambeth also devoted much time to Church Unity and the Church Universal. An important definition of the distinction between Full Communion and Intercommunion—especially important in the light of subsequent developments in this field—is to be found in Resolution 14 under the heading of Christian Unity:

'The Conference endorses the paragraph in the Report of the Committee on Church Unity and the Church Universal, which refers to the use of the terms "Full Communion" and "Intercommunion", and recommends accordingly that where between two churches not of the same denominational or confessional family, there is unrestricted *communio in sacris*, including mutual recognition and acceptance of ministries, the appropriate term to use is "Full Communion", and that where varying degrees of relation other than "Full Communion" are established by agreements between two such churches, the appropriate term is "Intercommunion".'

The Archbishop's comment on this again is of interest, in the light of later developments: 'I had, ever since the Cambridge sermon, realised the immense purpose and power that lay in working for Full Communion, and I was a little afraid that, as an immediate objective, it might be forgotten or overlooked; I was anxious to see it put firmly on the map.

Anyhow, that is what the Conference did: it took the words Full Communion and gave them the definition and the commanding position which they have held ever since. When they are lost sight of, ecumenists go astray.'

The highly complex matter of the scheme of Church Union in Ceylon, or Lanka, as a matter of potential controversy, was to the Lambeth of 1958 what the Church of South India issue had been to the Conference of ten years before, although there were marked differences between the issues involved and the circumstances displayed. It was discussed in conjunction with the Plan of Church Union in North India and Pakistan, The matter led to much involved debate, the clarification and guidance of which occupied Fisher greatly. The causes and outcomes belong to the inner history of the Ecumenical Movement, and have in any case passed over into other larger and more complex events. The point here is that once again Fisher's leadership and, especially in this context, his power of clarifying an issue and bringing it into the form of an acceptable draft, proved invaluable, and the essential harmony of the Conference as a whole was preserved.

A matter of more general interest and lasting significance—one indeed of even more pressing importance now even than then—was the report which the Conference produced on contraception. This came within the purview of the Committee on the Family in Contemporary Society. It is a masterly document, and to read now this clear statement of Christian principles on the matter, at a time when the population explosion is creating a situation of world anxiety, is both to marvel at its continuing topicality and to admire the firmness of its guidance. The attitude of successive Lambeth Conferences over the years had been, as regards contraception, first, and for a long time, totally condemnatory: then ambivalent. The 1948 Conference made no mention of the matter whatever. But now, in 1958, the Anglican Communion, insofar as its mind can ever be collectively expressed, came down firmly in favour of family planning. To quote from so closely reasoned a document as the Report on Family Planning is inevitably to leave out much that should be said. The key passage, however, as regards whether the Church did or did not accept the principle of family planning was this:

'Sexual relationships, scarred by fear, are tragically incapable of bearing either the strains or the joys of full and happy married life. But the procreation of children is not the only purpose of marriage. Husbands and wives owe to each other and to the depth and stability of their families, the duty to express, in sexual intercourse, the love which they bear and mean to bear to each other. Sexual intercourse is not by any means the only language of earthly love, but it is, in its full and right use, the most intimate and the most revealing; it has the depth of communication signified by the biblical words so often used for it, "knowledge"; it is a giving and receiving in the unity of two free spirits which is in itself good (within the marriage bond) and mediates good to those who share it. Therefore it is utterly wrong to urge that, unless children are specifically desired, sexual intercourse is of the nature of sin. It is also wrong to say that such intercourse ought not to be engaged in except with the willing intention to procreate children. It must be emphasised once again that Family Planning ought to be the result of thoughtful and prayerful Christian decision. Where it is, Christian husbands and wives need feel no hesitation in offering their decision humbly to God and following it with a clear conscience.'

Inevitably, some disapproval was expressed when the Report was published by those who professed to see in it a betrayal of principle, comparing it unfavourably with the inflexibility of Rome. Equally inevitably, many approved. But now, all these years later, when Rome after Vatican II can be seen to be deeply involved with this issue—more deeply than ever, perhaps, since Pope Paul's Encyclical *Humanae Vitae*— the rightness of this declaration of the Lambeth 1958 Conference can be seen. It was courageous and true; and the logic of subsequent events has shown it to be so.

Fisher himself described the Report as admirable, and went on to say that for it they owed 'an immense amount to Steve Bayne, who had not yet become Anglican Executive Officer. But it was there that he made his reputation, as chairman of that committee. And because of that reputation, we unanimously agreed that he should be the first Anglican Executive Secretary.'

This was another important outcome of the Lambeth Conference of

1958. Steven Bayne was, at the time, Bishop of Olympia in the United States. His appointment was announced by Archbishop Fisher in April 1959.

'At the request of the Lambeth Conference 1958, the Metropolitans of the Anglican Communion have appointed a new officer with the title of Anglican Executive Officer. The chief duties are, on the one hand, to act as controller of the Anglican Advisory Council on Missionary Strategy, and on the other hand to exercise a general supervision on behalf of the Consultative Body of the Lambeth Conference on all matters affecting the Anglican Communion which call for attention between the decennial Conferences. As the office is a new one, it will be for the first holder of it to discover how best to fulfil these duties, and to render his best service to the various Provinces of the Anglican Communion in their joint concern.'

The appointment proved highly successful, not least owing to the notable personal qualities of Bayne himself. By this time he has come and gone, his term of office expired. But that his appointment marked yet another stage, in the archiepiscopate of Fisher, by which the Anglican Communion was helped to become globally conscious of itself, there seems little doubt.

And so the Conference of 1958 ended. Fisher must have known it was his last. The closing session was marked by great warmth towards him, and the closing service at Westminster Abbey by one of the very rare occasions indeed when he allowed his feelings to break through. Of the closing session, Bishop Sherrill recalls: 'At the closing session of the 1958 Conference, it was my privilege to present a gift to the Archbishop on behalf of all the bishops. I said incidentally that, as I had watched His Grace preside, I had wondered what he had done before becoming Bishop of Chester, and that all at once an inspiration came to me: "He must have had something to do with a boys' school." The Archbishop in replying said that he never understood why people tried to belittle or denigrate what was meant by being the headmaster of a school, and went on to to make an interesting and amusing defence of schoolmasters. Then came the closing prayers and Benediction. The last words of the Archbishop were "Class dismissed".'

And of the scene after the closing service in the Abbey, Sherrill added:

The Archbishop always kept his feelings under control. But after the Benediction, outside in the cloisters of Westminster Abbey, at the closing service, his voice broke and he said with deep feeling: "Some of you I shall never see again." He and Mrs. Fisher had built such strong ties of friendship throughout the world.'

Fisher's memory of this may be given in his own words: 'Never in my life have I been so moved as at the closing service in Westminster Abbey at the end of the Conference, when Henry Sherrill preached the sermon, and we went in procession from the Abbey to the Chapter House, all the bishops of the Anglican Communion. There I bade them farewell. There immediately in front of me was Owen, Archbishop of New Zealand, who had been up at Oxford with me, and then headmaster at Uppingham when I was headmaster at Repton. There were all the others. I knew that I should never see Owen or many of them again. I did just say a few words of farewell to them all, a word of gratitude and love and affection, and had to turn away as they ended, because I could not trust myself to say more.'

.   .   .

However, the moment of emotion was brief. Behind Fisher, in the decade which had separated the two Lambeth Conferences, much had happened at home as well as abroad. In the years left before his retirement, much more was to happen. These events, of wide variety and scope, need now to be surveyed.

X

The Archbishop at Home

What we do in the course of Canon Law revision is not a piece of ecclesiasticism. It is trying out whether we can speak to the nation in terms which we have lived out first in our own society. This cannot be too much emphasised because, as I frequently find, if we begin to tell society how to reform itself, people say to us: 'Look at your miserable ecclesiastical quarrels; they are far worse than any strife or quarrel which is going on outside about economic matters.' We ought to have the answer to that, and we must have it before we can speak with power.

G.F.F., in a speech delivered in the Church Assembly,
12 November 1957

. . .

I sat through the Church Assembly more faithfully, I think, than anyone else then or since, because I didn't want to miss a thing.

G.F.F.

. . .

One great value of the Wolfenden Report is that it draws attention forcefully to the distinction between a crime and a sin. In a civilised society, all crimes are likely to be sins also; but most sins are not and ought not to be treated as crimes.

G.F.F., in *Canterbury Diocesan Notes*, October 1957

. . .

There is almost universal agreement that, while some manifestations of the gambling instinct are widely regarded as allowable, or even desirable, yet this instinct is, or is easily liable to become, a disturbing factor in social life.

G.F.F., in a speech delivered to the House of Lords,
26 April 1956

THE archiepiscopate of Fisher covered a highly important epoch, in ecclesiastical, in national and in international affairs. The full significance of these may well require the passage of time before they can be truly assessed, and placed in the context of subsequent developments. One difficulty, however, of giving any survey, now or at

201

any other time, even of the major concerns which occupied him, is their multiplicity and diversity. Some selectivity is therefore inevitable, and even that requires to be exercised upon clear principles. Those to be applied here will be, first, to distinguish the ecclesiastical issues which mainly occupied him, from those of society at large and, secondly, to look at what Fisher said or did from the point of view of the degree to which his actions add something to the portrait of him as a person.

To start, then, with the ecclesiastical affairs. Fisher's enjoyment of the Church Assembly, together with his assiduity of attendance, were often remarked upon. So was his mastery of its chairmanship. So, for that matter, have his occasional clashes with various personalities been remembered. He remembered them himself, as well as his relish of the whole thing. This is in itself revealing. He liked order, pursuing it as a positive good in itself, and he enjoyed authority, having from his earliest days had it presented to him in forms which he could respect, at home, at university, as a headmaster. And now, in Church Assembly, he was confronted with something to be brought to order, put into line, made to function effectively. Even the flatter moments of the Assembly—and some have found them very flat—for him had their value. He said: 'It was very often in the dull moments, or in the casual asides, that one got the best glimpses of where people's thinking was going. I thoroughly enjoyed every minute of it. There was nobody who didn't contribute something in his speech, and they on their side felt, I think, all of them, that I was a real member of the Church Assembly, not presiding, but in with them, in all the matters and business that they had to handle. And there was, I'm quite sure, a trust between us which had a very great positive value. I also was a good chairman in the ordinary sense of conducting the business. Lord Hugh Cecil said once that he and I were the only two people who understood the Standing Orders. This, from him, was a very high compliment.'

Then there were the battles, the earliest of which was with a redoubtable character, C. E. Douglas. He had 'an enormous amount of odd knowledge, which he could produce at any moment', as Fisher put it afterwards. 'He had a sharp insight into what was happening and an ability beyond the ordinary to see just where a point of advantage could be gained, or where a point of order could be exploited. It was a contest. I held my own, I think, because I knew the Standing Orders as well as he did. I could always feel when what he said was nonsense, and when in it was some point which I must not overlook. And so we went on, and I think the Church Assembly got both irritation and some amusement out of seeing us battle.

'It so happened that Douglas got elected onto the World Council of Churches, and was present at the great meeting at Amsterdam when we were to create this institution. When the matter was right in front of us, and I was there presiding, I was putting motions when suddenly up came C. E. Douglas and said, in effect, that he had a serious objection to raise regarding the election of the members of the Church of England. There was a flaw in their election. I forget what it was; but something had been misdone. This, he thought, rendered the whole of the proceedings as far as the Church of England was concerned null and void. As a Continental said to me afterwards, they were thankful I was in the chair—they would not have been able to make head or tail of what was happening. I knew it was C. E. Douglas, and I knew how to deal with him. I don't know how I did deal with it—I think very abruptly. I just told him that he was out of order.

'It was interesting to see how invariably the Church Assembly failed to be taken in by the poseur, or the self-advertiser, or indeed by the partisan, and came to wise decisions about most things, of a forward-looking and developing kind.'

There were, in Fisher's time, great developments in the workings of the Church Assembly, especially in the central direction. A great step was taken in direction from the top when the Standing Committee became not merely responsible for ordering the business, but also responsible for advising on policy. His own comment was: 'This was a grand step forward; it gave a new feeling to the Church Assembly, to have this amount of central direction. It might have been the beginning of a curia, around the Archbishop but, I think very wisely, after my time the Archbishop of York was made chairman of the Standing Committee, thus relieving the Archbishop of Canterbury, and giving the Standing Committee a valuable sense of independence. Matters of great importance came up, and if there had not been a Standing Committee to review them, and keep them together in a single survey I don't know where one could have got; and the fact that there were bishops, clergy and laity on the Standing Committee was a protection against it becoming a curia. Individualists of various kinds got in, and there they would fight their own battles and see to it that there was no kind of mere submission to official policy . . . Freedom has an enormous knack of coming to the fore.'

Second in importance to the work of the Church Assembly, which developed so much in his time, Fisher placed his involvement in all the affairs of Convocation. But as this comes into the picture of him particularly in relation to Canon Law revision, which was one of the great labours of his archiepiscopate, it may conveniently be left until that question is reached.

Third in importance among his many ecclesiastical concerns, he placed Bishops' Meetings. These regular gatherings aroused wholly unmerited dark suspicions, for a variety of reasons, including perhaps an innate suspicion by many of bishops as such, and by the fact that the meetings were held behind closed doors. As a matter of fact, as the Archbishop recalled, these meetings 'discussed a great deal of pure administrative detail, as well as matters requiring attention of a general kind, concerning which conflicts of opinion were developing in the Church. All this was done as part of our normal business, without any declared "sides", or interests. We co-operated as it was our duty and desire to do. Occasionally we would refer some little point to a group of bishops to prepare a report upon'. The Archbishop, deciding eventually that something should be done about this suspicious attitude to Bishops' Meetings, acted in a characteristically direct manner. 'I remember at last I called a group of Church Assembly critics to Lambeth. I said, "I want to talk to you about these Bishops' Meetings." I told them the kind of thing that we did there, why it was so necessary, why we could not do it except behind closed doors and so forth. Finally, I summoned a chaplain and said, "Bring me the agenda of the last two Meetings." I then read the items and the first was "Care of disused church-yards". The second was something similar, and I then let them look at the whole list. They were astonished to find that, in fact, what we were doing was co-ordinating our administrative actions, and discussing general lines of policy—nothing but what was good and helpful.'

For Fisher, the meetings in general were always interesting, as indeed were usually all gatherings of a consultative nature, where there was debate, the clash of minds and personalities. No picture of him, nonetheless, would be honest if it omitted to take note of the fact that some found him dictatorial. Indeed, it became part of his public image, however unjustly, as the years passed, and this feeling, it appears, was to be found in these Bishops' Meetings also. He was aware of it, and frank about it. Commenting later he said: 'I have no doubt that I was thought to be driving them too much because, as a matter of fact, inevitably, there are things in which one has to give a lead if one is to get anywhere at all. I never did try to drive them too much. Far from it. I had the greatest possible respect for their co-operative efforts and their corporate judgment. What happened almost always was that, in any matter of general concern, where it was coming up for the first time, or where a new point was coming up for the first time, I introduced it historically, if necessary, and then left it for discussion. And of course, people like Mervyn Haigh, George Bell and others, at once took it up and discussed it. The Bishop of Sheffield, Hunter, was a great discusser. The Bishop of Rochester, then Chavasse, was another, and there were plenty of people with individual reactions and opinions. Cyril Garbett, sitting by my side, as long as he was Archbishop of York, said very little indeed. He listened, and listened, and every now and then, towards the end, or when he began to see where the debate was going, he would get up and give a magisterial piece of advice. And if anybody was listened to with respect, it was he. All that was most useful, and at the end I did what I inherited from Archbishop Lang, I summed up and, no doubt, in the summing up, I pointed to what was my own conclusion as to the best next step. That was what I was there for, as chairman. And, of course, one did get, as an Archbishop, used to this kind of summing up of a long discussion, in some clear finality, to which there might be a general agreement. Archbishop Lang did far too much of it at Bishops' Meetings. I have no doubt that, as time went on, I got prosy. I never got indecisive; I hope I never got too dogmatic. But I did get, and this one of my chaplains told me, quite clearly (I was most grateful to him for it), that I was talking too much, and that some of the bishops were getting restive. Well, I think, that was probably a true case.

The more tired I was, the more it happened. I did not accept the charge that I was trying to drive them too much; I did accept the charge that I was talking too much, and that was one of the little things that went into my mind and contributed towards my resignation when I did resign.'

Meanwhile, there began, in the early years of Fisher's primacy, what he described as 'the most absorbing and all-embracing topic of my whole archiepiscopate'. This was Canon Law Revision, and the importance he attached to it, not always universally shared, is so deeply characteristic that a word on that aspect of the subject seems relevant. The revision of Canon Law involved the clarifying, modernising and generally bringing to order of a great code of Canons dating from 1603, which set out, in matters of faith, morals and discipline, the rules to which the Church required the clergy to give obedience. It was a gigantic puzzle; an enormously magnified version of *The Times* crossword which, day by day, the Archbishop delighted to solve. It was also a very serious and complex matter with a tangled history, and in the undergrowth surrounding it lurked many obstacles.[1]

There were anachronisms, disputed interpretations.[2] There were also explosive issues in plenty, likely to detonate at a touch, setting off a chain reaction of controversies reaching back into the past.

Here, then, was a massive tangle. That the unravelling of it would appeal, as a challenge, to the orderly side of Fisher's mind is clear. But behind that obvious fact lay, it would seem fair to assume, the conviction that to bring order out of the current disorder of Church discipline was

---

[1] 'Their language is often unnecessarily archaic, and their arrangement is not always clear.' Garbett, Archbishop of York, in his foreword to the report in 1947—*The Canon Law of the Church of England* (S.P.C.K.).

[2] Two examples are worth giving. Thus a mid-Victorian Dean of Ely, referring in Convocation to the discussion of the Canon on Lawful Authority by the Royal Commission, of which he had been a member, of 1864, which had been appointed 'to consider the Subscriptions, Declarations, and Oaths required to be made and taken by the clergy of the United Church of England and Ireland', asked: 'What is this lawful authority? The result of our discussion . . . was that it would not be right, and even would not be possible, to define what lawful authority was.' And Mr. Justice Vaisey, many years later, commented in a memorandum to the report of 1947 that: 'It is true in a sense to say that nobody can be sure what the words mean, either to himself or to anybody else, and that their effect has been to convert an obligation which was impossible to perform, into one which is impossible to understand.'

itself an objective of prime importance, deserving of the greatest effort, and that the achieving of it would necessarily bring about the desired end of a Church at reasonable unity with itself. Thus he set himself to this task, heavy as it was.

'It was somewhere in 1946 that the matter came before me,' he recalled. 'I had never made any particular study of the history of the Church of England or of the Convocations before my own personal share in their administration began. I had picked up a certain amount as I went along; and I knew that, for many years, in Convocation, they had been concerned with the possible revision of Canon Law. The Convocations finally referred the revision to a very strong commission, presided over by Cyril Garbett. They worked out in detail a complete set of new Canons, which was published in 1947. I had no doubt whatsoever that this report must be at once acted upon, even though it would be an enormous undertaking; first because here, after years of hesitation, a great commission had at last brought a proposal into practical politics. But, more than that, because (with the instincts of a headmaster) I knew that it was absolutely essential to the well-ordering and self-respect of the Church of England to have Canons which could and should be obeyed. The lack of order had become quite dreadful. Ever since the Royal Commission of 1906 appointed to deal with the disorders of the Church of England had reported, there had been a persistent demand that we should put our own house in order, particularly by ending the scandalous treatment of the Book of Common Prayer. If we took up Canon Law, we must recover a workable definition of lawful authority, and restore in the Church the will to respect it. That takes me to the oath made by ordinands at their Ordination, and to the Declaration of Assent, by which they vowed that 'in public prayer and administration of the Sacraments, they would use the form in the said book prescribed (i.e. The Book of Common Prayer), and none other, except so far as shall be ordered by lawful authority.' There it was, a solemn undertaking. But there was endless dispute as to what was meant by lawful authority, and to have a solemn oath taken at such a solemn time, which each could interpret to suit himself, was really ghastly. Archbishop Davidson, I am told, used at that point to say, "and as to what lawful authority means in this diocese, it means me!" This, in a real sense, of course, was true, but not in a legal sense and there were those, lawless at heart, who preferred that there should be no effective law.

'Then the Oath of Canonical Obedience, taken at the same time, bound the ordinand to pay true and canonical obedience to his bishop, in all things lawful and honest; which meant to obey him according to the Canons when Canon Law was in a state of complete confusion! Thus, at the very heart of the Church of England, at the moment when its new clergy were ordained, there was this cancer of disputed oaths and disputed loyalties and laws so out of date that they could not be obeyed. I could not endure this; I knew that from it sprang vast spiritual evils. Many of the clergy of the Church of England had completely lost all idea of obeying authority. Of course, because we are a sensible Church, and the clergy are sensible people, we got on; most of the clergy stuck to what was usual and acceptable to everybody, and in difficulties went to ask the bishop and took his advice. But for many years there had been rebels, many of them devoted men of very great pastoral powers and greatly beloved, which made it worse, adding a kind of benediction to disorder.' He added: 'The Anglo-Catholics of our day were deliberately standing out in an organised way for what they thought was authority, what they thought was holiness, and what they thought was the proper use of the sacraments and of the priesthood, and they were very powerful. To have argued this out on theoretical grounds would have been an endless and a fruitless process; we were in the happy position of being able to tackle the problem pragmatically, by revision of the Canons one by one. But as we did it, there were alarums and excursions all around us, both from the Anglo-Catholics and the evangelicals. That did not bother me all that much. All I knew was that here was a plain task that we had to fulfil by careful co-operation, and it was the kind of task, requiring a clear mind, a sense or order and orderliness and a power of reasonable persuasion which was native to me.'

By the time of Fisher's resignation, the work was almost complete, with only a few remaining points still to be fought out. But the undertaking was prolonged and testing. 'There were, inevitably, major clashes at certain stages. The question of vestments was a battle-ground; the matter of the Seal of Confession and the Ministry of Absolution led to immense complications. There had to be a complete overhauling of the Ecclesiastical Courts, involving repeal or amendment of some two hundred Acts of Parliament, going far back in history. The problem of Lawful Authority, with all that it implied, had to be fought over in a prolonged contest. An immense debt was owed to Sir Thomas Barnes, appointed by Attlee to act with us from the secular side. Often, however, I had to encourage him to persevere when he found the clericalisms with which he had to contend more than he could endure. There were, at times, dismay and discouragement over the time and labour being absorbed by the seemingly endless task. More than once, to the bishops or in Church Assembly, I had to hold forth at length about the central place of Canon Law for the renewal of the Church. I knew that it was vital that the work should be carried through to completion: and of course, carried through it was.'

An outward and visible sign of progress can be seen in the volume *Canon Law Revision, 1959*, published in 1960 by S.P.C.K. The revision will be completed before long, and authorised. Any reference to inner details and technicalities belong to another place than this, and possibly to a more distant time. But it is clear that the patience and determination which Fisher gave to Canon Law revision, together with the prime importance he attached to it, are all signs of that devotion to order and discipline which was always so marked a feature of his character. He knew well that once a new code of Canons was completed, they would need to be kept up to date year by year, since otherwise they would cease to be effective, or have real authority. For that, he foresaw a Standing Revision Body and that was eventually established.

.   .   .

These ecclesiastical concerns—and the Liturgical Commission and Prayer Book Revision should be included—were necessarily specialised activities of absorbing interest, which occupied the Archbishop. But he was also at the same time deeply involved in public life. There were few of the social issues of his time which he did not, as occasion offered, make statements upon and many of these are sometimes unconsciously illustrative of the speaker's own character, and of the values which underlay his judgments. In certain instances, also, the wisdom of the prophecies he was at times constrained to make, can now, after the passage of time, be seen. Thus, speaking at Brisbane in 1950, on the Welfare State, as by then created in Britain, he said, after welcoming the development, and pointing to its Christian roots: 'The Welfare State inevitably means much central control, and that means a large machinery of control. There is the danger that the machine will operate clumsily and slowly: but more serious by far is the fact that the power to control the machine passes to a few hands. Even sincere men may, by the use of power, do as much harm as good. Or again, the Welfare State has to deal with men's material needs, in bulk. It may come to think that is all a man is—a mouth, a body, an end in himself—unless somebody is going to keep another idea alive, that man has a greater end to serve than himself and a higher law to live by and deeper ends to be fostered and fed. In fact, the Welfare State calls at every point for a far higher level of citizenship from all of us than ever before. It requires citizens who put what they do for others before what they get for themselves; who are keen to put more into the common pool than they take out of it. This higher level of citizenship is essential if the Welfare State is to work: and if it does not, a successor state will almost certainly be some sort of tyranny.'

All these years afterwards, it would be difficult to maintain that these dangers have not to some extent manifested themselves. Whether 'a far higher level of citizenship' has emerged is, however, open to question.

The general election of 1951 was the occasion of an address in St. Paul's on 4 October of that year very typical, in its balancing of Fisher's Christian idealism with hard common sense.

'A general election is generally a very Christian way of ascertaining the will of the people, and choosing representatives to conduct the affairs of a nation. But because men are men, all kinds of stupidities, errors of judgment, false motives, false desires, injustices and deceits enter into a general election. Words become weapons and, like all weapons, may be misused: all the perils of false or misleading propaganda and promises press upon men, and the very keenness of men's convictions may increase the danger of them. It is the more necessary that all men of all parties should declare and hold fast to a true and sincere desire to govern all their political actions by justice, and to behave to all opponents or minorities with generosity and forbearance during the election and assuredly, whatever the result, after the election too.'

In another address in St. Paul's in 1951, the year of the Festival of Britain, the Archbishop revealed a fact about himself not always realised: that he was a great Englishman and a passionate believer in democracy, with a devotion to his own land, which, while again balanced always by common sense, was very real. 'The greatest creation of our nation,' he said then, 'has been a way of life, a tradition of how men and women and children may live together in the freedom of mutual respect and trust, free to be themselves, free to be generous to others—with a grand sense of proportion and patience and a grand power of laughing at ourselves.'

Along with this deep love for his own land went always a special affection for the United States. This affection was returned. Fisher went down well with the Americans from the start, and the long list of his honorary degrees from American universities is significant both of the esteem in which he was held over there, and of the extent of his travels about that vast continent. 'I never go to the United States,' he once said, 'without being exhilarated beyond measure.' The words occurred in a notable speech he made to a Pilgrims' Dinner given in London, in his honour, on 16 November 1954.

'Every friendship, if it is a reasonable one, means between the two friends, on the one hand a general identity of outlook and interest and controlling purpose and, on the other, a vast range of unidentical ideas, emotions and judgments which make the friendship interesting and alive, producing in turn despair of one another and delight in one another —but all disciplined, controlled and made fruitful by the unshakeable bonds of affection, trust and dedication to a common faith. I have not the slightest doubt that there is true friendship and enduring affection between our two peoples far deeper than any superficial differences or views. There is in both nations, beneath all their materialism, a real dedication to a common spiritual faith. Before a vast audience at which I had the privilege of welcoming President Eisenhower he gave a splendid expression of the kind of political, social and Christian faith which both nations share. During it, he turned to me and said: "I don't suppose the

Archbishop of Canterbury has ever read the Declaration of Independence.''
If reply had been possible, I might have said, "And I am sure that the
President has never read Magna Carta." The really important thing is
not that Englishmen of a sort wrote both, but that British and Americans
alike have inherited a faith which, in spite of failures always to live up to it,
they strive after and if need be die for—a faith in a free and responsible
society of free and responsible men as at once the gift and the challenge of
God to man.'

.   .   .

There was a number of social issues which arose during Fisher's time,
each of which led to grave and complex moral questions. To all he gave
much thought and had important, if at times controversial, things to say.
These issues were, to take but a few, the Wolfenden Report on the law in
relation to homosexuality, the practice of human artificial insemination
by donor (A.I.D.) and the question of lotteries and Premium Bonds.

It was a statement on the Wolfenden Report,[1] printed in the *Canterbury Diocesan Notes* for the October of 1957, which contained *inter alia,*
the valuable aphorism concerning the distinction between crime and sin:
'In a civilised society, all crimes are likely to be sins also: but most sins
are not, and ought not, to be treated as crimes.' He went on to define a
crime as 'a punishable offence against the man-made laws of society,' and
continued, 'What is a sin? The Report speaks of "a realm of private
morality and immorality" which is not the law's business. But it is each
man's vital business, the realm within which lies (as the Report says)
the personal and private responsibility of the individual for his own
actions, in his own home and outside it. Sin is then a misuse by men
and women of their own personal responsibility. By what standard is misuse to be judged? To be of any real use, the standard must be objective,

[1] The Wolfenden Committee Report on Homosexual Offences and Prostitution was
published in 1957. It represented the labours of a departmental committee, consisting of
two High Court judges, two Members of Parliament, doctors, lawyers, ministers of
religion and three women. It had been appointed on 24 August 1954 to consider the law
and practice relating to homosexual offences and to consider the treatment of people con-
victed of such offences by the courts, and the law and practice relating to offences against
the criminal law in connection with prostitution and soliciting for immoral purposes, and
to report what changes, if any, were in its opinion desirable.

outside and beyond man's fallibilities and self-illusions, not, like the law, man-made. The Christian religion gives the answer. Sin is an offence against God. Its measurements do not vary from age to age as man's laws do. Sin is always to be assessed, as man himself is always judged, by reference to the eternal and good God. So, then, whatever from time to time the criminal law may say, homosexual offences are sins . . .'

Those disposed to condemn as censorious so firm a condemnation, or to isolate it from its context, would do well to mark what followed. There was, he went on, 'a realm which is not the law's business'. Why was this so? 'Just because man's ultimate responsibility is to God alone, and in that responsibility no man can deliver his own brother. There is a sacred realm of privacy for every man and woman, where he makes his choices and decisions, fashions his character and directs his desires, a realm of his own essential rights and liberties (including, in the providence of God, liberty "to go to the Devil"), into which the law, generally speaking, must not intrude. Only God's love has an inherent right to entry there.' But he concluded with this: 'It is always hard to draw the line between what is private sin only, and what is an offence against public order and the general good. The standards of good order and good morality which prevail in a nation depend upon the degree to which its citizens, in the privacy of their own hearts and habits, value and live by integrity of character and sound moral standards. If the law can do anything without undue interference to strengthen the moral stamina of the people, it ought to do it. If in any matter of morality there are enough weak, misguided or evil-minded citizens to form, by their mere existence in the life of the nation, a centre of active poison of a serious kind, then the law could rightly invade their private lives to restrain them.' It was possible, he remarked, that society needed protection from the immoralities of some heterosexuals as well as of homosexuals. How that could be done without endangering essential freedoms was not clear. It might be added that the years since, if they have not answered the question, have certainly done nothing to diminish its relevance.

Artificial human insemination was the subject of a report of a commission appointed by the Archbishop to consider the moral aspects of this practice in the December of 1945, under the chairmanship of the then

Bishop of London, Dr. Wand. This body, which had included doctors, lawyers and theologians, published its findings in 1948.[1] In his Presidential Address to the Convocation of Canterbury in the January of 1958, the Archbishop made his own position clear, being moved to do so by his desire to comment on a judgment in the Quarter Sessions in Edinburgh in the case of a wife who, separated from her husband, gave birth to a child sixteen months later, conceived by the process of artificial insemination donor. Was this adultery? The judge appeared to have ruled that it was not, at the same time drawing attention to the serious moral and ethical questions involved. This drew Fisher back, in his Convocation address, to two of the findings of the 1948 Commission: the first that A.I.D. involved a breach of marriage, violating the exclusive union between husband and wife; the second that early consideration should be given to the framing of legislation making the practice a criminal offence.

Fisher strongly supported both findings. 'It is difficult,' he said, 'to suppose that the law can allow the standing and integrity of the family and of parentage of children to rest upon a deliberate deception, deliberately concealed. Either parentage by A.I.D. should be made a criminal offence altogether, as the Commission recommended, or if that cannot be, then the law should require that every case of A.I.D. be registered, and the register should be available for inspection under safeguard. In such a register should be recorded the name of the donor provided by the doctor. Indeed, the donor's share in this business is the most secret, the most responsible and the most hard to justify, since he begets children whom he will never be able to see or know, and for whose temporal and spiritual welfare he can never bear any personal responsibility. If that is not adultery on his part, it is something far less responsible and far less human than adultery. For these and other reasons it would seem that legislation of some kind is urgently needed to resolve doubts, and to preserve under control the integrity of marriage and of the family.'

The Archbishop appeared also before a Home Office departmental enquiry on A.I.D. Of this he recalled, years later, how 'they were very friendly and frank, and we talked about everything very openly. I think afterwards one or two of them agreed with me. When they made their

[1] *Artificial Human Insemination* (S.P.C.K., 1948).

report, all they said was that they hoped the practice would not grow. Indeed, they hoped it would never become more than very rare and might die out, and for that reason they thought it better not to legislate against it, since legislation would be tricky and difficult to secure obedience to.'

That was not the first encounter which the Archbishop had had with the State over a matter of public morality. During the war, he had been consulted, as chairman of the then Public Morality Council, of which he was chairman as Bishop of London, in the matter of contraceptive instruction to young troops. He recalled: 'All we could fight for, and we did, was that their instruction should not be just flung at them as a piece of knowledge that they would find useful; but that it should either be done by the chaplain or by a medical officer, in the context of "this is morally a very unhappy situation, and the advice you have been given is only of use to you if you do not obey the natural urges of morality to abstain from fornication altogether". We got a little way with that, and improved the situation a little. But the moral lesson of it did not get very far with the troops.'

The Archbishop's statement on gambling in general and Premium Bonds in particular occurred in the House of Lords on the Small Lotteries Bill on 26 April 1956. On gambling in general, he was, though opposed to it in principle, moderate in tone. It was when he touched on the question of Premium Bonds that he became formidable, launching out into a tremendous polemic, which was neither forgotten nor forgiven by some in the Government of the day. The whole passage is so revealing of Fisher speaking his mind when thoroughly roused that it needs to be given in full.

'My Lords, there is a wider reason which makes it, in my view, yet more important that the Bill should not proceed. This Bill might perhaps have crept through as a small, even if a small-minded, Bill. But the Chancellor of the Exchequer has now raised the same general principle on a far larger scale. I know that the Chancellor says that his Premium Bonds are not a gamble. But there will be all the paraphernalia of a national lottery, the sale of what are the equivalent of tickets, quarterly drawings, the publishing of winning numbers and all the rest. How long will the general public (or shall I say, future Chancellors of the Exchequer) be aware of some tenuous argument about "when is a gamble not a gamble?" or remember that because they are only gambling with the interest, they are not really gambling? The Chancellor has compelled us to consider the matter on a national scale. We all agree that we are engaged in a great struggle to preserve, to restore, to recreate the economic stability and the spiritual capital of our people.

'The Government knows as well as all the rest of us that we can only regain stability and strength by unremitting exercise, all through the nation, of the old-fashioned but essential virtues, integrity of character, strict honesty, the duty of honest work honestly rewarded, thrift, saving and the like. We all know that at present calls to such virtues fall on barren soil. Not enough people listen when they are told that it is their duty to work, or their duty to save.

'So what? The Government's duty is by every means in their power to restore the true coinage without which we cannot endure as a great people. It has chosen instead not a dazzling, but a rather second-rate expedient which may attract savings, but which adds nothing to the spiritual capital of the nation, and which insinuates on a large scale this undignified and unedifying adulteration of public duty by motives of private gain.'

.　　.　　.

Thus, with great affairs of both ecclesiastical and public concern, the Archbishop was occupied in these years to a degree which makes readily understandable the comments of those who, during these times seeing him in action, wondered at his astonishing capacity for work. And yet these home concerns are but a part of the picture. Beyond the seas, also, he had 'the care of all the churches' of the Anglican Communion, and no Archbishop, as has been said, ever saw as much of it, or became in the process as widely-travelled, as Fisher. On the trail of those travels, therefore, it is now necessary to follow him.

XI

The Archbishop Abroad

My presence here with you—Canterbury in Australia—cannot but lead us to think of the continuity of the Church's life through the ages, and through all the changes and contradictions of human history.

G.F.F. in St. Andrew's Cathedral, Sydney, 23 November 1950

It was dark, and by hurricane lamps we carried our little service through, and then I came out and found myself being lighted down the long flight of steps by a little African boy, who'd somehow got hold of a lantern. There he led me, looking up at me now and again with his face shining in the light of the lamp, his eyes fixed on me. I thought 'My word, here is a parable! Here was I, from old England, and a little child of Africa leading me.'

G.F.F. recalling a visit to Sierra Leone

It was very moving to shake hands with an old man and an old woman, Christians, who had been left for dead in their hut by Mau Mau, because they had refused to take the oath. Here were veritable martyrs for Christ before me.

G.F.F. recalling a visit to Fort Hall in Kenya

I have been constantly on the road . . .

II Corinthians xi. 26

ON 25 January 1951, the following letter appeared in *The Times*:

Sir,—I observe that the Archbishop of Canterbury and Mrs. Fisher have just returned to England. Much of their journey in Australia was completed before I left Australia to come here for the Prime Ministers' Conference, and I can, therefore, speak personally and

warmly of the effect of their work. It deserves to be widely known that
the Archbishop's visit stirred men's minds and hearts all over Australia.
He spoke, as did his gracious wife, to very many thousands; but his
appeal was always to the individual, and to the individual's duty in a
distracted and cynical world. His language was elevated and simple, his
message subtle and robust. At the very moment of my departure from
England, I am moved to pay this small tribute, politician and Presbyterian as I am, to a great man.

Yours faithfully,

ROBERT MENZIES.

London, 23 January.

It was a weighty tribute; but a deserved one. The foreign travels of the
Archbishop and Mrs. Fisher between 1946 and 1960 were extraordinary
both in extent and effect. As regards extent, they far exceeded anything
ever attempted by any of his predecessors. Apart from visits to the United
States and Canada several times, they went to Australia and New Zealand
in 1950, he thus becoming the first Archbishop of Canterbury to visit the
Antipodes, to West Africa in 1951, to Central Africa in 1955, to India,
Japan and Korea in 1959, to Nigeria for Independence Day in 1960 and to
East Africa in the same year. The great final journeys, to Jerusalem,
Istanbul and Rome, stand apart, both in nature and results, and will
be so regarded in this narrative.

As to the effect of the earlier travels, undertaken ostensibly for and on
behalf of the Anglican Communion, it can be said that their impact and
influence spread far beyond the theoretically narrow confines of their aim.
They were ambassadorial, in some cases almost royal progresses, and were
reported as such. For the man himself, they were remarkable as diplomatic
exercises. Always at his best in meeting all sorts and conditions of men, he
and Mrs. Fisher, delighted a great many people with their geniality and
accessability. The records bear witness of it.

In some ways, of course, the Archbishop was fortunate in the timing of
his travels. The Africa he visited, with many of its territories on the verge
of independence, was still warm in the long rays of Britain's setting
imperial sun. No one will see an Africa like it again. It is even possible

218

that no one will ever see again an Australia or a New Zealand so strongly bound by ties of affection and regard to what was still called the 'mother country' as those he saw. The list could be extended. But if he carried with him a British prestige, it is certain that he added to it greatly, and this great service that he did for his church and his country in these prodigious travels should not be forgotten. He did not himself forget them, and the memories remained with him in his Dorset village:

'In 1950, after the Lambeth Conference, I made my first visit to Australia, and this was a very great occasion. We went out by the *Dominion Monarch* to Fremantle, arriving on 16 October. At Perth, an old London vicar of mine, Moline, who had been at St. Paul's, Knightsbridge, was now Archbishop. It was a lovely visit. Perth, I still think, is in some ways the most attractive of the Australian cities; beautifully situated on the Swan River; less advanced than all the others, a thousand miles away from Adelaide across the desert, with a lovely little cathedral. The Mayor gave me a lunch and there, at the lunch, were all the notables of Perth, and an English cricket team, which was about to tour Australia. We made speeches, and in the course of his speech, the Mayor said: "I'm not much of a churchman—I used to go to church once, but since I was sixteen or so I've never been. But I am interested in it, and wish the church people all prosperity." So when I made a speech, I referred to the Test team there and then I said: "A word about my cricket. I used to play cricket until I was fifteen or sixteen. Since then I've never touched a bat, I never go to watch a cricket match, I do nothing to show my interest, but all the same I'm very interested and I wish the cricket team all prosperity." An Australian, sitting by the team, said "Well bowled!" and they all laughed to their hearts' content, and I felt that I had won that round.'

There was, in fact, a good deal more to this modest account of the opening of the Australian tour. Archbishop Moline, in a note of the whole of the Australian tour, gives some idea of the size of the operation, which was to continue on these lines throughout the whole stay.

'As soon as the gangway was lowered, my wife and I, accompanied by the Archdeacon of Perth and the Chancellor of the Diocese, went on board to meet our guests. There was a short press interview, and then the Archbishop and Mrs. Fisher were welcomed on the wharf by the Mayor of

Fremantle and representatives of Church and State. There was a happy informality about this exchange of greetings and then, with a motor-cycle escort supplied by the police, we drove in sunshine to Perth. We called en route at the university . . . and then at St. George's Anglican College. After morning tea at Bishop's House, the Archbishop and Mrs. Fisher were received at Government House . . . The Archbishop then went on to be interviewed at A.B.C. and to make a recorded broadcast. He then proceeded to Anzac House, where he was the guest speaker at a luncheon of business men. Meanwhile, Mrs. Fisher lunched with the executive of G.F.S. and spoke to them about their work. At 2.45 the Archbishop addressed 1,500 schoolchildren at a short service in St. George's Cathedral. No other engagements had been made for the afternoon, but both the Archbishop and Mrs. Fisher eagerly agreed to the suggestion that they should be driven to the Swan Homes for Children for tea.'

This they did, and the superintendent of the homes, Mr. Roy Peterkin, long remembered that visit. 'I recall it was a lovely warm afternoon. The spring was later that year and the fields were still green. Dr. Fisher turned and looked across our paddocks towards the blue hills of the Darling Ranges. "Look," he said, "it's like a little bit of England, but with a difference." But it was the human interest rather than anything else that really mattered. For a few minutes we would lose him out of the official party and when I found him he was surrounded by an enthusiastic group of autograph hunters. In the end, he had almost forcibly to be dragged away. Noticing a small group of girls looking disappointed because they had not secured an autograph, he collected the sheets and promised that he would sign these and see that they got them. He did so. Almost the last thing he did in this State was to hand to the secretary of the Archbishop of Perth the signed autographs for this group. I recall his pleasure and obvious delight at being provided with a police motor-cycle escort: "something that had never happened to me before." ' [1]

'From there,' Fisher remembered, 'we went across the Nullarbor Plain, most fascinating, those endless miles of pure desert, not a thing to see. Our

[1] This pleasure continued. In Sydney, he told the press that he felt like a registered parcel, and was never sure why they watched over him so closely. It could be, he suggested, either from fear he would get lost or from fear that he would take something. The escort themselves greatly approved of him.

first stop was Kalgoorlie and that was interesting. The glory of Kalgoorlie and its gold had gone. There was a thing called a Golden Mile which had nothing in it. I lunched with the whole of the clergy of the diocese—three clergymen and their wives. I remember we arrived in a blazing day. We got out, and there, in front of the station, was a platform and there in the blazing sun the Mayor, in full robes, greeted me and I made a speech back. I've never been so hot, nor could he ever have been so hot. But he was a good Methodist and we made great friends. On this Nullarbor Plain we stopped every forty minutes or so for water; wherever we stopped, the whole of the population of these fettlers and their families (fettlers were the people who kept the track in good fettle) came down, and we got out and we talked to them all. So we went across and we arrived in due course at Adelaide.'

There were old friends to be met in many places. A former headmaster of the Guildford Grammar School at Perth, Canon Freeth, had been at preparatory school with Fisher. The Bishop of Adelaide, Roben, had had a parish in the diocese of Chester in Fisher's time as Bishop there; the brother of another, Batty of Newcastle, had been Bishop of Fulham in Fisher's London days. There were new friends to be made everywhere. And in one place there was a major problem. It concerned a new constitution for the Australian Church, the framing of which had been delayed for many years by the extreme differences of churchmanship between some dioceses. Brisbane, among others, was 'high'; Sydney, the premier diocese, was 'low'. Bishop Moule, a man whose saintliness was as clear as his huge stature, was Archbishop of Sydney and Primate of Australia. He came from Canterbury, where the Moule family was very well known. Here was a situation for Fisher to deal with, where his powers of judgment and instincts for moderation were especially valuable. But, before he could come to grips with it, when he addressed the Synod in Sydney, he had had a tumultuous welcome to that city, in a cavalcade preceded by stamping horses, with ticker-tape floating down from office windows and a great service in the Cathedral. He also dined with the Cabinet of New South Wales. This was yet another occasion which gave a fascinating glimpse of the involved nature of the ecclesiastical scene. 'The place was full of Anglican Protestants and vast numbers of Roman Catholics. The

Roman Catholic Archbishop took great care not to come near me, unlike the Roman Catholic Archbishop of Brisbane, who was a grand man and came to a reception at which I was. We made speeches to each other, and nothing could have been happier.'

Eventually, in Sydney, he came to the matter of the divisions within the Church. Archbishop Moline recalled: 'He spoke seriously about the party prejudices which for so long had been a notorious feature of church life in Australia; and he helped us to look less at others and more at ourselves, to discover the cause of this trouble. This was a matter of grave concern to the Church at the time, because for over forty years party strife had frustrated all efforts to set up a self-governing constitution for the Church in Australia. The Archbishop, in his address to Synod, appealed for a renewed attempt upon the constitution. It was in this connection that the Archbishop made his outstanding contribution to the Australian Church. Not only did he bring new hope to those who were working on the constitution and spur them on to make another effort when they were tempted to despair. But he himself took an active part in the work by studying our proposals on the way back to England, and making some very helpful suggestions about a new approach to our task. In fact, his wise and impartial advice was one of the decisive factors in the ultimate achievement of autonomy by the Australian Church.'

The visit was enormously strenuous, conducted for the most part in great heat. Brisbane, Fisher remembered, was 'the only place where I prepared a sermon with not a stitch of clothing on, because I could not endure the thought of it'. In thirty-eight days in Australia, he in fact delivered ninety-eight sermons and speeches, travelled 1,500 miles by train, 2,000 miles by car, and 1,800 by air. In addition, even on the way out on the ship, he had had an office specially provided for him, where he worked through most of the days with his accompanying chaplain, the Rev. Clive Pare. He used only one labour-saving device, and this was a typed answer ready for the many who asked him about the 'Red Dean' of Canterbury. The typed notice said: 'Doctor Johnson cannot be deprived of his position unless he breaks a civil law or ecclesiastical laws. He has broken no law. He has only expressed his opinion. I violently disagree with them, but as long as we have freedom of speech in England, Dr. Johnson will remain.'

But, if the visit had been strenuous, it had also been enormously successful. The Archbishop of Melbourne summed it up in his Diocesan Paper of 13 November, 1950. 'I suppose no event comparable with the visit of the Archbishop of Canterbury has taken place within the diocese in its history. Both from the platform and the pulpit, truths were spoken which have made a very great impact in Victoria. I have heard the Archbishop quoted in a variety of places. His private dealings with individuals were no less marked. At once people felt at home with him, and he drew out so easily the confidence and goodwill of those he met.'

.   .   .

The New Zealand journey, including Tasmania, following straight on from the Australian tour, was an equal success. There again were old friends to be met, such as Owen, Bishop of Wellington, who had rowed in trial eights at Oxford years ago with Fisher, and many new ones to be made, such as the Queen of Tonga. This New Zealand visit had had its origin a hundred years before, when Archbishop Sumner had blessed the emigration to the other end of the world of the Canterbury pilgrims before their departure in September, 1850. Three months later, the famous First Four Ships reached what was to become New Zealand. Fisher, at a luncheon given by the then High Commissioner, W. J. Jordan, in London in 1948, had been invited by the Primate of New Zealand, West-Watson, to go out for the centennial celebrations.

After visits to Auckland and Napier, each with its special features of interest, came the visit to the capital, Wellington, which began coolly, with no particular warmth at the civic reception. Yet, two days later, Fisher was having to be protected from the pressure of crowds seeking to shake his hand. The Archbishop found New Zealand 'absolutely fascinating. We had expected to like the New Zealanders and rather dislike the Australians. In fact, we fell in love completely with the Australians first, and then went on to New Zealand, and found the New Zealanders as lovely as we had expected. It was a peaceful, quiet life, which some New Zealanders found too peaceful for them. But they were happy, and we enjoyed them very much indeed. There was the Maori population, too, immensely interesting.'

It was a Maori dignitary who was the centre of an incident which the Archbishop recalled. 'We went to Lyttleton, the port at which the settlers had originally arrived, and there was a general luncheon in the railway sheds. At it, the best speech of all was made by a distinguished Maori gentleman, who had been in the government, and had an immense power of Gladstonian oratory. He was really splendid, and we were duly impressed. The next day, there was a kind of fête, and a great procession all through the streets of Christchurch. There, in the middle of this array, came a float, and on it a Maori war canoe, manned by Maoris, looking terrific, half-naked, with their paint and their expressions terrifying. In the bows, gesticulating and making all the appropriate Maori faces—a wild man from the past—was the very distinguished statesman who, the day before, had been making the Gladstonian speech in Lyttleton. It was a lovely combination, and shows how the Maoris have taken their place, without any trouble, in the life of New Zealand. Part of the reason at least was because they were already Christian, thanks to missionaries from Britain, before they came into conflict with the white settlers.'

Before it was over, this visit became extraordinary. A mid-week Communion service of the Mothers' Union, held in Auckland, was so packed that the administration alone took three hours. And in Christchurch on the centenary day, Fisher preached to the largest congregation he ever had, packing the streets in the heart of the city, whom he addressed from a pulpit jutting out from a balcony erected over the west door of the cathedral. He said: 'In front was the square, packed with people, and down every street as far as I could see, were people standing, and I was told that there must have been thirty thousand people or more, all around, as far as the eye could reach.'

. . .

The following year, 1951, he was off again, this time to West Africa, for the inauguration of the province. That province-creating which had occupied him as one of his first tasks as Archbishop, came to life now in these African travels, fascinating and incident-packed, so that what had been an administrative matter now became flesh and blood reality. There was an interesting incident even before Fisher arrived in West Africa, when he was *en route* for Dakar via Lisbon.

'At Lisbon, there was something which had to be rectified on the plane, and there was a delay of an hour. I went out of the airport, and walked up and down a longish road, which was an approach road to the airport. As I walked one way, I passed a group of twenty or thirty seminarians, young Roman Catholic trainees for the priesthood, walking the other way. As we walked to and fro, we looked at each other. Then we finally began to bow to each other. I was in full episcopal dress. Finally, I went across to talk to them. It was very difficult because they knew no English, and I knew no Portuguese, but we got on, with a mixture of a word or two of Latin. I said I was the Archbishop of Canterbury. It didn't mean anything to them at all. They didn't seem ever to have heard of the office. After a while they said to me, "Are you a Catholic?" I said: "Yes, but not what you mean by Catholic." They looked surprised and said, "Are you a Protestant?" And I said: "Yes, but not what you mean by Protestant." That bothered them still more, and they grinned and scratched their heads. They ended by asking whether I would visit them in their seminary, and I said they had better ask their head before they started inviting heretics like me to see them. It was an amusing little meeting, which both sides thoroughly enjoyed.'

The origins of this journey to start the province of West Africa in Sierra Leone lay in a meeting which had taken place in Lambeth Palace in the early autumn of 1950. An account of it, and what followed, came from the Right Reverend J. L. C. Horsted, Bishop of Sierra Leone at that time.

'Three of us who were bishops in West Africa, John Daly, of the Gambia and Rio Pongas, Leslie Gordon Vining of Lagos, and I went to Lambeth Palace to discuss with the Archbishop possible steps forward in the formation of the province of West Africa. After some very careful discussion, it was agreed that the province should be inaugurated in 1951. I well remember the astonishment on the faces of all three of us when the Archbishop remarked: "Let me get my diary and see when I can come." The idea of the Archbishop of Canterbury coming in person to West Africa had never entered our heads. Such a visit would make history, for never before had a Primate travelled to inaugurate in person a new province of the Anglican Communion.'

The words should not be taken, however, to imply grandeur. This was a visit to an area of African, rather than European standards of material wealth, where the Church, often small-scale, was the result of heroic missionary endeavour in the not-so-distant past. 'Sierra Leone,' wrote its Bishop, 'was small and poor, though the Church members were very loyal and intensely proud of their Freetown. Bishopscourt was spacious enough to entertain visitors, but it was without modern conveniences, and the month of April, the time chosen for the visit, was the month when water was scarce. Indeed, the first day that year when the water was turned off from the mains was the day of the Archbishop's arrival. For transport, we had at the time an old Ford Prefect which I had brought home on leave in order to have a reconditioned engine replacement. I still had to learn that the Government of Sierra Leone would be so responsive to the privilege of receiving such a visitor that arrangements would be made to put at the disposal of the Archbishop a comfortable car and a police outrider.'

This kind of background needs always to be borne in mind in relation to many of Fisher's African travels. It helps to explain the excitement his visits occasioned, and makes more moving the love with which he was received. Two years after this visit, came the Queen's Coronation. The Bishop of Sierra Leone recalled how 'We took the Bishopscourt "boys" to see the film. Their comment afterwards was: "We saw Pa Canter put the crown on the woman's head. We know that it was him. We know his voice." '

.   .   .

He was in Africa again in 1955, after two visits to the United States in the meantime, for the inauguration of the province of Central Africa. This was a memorable journey, not least for the Fishers themselves. The records of it abound in names now vanished from the scene: in Governors, Provincial Commissioners and the like; in hints of events which were to have great consequences within a few years as Africa changed. And, all through, there is a sense of the strong African sunlight, and of the memory of missionary pioneers and their living successors who had toiled under it to sow the seeds of the Church which Fisher saw on this visit. The impact of it all on him was clearly very considerable. There is almost a euphoric quality about his memories of it years later.

'In 1955, I went, via Capetown, to Central Africa. My brother Leonard, the next brother above me, had been Bishop of Natal—a grand bishop he was, too, universally loved and trusted. He retired to Grahamstown. We flew there. Grahamstown had a great attraction—its great Broad Street, so broad because their ox-wagons, with their eight pairs of oxen, had to swing round when the wagon turned, and there had to be room for the team to do the turn with their wagon. There was the university at one end, St. Andrew's School, and many other happy recollections there. Thence we went to Central Africa, and this was a great thing. We went first to Livingstone and the Victoria Falls; then to Mapanza, our first introduction to a Central African mission. At Livingstone Mr. Clay, the Provincial Commissioner, was a splendid host and before I left I celebrated in a little church there, at seven o'clock in the morning, using the 1662 Liturgy, as used in England, with little alteration. There were about sixty communicants, including about fifteen or twenty Africans. It was a joyful and moving service and the Provincial Commissioner said he was genuinely grateful for it.

'At Mapanza we had tea with the Sisters of the Community of the Resurrection from Grahamstown. Then there was an open-air service, wonderfully happy and domestic, with all the mission people there. I spoke to the headmaster of the school, who interpreted me, sentence by sentence. It went very well. Towards the end of my address, I said these words: "And so, I am very happy to be here with you." The men in the audience applauded loudly, most unusual, I was told, but very encouraging, and the interesting thing was that they applauded the sentence before it had been interpreted to them. Then in the evening, there was a terrific entertainment in the darkening twilight, with great bonfires burning and everybody sitting round in a great circle, then tribal dances by schools and others, with the drums beating, which first introduced me to African drums. They moved me more than I can say. In fact, I wanted to leap out into the middle and join in the dancing, but was wisely restrained by my neighbours. And then at the end, the Bishop told me just a sentence I could say by way of thank-you and good-bye.

'From there, we went to Lusaka, and I planted a great cross on the place where, in due course, the cathedral was built. Lusaka was interesting, with a wonderful Governor, Sir Arthur Benson. His wife was a Roman Catholic but she came to everything with him, and I got the feeling there that Benson was on very friendly terms with the leading Africans, and that there was a real process of integration going on. I have memories of a great service in the open-air, as the sun came up early in the morning, where there was to be a church. All that was visible were the walls, up to a few feet, running round and a great congregation, Africans and Europeans mixed completely, the Governor kneeling next to African women, and then his staff, and then more Africans. It was a most moving thing. I remember preaching to a congregation on the Prayer for the Church Militant, and Bishop Thorne, who was there, being deeply moved and saying to me: "It must have taken you a long time to prepare that sermon." I said, "Well, no, I've just grown into it through a great part of my life."

'From Lusaka we went to Kota Kota, and then from Kota Kota to Likoma. There, in the middle of Lake Nyasa is this island of Likoma. You go there by steamer, and it's removed from everywhere. Its lovely Cathedral is there, and Likoma itself is a sort of holy island. There is this great Cathedral and a population very largely Christian. As we came in the early morning, the road running up from the landing-stage towards the Cathedral was thick with people. As I came out of the ship, they knelt and I gave them my blessing, and then I walked through this mob of friendly, shining, lovely faces, up and up and up, and so to the Cathedral. There I celebrated. There were, I think, nine hundred communicants. It was a terribly moving service. I preached a little sermon and the interpreter, an African, said he would rather wait until I had finished and then give the whole address, than give it sentence by sentence. So I talked for about ten minutes and then stopped. He then delivered the address to the people, and the white missionary said that he had not missed a point that I had made, or altered the order, but had the whole thing in his mind, so that it came out a perfect interpretation of what I had given.

'It was there that I was told the entertaining story of a rather pompous visitor who was being interpreted, and who began his sermon by saying, without any other introduction or text or anything, "I am the Good

Shepherd". The interpreter said, "He says he is a good man, and keeps goats", which rather destroyed the atmosphere. Well, immediately after this great service, we had breakfast outside, in the open air, and then a gathering of all the men, while the women went elsewhere, and my wife talked to them. There I was presented with gifts: a ram, eleven chickens, tied together and laid at my feet, who blinked at me; an elephant tusk; and last of all an African came up and gave me a little envelope, in which was thirteen-and-a-penny-halfpenny. It was all very moving. Then we heard a noise approaching, and there was a great ululation going on. These were all the women coming in, with my wife in the middle, ululating with them all! What a time!

'This did not end the Central African tour. From Likoma we went down to Mpondas, and then on to Zomba and Blantyre, with a pause at a tea-planter's, living near, for a night. And I think it was at Blantyre, or Zomba, that a reception for the Europeans and Africans had to be held in private grounds. When they tried to get the club grounds, they were refused, because some white settlers said they were not going to have Africans plunging about their gardens and their club-house. This was just a reminder of the schizophrenia present among the white population.'

Thence the Archbishop went to Salisbury and, after various visits to other areas, back there for a great ceremony at which he and the Archbishop of Capetown combined to surrender their respective jurisdictions over Central Africa into the hands of the new self-governing province. After that, 'We went up to Kenya and I made my first visit to Fort Hall. That, indeed, was memorable. The Mau Mau business was still going on; and I was to lay the foundation stone of a new church to be built in memory of the African martyrs at the hands of the Mau Mau. When robed, we went in procession through Askaris lining the route, down to the place where the foundation stone was to be laid. We had a canopy over us to keep possible rain off, and there was an oblong space roped off, and round it a mass of African Christians of the diocese of Fort Hall, each with a little board in front of him, saying the mission from which they came. They were all on the level, but from them the ground rose steeply, and this rising ground was crammed with Africans. I said, "Who are these?" and they said, "They're gate-crashers from all the districts around, probably Mau Mau to a man. They must all have taken the first oath." We had a lovely service. I laid the foundation stone; I gave an address. And then, as we moved off, walking in procession right round this oblong, I was greeting the Christian groups on the other side of the ropes when I looked up and saw the Africans above. I said to myself "Why not?" and I started waving to them. They waved back with delight and joy, and I went round a sort of triumphal gathering, not only of the Christians below but of the un-attached, and probably Mau Mau, above. It was a grand feeling that, for a moment, they were all united in a kind of temporary harmony. The Bishop told me later on that a message had come from the Mau Mau in the forest that if I would come and rule over them, they would come out and live at peace.

'From Kenya, we went on to Uganda. The highlight was the consecra-tion of four African bishops in the Cathedral at Namirembe, a wonderful service. The African voices singing the Litany was one of the most im-pressive things I have ever heard.'

It was on this visit that the Archbishop encountered again the 'unhappy, unfortunate Kabaka of Uganda', since deposed, who in earlier years had stayed with the Fishers in Canterbury at the time of his wedding to the girl who became his queen, the Nabagerika, educated at Sherborne School for Girls, highly intelligent, a commanding figure, but doomed to a terrible life of frustration and isolation. There was to be an echo of this visit when the Archbishop returned to Uganda in 1961. On that occasion, in the words of the Archbishop of Uganda, 'It was a mark of most singular con-fidence and recognition of Dr. Fisher's persistent and careful interest in the affairs of Uganda that he was asked to address the great Lukiko at Mengo at a time when British people could hardly expect to be welcomed in that particular assembly.'

. . .

Meanwhile, in 1959, the Archbishop with Mrs. Fisher, visited India, Japan and Korea. In the first, there were past splendours and dreadfully present realities to be seen: the pavements in Calcutta on the way in from the airport, covered with men, women and children, whose only home was there. 'Babies were born: people lived their whole lives there: they died there. It was a ghastly thought, and no one can say how it can ever be tackled, or redeemed. That,' as Fisher recalled, 'made its indelible memory.' So did another view on the approach to the city: on the right the racecourse, in the middle the huge memorial to Queen Victoria, with Curzon standing at a respectful distance, bowing his head to majesty, and then, on the far left, St. Paul's Cathedral. 'Racing, Empire, Church,' Fisher recalled, 'all were in one view. And the stately road by which we approached had on every side statues of soldiers and administrators from Great Britain, who had done great things in their time, and the Indians had had the sense to leave them there. We stayed with the High Commissioner. I had stayed with him in Germany a long time before, when I first did a tour in Germany just after the war from Dusseldorf to Kiel; he was a grand administrator during that difficult period. They made our visit to Calcutta very happy. I remember great services in St. Paul's Cathedral. On Good Friday I preached, in English, a sober sermon. A Bengali priest listened to it; and when I had finished, re-preached the sermon from memory to this great audience, and delivered it with a vigour and a fire and an impressiveness which my little effort, by itself I am sure, did not possess.'

From Calcutta, the Fishers went, via Hong Kong, to Japan. To go there, in fact, was the main purpose of the whole journey to the Far East, since the Archbishop had been invited to attend celebrations organised by the Nippon Sei Ka Kai, marking the arrival in Japan of the first Protestant missionaries. In Bishop Yashiro, Presiding Bishop of the Church of Japan, Fisher had a great friend from the time when the bishop came to the 1948 Lambeth Conference. He had been sorely tried in adversity during the war. The Japanese government had attempted to compel all the churches to amalgamate, and some bishops of the Anglican Church had given in. But Yashiro stood out and refused to let the Anglican Church be absorbed in this newly-created national church. After the war, Yashiro had to decide how the bishops who had surrendered their trust were to be treated—a problem which Yashiro had come to put before the Lambeth Conference, which gave its best advice. So advised, Yashiro was able in due course to bring them back and restore them to the service of the Church. Now Fisher was able to see this friend on his own ground. In Kobe, the diocese over which Yashiro presided, he consecrated the new Cathedral. In Osaka he visited St. Andrew's University, and schools, and gave a public lecture.

There were entertaining incidents during this visit, too, in addition to the great events of the centenary programme. There was the occasion when he was about to receive an Honorary degree and discovered, only when on the platform, that it was to be a D.C.L. and not a D.D., and had minutes in which to adjust his speech accordingly. There was a dinner when, to the Archbishop's surprise, he found himself with Geisha girls on either side of him. There was a distinguished Anglican who, entertaining the Fishers at lunch in his own house, introduced himself with the words: 'I am a member of the Japanese upper middle class'; to which greeting Fisher said in reply: 'I am so glad to meet you. I am a member of the English upper middle class.' And there were, unforgettably, the Noh Plays, where he sat entranced by the queer music, the male actors producing their voices strangely from the stomach, hardly moving, highly stylised, and yet dramatic and fascinating with their white-plastered faces. Years afterwards, hearing that these Noh Plays were on in London, he and Lady Fisher made a special effort to see them.

So ended this Far Eastern journey. It was the first tour of Asian countries ever made by an Archbishop of Canterbury. He had left London on Palm Sunday, 1959, with Mrs. Fisher and Canon Sansbury, Warden of St. Augustine's, Canterbury, and Mrs. Sansbury. In five weeks, they had travelled 20,000 miles, and visited Pakistan, India, Hong Kong, Japan and Korea.

.   .   .

1960 saw the Fishers back in Africa for the inauguration of the province of East Africa at a service in Dar-es-Salaam when Leonard James Beecher — 'One of the great, creative persons in East Africa', as Fisher described him—became its first Archbishop. This African visit followed the adventurous, tumultuous pattern of the earlier ones; with the same wild welcomes from the people, the same stirring moments the same mutual appreciation and, on Fisher's part, the same unfailing pleasure in meeting all sorts and conditions of men. He never seems to have tired of this—an extension on a global scale of that gift for genuine, unaffected cordiality which many had noted even in his Chester days long ago.

Nor, for that matter, does he seem to have become physically tired as the years passed. Now, in 1960, at the time of this visit, he was seventy-three. Yet for some of it, he travelled, with Mrs. Fisher, in what she described as 'a very small plane, called a Cessna. This just held the Arch-bishop and myself, the chaplain (Mr. Adie) and the pilot and one other.' A Cessna, it may also be added, has only one engine. But they flew quite imperturbably, it would seem. Of one journey, Mrs. Fisher noted, 'We flew on to Dodoma, the Diocesan Centre of the diocese of Central Tan-ganyika. This flight of about three hundred miles was over completely featureless country—no roads, no rivers, no noticeable mountains, very sparsely inhabited, I suppose because of lack of water.' And of the con-clusion of another flight, she wrote: 'We flew on right across the southern part of Tanganyika to a Mission on the shores of Lake Nyasa. This little place, Liuli, had not had an aeroplane land on its strip for nine years, and before permission could be obtained for our plane to land, the Mission's schoolboys had to rake and hoe its surface to make it fit to land on. As we came in, we saw people running from every direction, along paths, through the bush and the mealie fields, full of excitement and wonder at seeing a plane. We were escorted from the airstrip for about three-quarters of a mile along a sandy track by all the children in the three Mission schools, the boys playing pipes and drums, and marching steadily and well, with fine African sense of rhythm.'

Such are some of the memories of these travels. They could be endlessly added to. It would be a pity to lose forever the picture contributed by the Archbishop of Uganda, of Fisher arriving at a certain airport, on one of his earlier African visits, at about six-thirty in the morning: 'I was astonished to see a rather wan-looking Governor and his A.D.C. waiting to greet him. H.E. clearly needed his breakfast, but nothing could restrain Dr. Fisher from greeting, with great satisfaction and affection, everyone he saw, while the Governor rested on his stick and still longed for breakfast. The climax came when Dr. Fisher turned to a number of Sikhs standing on the airport staircase. They had no connection whatever with our party, but they were greeted with the same cordiality, and then the Archbishop seized me by the arm and whispered "Always be polite to a man with a beard." '

But there the matter must rest, except for two questions. What did it all add up to, this prodigious and courageous journeying over so many years, and what does it add to the picture of Fisher? Two answers may be given. The one, relating to an earlier visit to Africa, can be found in the *Nyasaland Chronicle* for May, 1955. 'To the Africans, as appeared in all the speeches of welcome they made to the Archbishop, what delighted them most was that it had been granted to them to see with their own eyes "Geoffrey our Archbishop" for whom they had prayed by name in the prayer for the Church, Sunday by Sunday, for so many years, and to find him a real father in God, full of joy and love, as one of them said. Indeed, it may well be that when history comes to be written in its proper perspective, the constructive imagination that has inspired Archbishop Fisher to see for himself so much of the world-wide Anglican Communion and make personal contact with so many of its members, will prove to be his characteristic contribution to the growth and development of the Anglican Church.'

The second, following what was perhaps the greatest honour that came to the Archbishop out of Africa—an invitation from the Nigerian Government to go there for their Independence celebrations in the September of 1960—speaks for itself. The writer's name was Okwudili Orizu, and he was describing Fisher's visit to Onitsha, Nigeria.

'Accepting an invitation to our Independence celebrations, the Archbishop of Canterbury came to Nigeria. While there he paid an epochal visit to the town of Onitsha on Sunday, 25 September 1960, a date never to be forgotten by all Christians in the eastern region in particular, and by Nigeria as a whole. It is now a date that has become a household word. In his usual simple manner, His Lordship never made a triumphal entry into Onitsha. But, for his being extraordinarily learned, with his wide experience and understanding that are beyond the average man's estimation, and for his other divine gifts that make him what he is, Onitsha town indeed possessed the look of a Resurrection Day. No throne was erected to make his seat spectacular; and when I asked a top member of the Church to explain why His Lordship was not given a special seat, he replied: "He is a humble man. He does not believe in having himself glorified." '

XII

Archbishop and Crown

Must we not be humble and thankful that when the call, unwanted and unexpected, came to him whom we then knew as the Duke of York, he answered it with a resolute and faithful heart, and depending upon God, grew year by year in strength and wisdom—providing us with just what his people needed?

> G.F.F. in a broadcast from Lambeth Palace preceding a memorial service to King George VI, 10 February 1952

. . .

Let us thank God that we have an hereditary monarchy, fashioned by the wisdom of sovereigns and the sturdy independence of our people into a matchless instrument for expressing, in the one person of the reigning sovereign, our natural unity.

> G.F.F. in a broadcast from St. Paul's in preparation for the Coronation

. . .

Millions saw the culmination of the tremendous drama when St. Edward's Crown was uplifted in a majestic gesture by the Archbishop of Canterbury and descended gently, in all the flashing splendour of sovereignty, on the youthful brow bowed to receive it.

> *The Times*, 3 June 1953

. . .

He must be a good man, this Archbishop of Canterbury, for every part of the service which he conducted he endowed with a warm, sincere and paternal touch.

> Paul Gallico in *The Daily Express*, 3 June 1953

. . .

I, who am no courtier by nature at all, found myself at ease with them, and never pretending to put myself as Archbishop, still less myself as myself, across to them in any kind of way: but being myself to the best of my ability.

> G.F.F. speaking of his relationships with the Royal Family

THE relationships of successive Archbishops of Canterbury to the Royal Family of their day make a fascinating study. History links them by a constitutional bridge: circumstances determine how often, as on great occasions of State, they must meet upon it. But personalities and opportunities combine to affect the nature of the less formal relationships which each has with the other, and what the Archbishop of the day makes of these relationships can be revealing of some aspects of the man himself. Thus Davidson, all through a long life of service to the Crown, found his relationship changed from those of the remarkable intimacy which he had with the ageing Queen Victoria when he was Dean of Windsor, to those of a trusted adviser, faintly resembling at times an immensely respected family solicitor, of her successors. After him came Lang, by nature and predilection a courtier, who built extensively upon the foundations laid, early in his career, as Vicar of Portsea, when his royal neighbour at Osborne formed the habit of inviting him over to preach. Thereafter, through all his years, he was to be found much about the court, and with George V, indeed, formed a personal friendship. Temple was on the scene as Archbishop too short a time to make any particular mark in this respect.

But with Fisher it was different. He was not a courtier, as he said himself. He was certainly not a cautious family solicitor. He was Geoffrey Fisher, personally devoted to the Royal Family; but completely natural and uninhibited in his relationships with them. It was the chance of history that these relationships were frequent and deep: ranging over the whole field of family deaths, family marriages, family births, a coronation and one resounding controversy. In other words, a lot happened to the Royal Family in his time, and he was involved with most of it. The list of these happenings is some indication of the opportunities for close and pastoral contacts thus presented to him. In 1947 Princess Elizabeth married the Duke of Edinburgh: Prince Charles was born and baptised in 1948, Princess Anne in 1950. King George died in the February of 1952, Queen Mary in 1953. The Coronation of her granddaughter followed three months later. Two years afterwards, in 1955, there occurred the extraordinary furore over the matter of Princess Margaret and Group-Captain Townsend. And then, in 1960, Prince Andrew was born, and Princess Margaret married to Mr. Antony Armstrong-Jones. Thus circumstances brought the Archbishop into close and intimate relationships with the Royal Family at an exceptionally eventful time in their affairs, when one generation was giving way to another, and a young queen coming to preside over all.

Thinking at large, long afterwards, over these concerns and his part in them, the Archbishop said: 'On two occasions I met the whole Royal Family and in the most solemn and intimate way. The first was when I took a little service in Marlborough House the morning after Queen Mary died: they came together in the Drawing Room and I said a few prayers and read from the Bible with them. This is the kind of thing that one never forgets. Whether I did it properly or well I haven't the slightest idea. But at least it was done, and it was a bond between us. The other such occasion was in the chapel of Marlborough House, before the funeral of Queen Mary, when they were all present and I spoke a few words to them, and celebrated the Holy Communion with them. There were, of course, many wonderful occasions when I was associated with the Royal Family. The glorious Silver Wedding celebration in St. Paul's of King George VI and the present Queen Mother was most moving. I had always been overwhelmed by the vastness and grandeur of St. Paul's. But on that occasion, I felt that the whole great St. Paul's was as intimate as a domestic chapel, with the beloved King George and his wife, the Queen, present there as their family. One could not but feel the sympathetic domestic affection carrying us up to almighty God.'

The funeral of King George VI, which took place a year before the death of his mother, was an occasion rendered particularly poignant by the comparative suddenness of his passing, by the deep impression he had made on all his people by the manner in which, unexpectedly called to the Throne after the abdication of his brother, he had triumphed over considerable natural handicaps, to become a much-loved king, deeply identified with his people by the simplicity and devotion of his leadership through the long years of war. The occasion drew from Fisher, in a sermon in St. Paul's after all was over, an example of very fine oratory, a stylised use of English of which, when occasion offered, he was a master. He was speaking of the Committal Service at St. George's, Windsor.

'The nation, the Commonwealth, the world, with measured tread and muffled drums and solemn hearts, brought to the chapel the mortal remains of the King, all that still belonged to the world, and stopped there, away from the world in which the battle had been fought, into the profound and powerful peace of the House of God. There, in that shrine of our history, we felt upon us what the King had been for us in history, taking his heavy burden and bearing it without a fault, leading his people through dark and perplexed days by the self-forgetting example of his courage and sacrifice, and steadfast devotion to duty. But there in that shrine, we passed beyond history. The trumpets of faith were resounding all about us, touching human sorrow with their comfort and translating time's utterances into eternal truth . . . So were committed to the ground in Christian hope the mortal remains of a faithful king, a faithful man, with the same faithful prayer for "this our brother" as for any man at his latter end. And already the boundaries of this world were broken, and we had passed out of the confines of the chapel and of this world to the eternal Kingdom of God, by whom all history is judged and to whom every child of man must render his account.'

But the great central event of the Archbishop's public contacts with the Royal Family was, inevitably, the Coronation of Queen Elizabeth II on Tuesday, 2 June 1953. A coronation, by its very nature, is an occasion involving the Primate very closely indeed. Particularly at the service itself; long, involved, glittering, a complex pattern of symbolism and splendour, and yet at every moment rich in spiritual truth and national dedication, he is, after the sovereign, the central figure, and this time, for the first time, television cameras were there to reveal how he carried out this daunting and yet exhilarating duty. That he did it extremely well was the general judgment. Everything went off perfectly, without a hitch, and the youth and grace of the monarch—the first queen to be crowned sovereign since Victoria—added vastly to the impression made upon those who witnessed it in the Abbey, or by television. So did two other facts: the supremacy throughout of the religious aspects of the ceremony, in particular those of consecration and dedication of the sovereign to the service of her people, and the extremely careful preparation which, never intrusive, yet created the unity of spirit which dominated the whole. This included an informing of the public, through mass-media never before available in such variety, of the meaning and symbolism of the service. Thus, before the event, many had been made familiar in some measure with the structure of the ceremony: the Recognition, the Oath, the Anointing, the Investiture, the Crowning, the Enthronement; and had heard for the first time of such recondite matters as the Ampulla, the Spoon and the Armills.

As a headmaster, Fisher had a special interest in and flair for arranging special services in the School Chapel, and so too when he became a bishop. Now he entered into every side of the Coronation with trained enthusiasm. Thus, *The Manchester Guardian* (as it then was) of 3 March 1953: 'Dr. Fisher is taking the Coronation preparations in his stride, and shows every sign of enjoying the detailed negotiations which precede each minute change in the order of the ceremony. After a lively explanation to the Press this morning of the history of the armills (or bracelets) which are to be reintroduced among the ensigns presented to the Queen, Dr. Fisher said: "You can see how absorbingly interesting it is to prepare the Coronation rite." '

Long before this, however, in March of 1952, the preparations had started. The Archbishop was concerned with the spiritualities, the Earl Marshal, the Duke of Norfolk, with the ceremonial. 'Both of us,' Fisher said, 'trusted each other completely, and worked together in complete harmony.' But there was much other business, and wide areas where the concerns of the two merged, as in the matter of the television coverage. In the July of 1952 the Archbishop set up an Advisory Committee on the Rite, a field in which precedent and historical continuity were of the utmost importance. This Committee included Wickham Legg, who had been present at the coronation of Edward VII in 1902, and Claude Jenkins, who had a great knowledge of the 1911 coronation of George V, together with E. C. Ratcliffe, Ely Professor of Divinity at Cambridge, Norman Sykes, Dixie Professor of Ecclesiastical History at the same university, and A. C. Don, Dean of Westminster. This committee drew up the service, the final three-hour meeting in January being conducted by the Archbishop from his bed, to which one of his rare minor illnesses had confined him. There were some changes in the service, one being of very great interest and significance. The presentation of the Bible to the Sovereign had been introduced for the first time for the coronation of William and Mary in 1689 and, oddly enough, took place along with the investiture with all the other insignia of temporal power. Fisher, with the warm approval of the Dean, who had once worked as an Episcopalian in Scotland, transferred the presentation of the Bible to the beginning of the service, along with the Oaths, where it was evident that they rested on the

Bible and the Kingdom of God to which it bears witness. And so another thing became possible. In this new position it became possible and pro-phetic that the Moderator of the Church of Scotland should be joined with the Archbishop in presenting the Bible to the Sovereign, representing the only two Established Churches in the British Isles, or in the Common-wealth. Otherwise, precedent was largely followed, and Professor Ratcliffe wrote an historical introduction and explanation to it.[1]

In the following April, Fisher had to think of the occasion in a much more personal way. 'I was very conscious of the fact that it was part of my duty to do what I could to prepare the Queen for the personal dedication which gave meaning to her coronation,' he said, 'and there was no pre-cedent known to me to help me to know how to prepare a queen for such an event. I decided there was only one thing which seemed to me to be natural and necessary: that was that I should prepare a little devotional book which she could have and use for herself, day by day, in the weeks before the Coronation. It was hardly before the beginning of April that I thought of this. Before I began, I asked two friends, two wonderful women, Miss Potts, of St. Julian's, and Mother Clare of St. Andrew's Community, to make suggestions to me, and from them came suggestions which greatly helped me in tackling this task. We were going away for a holiday in Dovedale, Derbyshire, at the Isaac Walton Hotel; and there I practically remained in the hotel for the whole time till I had completed the task. The little book took the form of a simple meditation and prayers appropriate to the part of the Coronation Service, for each day, covering a whole month and leading up to the Coronation itself. Each day had a theme; with the little meditation and one or two prayers. I completed it all, working intensively, in not much more than a week. The Cambridge Press printed it wonderfully and bound it beautifully. I gave four copies, one to the Queen, one to the Duke, one to the Queen Mother and one to Princess Margaret. When I had done it, I felt that I had done all that was in me, all what I had, to prepare the Queen for her coronation. This was the most precious thing that I ever did, in a kind of way.' Seventeen copies of this book were printed.

A word more might be said about the armills. From previous services it

[1] *The Coronation Service of Her Majesty Queen Elizabeth II* (S.P.C.K. and C.U.P., 1953).

appeared uncertain whether the armills were bracelets or some kind of stole. Investigation showed that they were bracelets to be put at the appointed place on the wrists of the Sovereign. The accompanying prayer was easily adjusted. But the only bracelets were those presented to the first Queen Elizabeth, too cumbrous for use. What could be done? Fisher, who had established that bracelets were needed at this point, suggested that new bracelets of gold should be made, and that the gold should be a gift from the Commonwealth, so that the bracelets would have a great symbolic value. This idea was accepted and the golden armills were thus given by the Commonwealth.

Rehearsals began on 15 May and there were many of them, sometimes twice a day, on at least one occasion at short notice, as a certain bishop had cause to remember when, having gone on holiday, he was sought out by the police and sent forthwith to London. At last all was ready, and Fisher felt satisfied that every adjustment to detail had been made which could add to the dignity and spiritual atmosphere of the ceremony. Finally, on the evening before, the Archbishop went to Buckingham Palace for a short private service of preparation. The following morning he breakfasted at eight, was at the Abbey by ten, and thereafter went through the whole vast ceremony, as indeed did the Queen, without any hesitancies or apparent difficulty, or any signs of tension.

The rest is history. The Coronation was in every sense a triumph, enormously impressive, and admirably shown on B.B.C. Television for the first time. Thus millions were able to see the splendours and share the drama from the moment when the Archbishop, at the Recognition, presented the Queen at the four sides of the theatre, or platform, set up at the crossing of the Abbey transepts with the words: 'Sirs, I here present unto you Queen Elizabeth, your undoubted Queen: wherefore all you who are come this day to do your homage and service, are you willing to do the same?' Then, as the rubric put it: 'The people signify their willingness and joy, by loud and repeated acclamations, all with one voice crying out GOD SAVE QUEEN ELIZABETH. Then the trumpets shall sound.'

The press of the day following was lyrical, each paper in its several style. Thus *The Times* of 3 June 1953: 'A lustre which no clouds could dim and no torrent could tarnish glowed at the heart of yesterday's tremendous events. It was not the splendour of sovereignty so much as its high solemnity, which enriched the long and lovely pageantry of the day, and set the mood which held the multitude enthralled. That was the reward and the fulfilment of the vigil gladly endured through many comfortless hours, a benison which all could share with the young queen who came to her sacring so richly dowered with the prayer she had herself invoked from her people.' Or the *Express* of the same date: 'I saw a mystery enacted today. I watched a queen, uncrowned, come to church. I watched a queen, uncrowned, at prayer, and felt that I should not watch.'

The Archbishop, who kept a diary of the events, recorded more soberly that he thought the religious significance of the Coronation had been much more generally appreciated than formerly, and that the Queen's request for prayers in her Christmas broadcast had contributed to this end.

.   .   .

All that was in 1953. Two years later, some sections of that same press which had been unanimous in appreciation of the Archbishop's part in the Coronation were condemning him for his alleged part in another Royal affair—the question of the possible engagement of Princess Margaret to Group-Captain Peter Townsend, an officer who, once of the Royal Household, had been involved as an innocent party in divorce proceedings. This was an unhappy affair, not rendered any the less so by the inability by reason of their positions, of the principals to speak for themselves, although the Princess did, in due course, issue a powerful, personal, and decisive statement. But for Fisher the only thing to do was to ride out the storm, knowing all the time, but being unable to say so, that he had not in any way done that which he was stated to have done—brought pressure to bear upon the Princess at any stage in the making of her decision. But press and public seemed to think that he had, and the ghost of Lang and the abdication, which that archbishop in his day had been thought to have influenced, walked again. The winds of disapproval for a time blew very hard indeed upon Fisher. Characteristically, he found some humour in the situation, especially in the combination of two headlines, current at the time, the one saying 'The Archbishop Must Go', the other proclaiming that 'The

Archbishop Has Gone Too Far'. Even so, the experience was not pleasant and the only reason for referring back to it now is that the truth about Fisher's part in the matter may be made plain for all to see.

But first it is necessary to give, however briefly, something of the background to this storm. Romantic speculations about the Princess and the Group-Captain had appeared in the foreign press before they were taken up by British editors. The first mention in the British press was made by a Sunday paper in the June of 1953, just after the Coronation. Shortly afterwards, Townsend left the Queen Mother's household to go as an air attaché at Brussels. Henceforth for two years, in spite of being constantly harried by reporters and crowds, he carried himself with dignity and friendliness and got on with his work.

Meanwhile, speculation continued, and the issue became an extremely sensitive one. Fisher discovered how sensitive it was when, during his journey to inaugurate the province of Central Africa, he gave an address during a communion service in a country church in Nyasaland at 6.30 a.m. to a congregation of some forty or fifty people on the text 'Whose service is perfect Freedom'. There were several threats to freedom in the modern world, he said, and one of them was made up of some sections of the press. Concerned about preserving their own freedom, they limited that of others by making people hesitant to speak in case their remarks were taken up and misrepresented. That anyone present should wish to report such a remark in such a setting to a London newspaper would seem utterly unlikely. But in the circumstances, it was enough to cause ticker-tapes to chatter in Fleet Street and Fisher found himself henceforth hard-pressed at various press conferences. In Capetown on 7 April he was reported as discounting recent speculation about Princess Margaret; in Grahamstown the following day he was saying that 'the rumour was a stunt, and a most offensive stunt at that, by a few English newspapers.' When he returned to England, he had to face a fairly hostile press conference at which he said he had no comment in reply to questions concerning the Princess. He added, according to *The Times* of 24 May 1955: ' "If you can convey to your editors that my answer was 'No comment', that I made no comment, and that is the end of the affair, it would be a good thing all round." Asked if he would clarify the report which followed his remarks, he replied: "I do not see why I should clarify the minds of people who think I have said things which I never said." '

There, for the moment, the issue smouldered as far as the Archbishop and the press were concerned. It flared up again in the October and November of the same year as a result of four press statements concerning the Princess, and two actions of the Archbishop's. The statements followed each other in quick succession. Thus *The Times* on 14 October: 'Group-Captain Townsend visited Clarence House last night. His visit lasted two hours.' The following day, there was this: 'In view of the varied reports which have been published, the press Secretary to the Queen is authorised to say that no announcement concerning Princess Margaret's personal future is at present contemplated. The Princess Margaret has asked the Press Secretary to express the hope that the press and public will extend to Her Royal Highness their customary courtesy and co-operation in respecting her privacy.' Then, on the 28th, there was this: 'Princess Margaret went to Lambeth Palace yesterday afternoon and was received by the Archbishop of Canterbury, Dr. Fisher. She stayed there nearly an hour. Later the Archbishop's chaplain said: "It was a private visit. I cannot give any information about it." ' Finally, on 1 November, the Princess issued from Clarence House the following statement: 'I would like it to be known that I have decided not to marry Group-Captain Peter Townsend. I have been aware that, subject to my renouncing my rights to succession, it might have been possible for me to contract a civil marriage. But, mindful of the Church's teaching, that Christian marriage is indissoluble, and conscious of my duty to the Commonwealth, I have resolved to put these considerations before any others. I have reached this decision entirely alone, and in doing so I have been strengthened by the unfailing support and devotion of Group-Captain Townsend. I am deeply grateful for the concern of all those who have constantly prayed for my happiness.'

Meanwhile, without any intention whatsoever of doing so, the Archbishop appeared to stoke the fires of controversy by two actions, the occasions of which chanced to come his way at this time. The first was that at what some papers called a society wedding he was said to have made remarks, pointed at the Princess, on the permanence of the marriage bond. The only factual part of this was the wedding. That his remarks should be interpreted in the way they were was as far from his intention as it was far from his expectation. He said long afterwards: 'When the trouble was fully on in the papers, it happened that I was taking a wedding in St. Martin-in-the-Fields. I gave an address in which I said simply what I always say at any wedding: that marriage was for life and so on. One or two of the papers said that it was "very improper" of me to say such a thing just at that time, and that obviously I was aiming it at Princess Margaret. I wasn't, of course, aiming it at anybody at all. It just happened at that time.'

The second occasion of controversy arose out of a television programme, long pre-arranged, in which Fisher had agreed to be host at Lambeth Palace to Richard Dimbleby for one of the 'At Home' programmes in which famous houses were visited. Fisher's own memory of this occasion was that: 'After the thing had finally been finished by Princess Margaret's own public statement, Richard Dimbleby came to Lambeth to interview me in one of the At Home series. Before the broadcast began we talked about everything in my study, and he mentioned Princess Margaret, saying that he proposed to ask me a question about her. I replied in what I thought was a completely suitable way. I said that nothing need be added to Princess Margaret's own statement.'

He did, in fact, add this, reported in *The Times* of the following day: 'I can say, perhaps, just three things. These underline the things Princess Margaret herself said. First, she said she took this decision alone. That means by her own free will. Of course she took advice. She got plenty of advice, asked for, and a good deal more unasked for. In the end, it was her own decision and she was under no pressure from State or Church.

'The second thing I can say is that her decision was purely on the grounds of conscience. She was seeking all the time what God's will was, and when it became clear what God's will was, she did it, and that is not a bad thing for people in general to take note of.

'The third thing, again from her own statement, she especially thanked those who prayed for her. Only people who have been praying for her can really understand the decisions demanded of her, the problems she had to face, and the tearing of the heart one way or another. Those who prayed for her know what she has been through, and those who have not do not.'

He also—and this was what appeared to infuriate those sections of the press which now turned upon him—said that he did not mind 'two hoots' what people might be saying and that much of it represented 'a popular wave of stupid emotionalism'. That was on 2 November. On 4 November, the *Daily Sketch*, accusing him of having thrown words 'like a bundle of incendiaries on a dying fire', was hinting at the necessity of disestablishment, no less. The *Daily Mirror*, by 5 November, under a banner headline A RISING TIDE OF ANGER (CRISIS HAS COME TO THE SERENE CLOISTERS OF THE CHURCH OF ENGLAND) was positively demanding it. 'Slowly,' it asserted, 'a wave of anger mounts against the Primate, bringing with it a tide of doubt about the teachings of the Church on divorce.' It also published a selection of readers' letters, remarkable in some instances for their vitriolic character.

What had happened? The answer would seem to lie, as regards public feeling, in the widespread notion that the Princess's romance had been, as the *Daily Express* put it, 'broken by ecclesiastical influence'. But this was not so. What actually had happened, so far as the Archbishop was concerned, was very different. He had at no time pressed his advice upon the Princess, nor been invited to do so. What he had done was to receive her decision, which he greatly respected and was thankful for. At the same time, it did not surprise because he had reason to know and admire the character and convictions of the person making it.

Of Princess Margaret and of this particular matter he said, years later: 'I saw a lot of her, of course. In fact, my first contact was when I confirmed her. From then on, I used to meet Princess Margaret fairly often, and always enjoyed it immensely, for the simple reason that every meeting with her was a challenge, a sort of friendly engagement in argument which I think we both enjoyed. She was always friendly, always intelligent, always entertaining all through my experience of her. So it was that I came to be especially devoted to her; and of course I knew what a genuine concern she had in the life of the Church and the life of a churchwoman. About the episode concerning Group-Captain Townsend, I can say no more than is known publicly. Throughout it, Princess Margaret was still what she always has been—a frank and utterly open person, who concealed nothing, but would state her views and would let me state my views, which we would discuss and argue, enjoying each other immensely in the process of talking things over in this free and open way. We never discussed this particular problem.'

It should be added that not all the Press, by a long way, was hostile to Fisher during this controversy. The *Daily Express*, for one, though critical enough at times, now and later, on 11 November was saying 'The Archbishop of Canterbury is being unfairly attacked', and went on to make the point that, although it did not agree with the marriage discipline his Church maintained, he yet had the right to proclaim it.

Eventually, the furore died away: but not before the Press Council at its quarterly meeting on 18 October had severely rebuked those sections of the press who had, it felt, conducted themselves ill in the matter. 'The Council feels,' the statement ended, 'that certain papers have offended against good taste and have done a considerable ill-service to the reputation of the press.' Oddly enough, no one seemed to find it necessary to apologise to the Archbishop who, if his private life had not been invaded, had at any rate been grossly misrepresented. It was left to Randolph Churchill, in a letter to *The Spectator* on 23 May 1958 to put the matter straight:

'A large section of the gutter press has in recent months squandered acres of newsprint by writing in an impertinent, untruthful and offensive manner about the private life of Princess Margaret. And a number of newspapers have sought to suggest that Her Royal Highness was thwarted from marrying the man she wished by the Archbishop of Canterbury. Some have persisted in this falsehood after Her Royal Highness had already given the story the lie. A similar *canard* was spread about the abdication of King Edward VIII, and the public was invited to believe that the King was chased from his throne by a conspiracy organised by Archbishop Lang. The recent biography of Mr. Geoffrey Dawson by Sir Evelyn Wrench has utterly disproved this story, and we now know for certain that the Archbishop played virtually no part in the abdication.

'However, since so many journalists believe that history repeats itself, and therefore think it safe and profitable to parrot each other's fabrications, the public has had this further legend of archiepiscopal intrigue foisted upon it.

'What is the truth? Princess Margaret had made up her mind that she did not wish to marry Group-Captain Townsend before she went to visit the Archbishop at Lambeth Palace on October 27. The Archbishop, however, supposing that she was coming to consult him, had all his books of reference spread around him carefully marked, and cross-referenced. When Princess Margaret entered, she said, and the words are worthy of Queen Elizabeth I, "Archbishop, you may put your books away; I have made up my mind already."

'It seems in the interests of Her Royal Highness, of the Archbishop, and not least of history, that this fact should be known.'

It was a spirited and, in the circumstances, a necessary putting-right of the record. Only one thing about it puzzled Fisher. This was the reference to his having books set out ready for the Princess' visit. His comment was: 'I had no books of any sort spread around. The Princess came and I received her, as I would anybody else, in the quietness of my own study. She never said "Put away those books" because there were not any books to put away.'

So ended a memorable episode. Left outstanding, however, was the whole question of the Archbishop's relationships with the press, which had not been good. It is clear, in this instance alone, that the services of an expert press-officer on his staff would have been invaluable, and would have prevented much misunderstanding on both sides. Eventually, before the end of Fisher's archiepiscopate, that need was met, with brilliant success. But for the moment, the story of how that came about must wait.

Other encounters with members of the Royal Family, quite apart from those on formal occasions, all had their interest. The Duke and Duchess of Gloucester who, at one time, had two sons at school at Broadstairs, used to lunch with the Fishers on their way to visit their children. They would bring them, sometimes, to the Old Palace, in Canterbury, and that meant that the Fishers came to know them rather well. 'I think,' Fisher recalled, 'I was also rather helpful to the Duke, who was not always an easy conversationalist. I can generally make people laugh, and I knew how to make him laugh. That was all that was necessary; for once he started thus, he became genial to those around him and conversation flowed. Now and again, I performed the same service for the Queen herself. She is in every way a glorious person, full of wisdom and wit. She is of course an adept at starting conversations, and being on terms with everybody she meets. But occasionally at the beginning there is a moment or two of hesitation to overcome. The Queen and Prince Philip did Repton School the honour of coming to the School for its four hundredth anniversary. It was, of course, an immense occasion for the School, and so very personal to me, as a former headmaster of it. They had lunch in the dining hall of the Hall, which is the headmaster's house, with ninety boys or so in it. On this occasion, the High Table was occupied by the Queen, in the chair usually occupied by the headmaster. Opposite was the Duke, then, alternately, boys and adult visitors all round the table. I was next but one to the Queen, and I listened to see how things were going. Just at first they were not flowing, and once or twice I came in to make a remark to help things along, and then, after a very few minutes, I heard the Queen burst into a peal of laughter, and I knew that all was well, as indeed it was.

'The Princess Royal was always very kind and gracious to me, while Queen Mary stamped every word and gesture with the mark of her own individual character and excellence, and was kind enough to address me, in writing, as her friend. The Duchess of Kent was always most interesting, and on the spot in everything she said. She revealed a delicacy of judgment and taste which was most refreshing, and more often than not we ended by discussing the truths of the Christian religion. If I say nothing of the Queen Mother, it is simply because everyone knows her boundless charm and sympathy as well as I do.'

The frank and open relationships which Fisher had with the Duke of Edinburgh have been mentioned earlier. As the Archbishop said, "Freedom and openness were exactly characteristic of my dealings with him.' One pleasing story, however, remains to be told. 'During the Coronation service,' the Archbishop recalled, 'the Queen makes an offering of gold, which is presented and placed upon the altar. The Duke once asked whether he could make an offering, also. I welcomed the desire and said I hoped that, just as the Queen's gift goes to Westminster Abbey, so the Prince's gift might come to Lambeth Chapel. It did. A chalice and paten— the chalice a very remarkable one, glass encased in gold work. He took a great interest in it; he discussed it with the artist and was partly responsible for its design. There was an occasion when my wife was seeing some people out of the front door, when suddenly there was Prince Philip, running up the stairs, with a parcel in his hand. He was bringing this chalice and paten as a gift to Lambeth Chapel, which he wished himself to show me—an example of the generosity of all his relations with everybody.'

Such were some of the Archbishop's contacts, formal and informal, with the Royal Family, the warmth and extent of them still indicated by the autographed photographs in Trent Rectory, the place of his retirement. It was there that he made this final reflection on the matter of the Crown and the Royal Family: 'One of the things that stand out to any observing person is the astonishing sequence that has been given to this nation. After the rather worldly setting of King Edward VII's reign came King George V and Queen Mary, remarkable examples of plain and humble Christian duty. Then there was the interlude of Edward VIII, so full of promise and yet so full of frustration. After that came King George VI and Queen Elizabeth; again extraordinary examples of plain Christian grace and duty with, in the case of the King, a triumph over the natural disabilities of shyness and stammering. They were just the people to restore again the quietness and happy confidence of the people in their Royal Family. And then, following them, came the present Queen and Prince Philip, each in their respective ways and duties absolutely superb. I never forget that, Sunday by Sunday, in every parish church of the land we pray for the Queen herself in her own person, as well as for the Queen and all who are in authority under her.

'If there are to be monarchs at all, there could not conceivably be any more fitted than our Royal Family to represent their people, and to represent to their people a sane, progressive, keen, creative, and godly outlook on life. I am glad that I am not one of those enterprising publicists who think it is a useful thing to be always asking what is the value of the Monarchy. Its value depends partly on successive sovereigns, partly on the good sense of our people. It lives because, from both sides, it is constantly being vitalised.'

XIII

Archbishop and State

My relations with the Press, I gather, were bad. That is to say that parts
of the Press made the worst of me whenever they could. I must accept
that. It was not intentional on my part; I always had the friendliest
relations with the reporters. They came: I talked, and I'd say what I
thought. And if they were surprised at something, I'd say what I meant.

G.F.F.

•   •   •

Dr. Fisher's invitation to Archbishop Makarios to come to London is
imaginative and admirable.

The Star, 22 May 1958

•   •   •

By inviting Archbishop Makarios to London to a Church conference at
the end of June, the Archbishop of Canterbury, Dr. Fisher, gravely
embarrasses the Cabinet.

Daily Express, 14 June 1958

•   •   •

I think I was generally listened to in the House of Lords with interest
and with respect, partly because they never quite knew what line I was
going to take.

G.F.F.

INEVITABLY, an Archbishop of Canterbury comes into frequent, and
at times critical contacts with the Governments of his day. It was
certainly the case with Fisher, though here again, as in the case of his
relationships with the Crown, his actions and attitudes came from himself.
In other words, if he was not a courtier, he was certainly not a politician:
he was himself, accustomed by training and habit to scrutinise any
particular issue with a powerful intelligence, and then to speak his mind
upon it. It was therefore not to be expected that all his contacts with the

State were smooth. He had, in fact, some considerable differences with the Government from time to time. Suez and Cyprus were two among several great issues which led to clashes.

Fisher's relationships with what has been called the Fourth Estate of the Realm, the press, with which nowadays other mass media such as television must be included, were of a different order. In this area, his habits of outspokenness and of assuming that everyone was necessarily capable of grasping a lucid argument very quickly, or of not misunderstanding a plain statement, sometimes led to misunderstandings. The case of the American reporter and the H-bomb illustrates the difficulty clearly. This reporter came to see the Archbishop about the bomb. He said how dreadful and horrible it was. Fisher replied: 'Yes, isn't it?' But he did not, as he recalled the incident, show any obvious alarm. His interviewer clearly thought he was very light-hearted about it all. 'Just think,' the reporter said, 'the whole of humanity might be extinguished!' Fisher replied that he supposed it might. 'But they've all got to die sometime, and it shouldn't be all that dreadful if they all died at the same moment.' This his interviewer thought was an absolutely ghastly thing to say. 'But I explained to him that it was a perfectly sensible thing to say, and that the great thing was not to get alarmed at what might happen, but to deal as best one could with the situation in front of us. I was able to explain to him enough to stop him going away and making a song out of it.'

Then there was the case of 'Cassandra' of the *Daily Mirror* (the late Sir William Connor, in his day a most notable and able journalist, who was often particularly severe with Fisher). 'I remember,' the latter recalled, 'one time when I got across Cassandra. I was opening new buildings at a domestic-science college. In my speech I not unnaturally talked about the fact that cooking and feeding the family was a very important thing, with godly implications. Thus talking, I said, "Of course, in the family and in marriage, mother and father are a partnership." I added, because I think it's perfectly true, that the man ought always to let his wife know what his earnings were, and they should arrange mutually how much should be given the wife for housekeeping. This Cassandra took note of and thought dreadful, and he had a whole article denouncing me for saying something which would, he said, "destroy the harmony of every working-class household". I should say it would develop the harmony. But there is one instance I happen to remember where I got into bad odour.'

Fisher's attitude to such incidents was outwardly, as the Archdeacon of Maidstone, J. A. M. Clayson, noted, one of unconcern. But 'he was in fact sensitive of the criticisms, particularly if the statement was obviously inaccurate. Pope John was a popular figure, and the *Sunday Express* made the most of it. One Christmas the paper stressed the fact that the Pope had visited a prison in Rome and went on to say it was a pity the Archbishop of Canterbury didn't match up to this pattern. The Archbishop was hurt by this, for he had himself visited Maidstone Prison on several occasions to confirm some of the prisoners.'

Such matters are not trivia. If any section of the press presents a consistently unfavourable view of a man, at least two results can follow: it can distort his public image, and it can cause the person concerned considerable distress. Both happened in the case of Fisher. Eventually the difficulty was resolved and an excellent press relationship was established. Meanwhile, it is worth asking why such difficulties ever arose at all. There would appear to have been quite a number of reasons. First, there was Fisher's own attitude towards the press, about which he was frank, as always.

'I have no doubt that I said rash things about the press, in public, when I ought not to have done so. But if I did, it was because I thought then, and I still think, that the press uses its freedom very often in ways that are damaging to the morale of the nation. However, if I did, I was fair game for them to hit back at.'

Second, there were his own occasional sharpnesses with members of the press, quite apart from his combative reactions, at times of stress, to their probings. There was, for instance, an occasion in Australia when two young men came to interview him, and it became obvious at once that they knew nothing at all about ecclesiastical matters, or the Christian religion. The Archbishop asked them if they had had any training. They replied that they were only just beginning. Fisher said: 'Will you tell your editor that it is scandalous to send out two men like you, who know nothing at all about the Church, or any church, to interview me, and that he had better take more care in the future.' He then sent them away.

He also did not conceal his irritation when, on one American tour, he was asked beforehand, at the very entrance of the hall, for the script of an important address which he was proposing to give from notes only. In this case his interrogator knew no shorthand, and Fisher was annoyed, both by the presumption and the incompetence. At other times, his bantering of reporters, although often well received, was not always so.

But, basic to the whole question of the Archbishop's relations with the press was the fact that no adequate organisation whatever existed until the later years of his archiepiscopate, to assist him in this field. This was a major weakness which led to much misunderstanding on both sides. Eventually, in 1960, Colonel Robert Hornby, who had been Director of Public Relations for the British Army in the Far East, was appointed Chief Information Officer of the Church Assembly, a position which he held with great distinction and success until 1965. This officer was astonished at the amateurishness of the long-established situation at Lambeth. He found, for example, that it was possible to ring up Lambeth Palace from Fleet Street late at night, when the papers felt in some need of a story and for a reporter to find himself talking to the Archbishop himself, though often, to avoid being quoted, the latter let it be assumed that the reporter was talking to the chaplain. There might then ensue a long discussion on the precise implications of the Archbishop's latest statement. With a soldier's simplicity, Hornby marched into Lambeth Palace and demanded that no further question should ever be phoned direct there, but should be put through to his office. This was not very well received at first; but was at last accomplished.

The results were astonishing. In Fisher's words: 'After we got a Chief Information Officer, and Hornby had got into touch with the press, the whole situation altered. It was miraculous. He would explain to them what the occasion was at which I was speaking, and if I dropped some kind of brick, he would put it right at the end of the meeting before they went. As a result, the publicity given to the Church of England improved out of all knowledge. The illustrations and numbers of pictures increased greatly, and the kind of friendliness of reference to the Church of England was a joy to behold, instead of the critical, cold relationship which was evident beforehand.'

Colonel Hornby's own account of the matter not only gives a more detailed picture of this important development, but adds something to the picture of Fisher himself.

'I understood that there was apprehension about the relationship between Lambeth and Fleet Street, and I was told that the Archbishop of Canterbury was frequently misquoted and, indeed, that press relations generally were not all that people would like them to be. Of course, I knew then very little about Archbishops and in my first interview I said to him, "Well, Your Grace, I would like to have a copy of everything you are going to say before you say it," because I had suspected that the difficulty really lay in the fact that the press did not have sufficient warning of what the Archbishop was going to talk about. His Grace said to me: "I have never put this kind of thing on paper in advance yet, and I don't propose to start for you. I always have notes, but I do not always follow them."

'At this point, I thought I had better retire, having made a few more noises about the importance of letting the press have a preview of important statements before they were made public. This was early in January 1960. The first public occasion on which the Archbishop was to appear after that interview was the Convocation of Canterbury, at which he gives a presidential address. This was normally finally finished by the Archbishop just in time for the meeting of Convocation, and reporters had to take it down as best they could. On that particular morning, a messenger from Lambeth arrived at Church House, quite clearly having never been inside the place—he lost his way—came to my office eventually, and presented me with a carbon copy of the address. This was ten minutes before the Archbishop was due to speak, and therefore was not much use. But it showed that His Grace had firmly taken the point that I had made. In fact, I went down to meet him at the steps to Church House and as he came up the steps he nudged me in the ribs with his elbow and said just two words: "Got it?"

'From then on until his retirement he did prepare for me, well in advance, the major speeches and sermons he had to make. Basically, the trouble was the technical point, which had not been understood by any of the Archbishop's advisers, nor indeed by His Grace himself that, with the best will in the world, the most brilliant shorthand writer becomes exhausted when, after listening for twenty-five minutes to an exposition on a particular subject, he is then expected to summarise it and telephone it to his office within ten minutes of the speech ending.

'Of course, the Archbishop had a brilliant mind and was quite capable of composing speeches or sermons without much time for preparation, and it was this gift of being able to think on his feet that in many ways laid the traps for the misinterpretation and misquotations which subsequently appeared. Also the Archbishop has a very fine, beautiful voice, but a deceptive delivery. Try taking the Archbishop down in shorthand and you will realise how quickly he speaks. He also had a habit of stringing the important words in a sentence rather towards the end of a phrase so that it was necessary to go back over what he had said in order to grasp the full meaning. It was quite easy, particularly if you were trying to take it down, to misinterpret. Also, of course, he thought about three or four times as fast as the people who were trying to report him. So this really was a technical difficulty. It certainly was not a personality difficulty. His personal relationships with the press were excellent. It was that there had been no machinery available to enable what he was going to say to be presented to Fleet Street in such a way that it could be assimilated.

'A classic example arose at the birth of Prince Andrew. I arranged for the press, television and radio to be at Lambeth Palace because the Archbishop of Canterbury, taking precedence before the Prime Minister, is usually expected to comment first on a Royal birth.

'The interviews were due at five p.m. I arrived at four p.m. and got into the Archbishop's study at about four fifteen. I said that the press were expecting him to comment about five o'clock, whereupon he looked up and said, "What is it, a prince or princess?" adding, "Well, I'm going to have tea now. I'll write something when I'm having tea." This, I think, is a measure of his intellectual capacity—that he was not at all daunted by having a dead-line twenty minutes away, ten minutes of which would be taken up having tea, before he commented on a national occasion. I was handed what he was going to say on the back of an envelope. He then memorised that, perfectly, word for word, and I was left with the envelope, after which I had to dash into one of his secretaries to get it re-typed and issued to the press. This was the sort of arrangement which went on for the first few months when I took over. I remember one of the secretaries at Lambeth commenting to me when I said that the newspapers must have something: "I thought the press took the news down from the B.B.C. at six o'clock."'

If such expert aid as Hornby's had been available even two years earlier, the Archbishop would almost certainly have been saved from what was perhaps the biggest clash with the press he ever had—the Makarios affair. This gave him much anxiety. He felt it, as he put it years later, at one point 'almost more than I could stick'. The facts were simple, and arose from the issuing of invitations by the Archbishop for the Lambeth Conference of 1958.

Among these invitations were some to the leaders of the Orthodox Churches to attend the opening of the Conference. This was according to precedent. The first day was an open day, before the Conference proper began, and it was a habit to receive there leaders of other churches. The question which had previously faced Fisher was whether he should invite Archbishop Makarios, head of the Orthodox Church of Cyprus, with the other Orthodox heads. There were two difficulties. The first was that not to do so would have been a direct insult to all his fellow heads of Orthodox churches. As one newspaper, *The Manchester Guardian*, later commented when the uproar had died away, 'To omit him would have been even more of a political act than to include him.'

But the second difficulty was that Makarios had been involved in the troubles in Cyprus which for several years had been engaging British troops in that island, and inflaming public opinion in this. He had also been deported and had not denounced, as many felt he should have done, the activities of the Eoka terrorist organisation.

Well aware of these difficulties, Fisher had, a year in advance, asked the Foreign Office for guidance in the matter. They had replied that so far as they were concerned an invitation to Makarios would be in order. He then asked the Colonial Office which was directly in charge; but they had delayed giving any answer. Finally, however, they informed Canon Waddams, the Secretary of the Council of Foreign Relations, that the question was one for the Archbishop of Canterbury to decide, and was entirely a matter for him. This meant that, on the civil side, there was no objection. On the ecclesiastical side, Fisher felt quite clear that he had to invite him, and did so.

An extraordinary rumpus then began. As Fisher recalled, the beginning came at a press conference which he chanced to be holding on quite another matter, at Lambeth on the day the invitation was announced. 'I had to refer to this question of Makarios, and I hurriedly prepared a statement. It made perfectly clear that I had sufficient approval from the Colonial Office, and that my reasons were entirely ecclesiastical. That was a plain statement of fact; but it released a vast amount of misrepresentation and of stupid abuse about me.' It did indeed. One paper, discovering that the Archbishop had had correspondence with Makarios beforehand, which was indeed the truth, pursued him to know what had been in the correspondence. This information the Archbishop naturally declined to give, as a matter of principle. The refusal gave rise to suspicions of a mysterious plotting between the two.

This was serious, and there was no doubt that the Archbishop had a very bad press. Thus *The Times* of 23 May 1958: 'Although the Government were informed about the Archbishop of Canterbury's invitation to Archbishop Makarios to visit the Lambeth Conference, there is reason to think that it has deeply embarrassed and displeased them. The Government anxiously realise that any visit that Archbishop Makarios might pay to London in his capacity as a religious leader must involve the possibility of political overtones that might not be happy.' The *Express* quoted a clergyman in Exeter a few days later, as saying that the invitation to Makarios was 'an outrage on our Christian consciences'. The General Assembly of the Free Church of Scotland heard the invitation denounced as an act 'bringing religion into deserved disrepute'.

The whole business indeed gave Fisher great anxiety and distress. Nor did his action, possibly suggestive of overstrain, of saying on television to Richard Dimbleby that he regarded with abhorrence the general political behaviour of Makarios and his association with terrorism, win any approval of him in Orthodox circles. The Archbishop in this context had said, in answer to one of Dimbleby's questions, that Archbishop Makarios was 'a bad man'. For this, which enraged the Greek Church, he later apologised in a cable to the Archbishop of Athens: 'Archbishop Makarios's ecclesiastical office highly honoured by me. My remarks expressly excluded reflections on his personal character. Criticism confined strictly to certain political aspects . . .'

This again was featured in the press. But eventually the affair was settled in a manner made clear by a passage in *The Times* of 25 June 1958: 'Archbishop Makarios announced today that he would be unable to attend next month's opening ceremonies of the Lambeth Conference, to which he has been invited by the Archbishop of Canterbury. He said that other preoccupations required his continued presence in Athens.'

Fisher's own comment long afterwards was: 'I felt there was no reproach on me whatsoever. I had merely done my duty and done it in a proper way. In the end, of course, Makarios refused the invitation, to my great delight, and a fellow bishop said to me, "I'm very glad that you issued the invitation; and greatly relieved that Makarios did not accept it." And that is the truth.'

So ended the Makarios affair, a classic instance of the dangers which, in public life, can wait upon the best intentioned of actions once their motives are misinterpreted. Yet only two years before, in 1956, Fisher had been to the forefront in making a plea for constructive action over Cyprus by the British Government which, if it had been taken up, might well have lessened some later bitternesses. *The Times* of 16 March of that year described his speech in the Lords as one of 'a quality and content which placed it in a class apart from anything which the Commons offered.' Fisher had been pleading, with great urgency, for three measures which he begged should be taken quickly. The first was that the British Government should appoint a person, or persons, to draft a constitution on the lines of the correspondence between the Governor and Archbishop Makarios; secondly, that the Greek and Turkish governments should join with the British Government in an immediate appeal to the Cypriots to end terrorism and, thirdly, that Archbishop Makarios should be informed that his exile was temporary (this was at a time when he had been deported to the Seychelles) and would end as soon as public order in Cyprus had been restored. All this, as *The Times* recorded, made a deep impression on the House.

It also led to a sharp clash with the Colonial Secretary of the day. The incident was described by Fisher. 'This matter arose out of a speech I was going to make to the British Council of Churches. I had been trying to ginger up the Government to get on with the thing and take some further action. I was going to tell the British Council of Churches that, while Eden had made a statement on Cyprus that was perfectly in order, I had every hope that the Colonial Secretary, who was keenly interested, would be able to find a way of suggesting some fresh opportunity for advance. I sent the speech to him for his approval on the Thursday of one week and heard nothing. On the Monday afternoon, Slack[1] rang to ask whether he could release it to the press for delivery the next morning. I said: "Yes. I haven't heard anything from the Colonial Office; I must assume that it is all right." That evening the Colonial Secretary rang up. He said that he had been in Italy and only just come back and found my manuscript and that he did not at all approve of what I was proposing to say. I said that it had already been issued to the press. I delivered the speech. It was meant merely to encourage the Government not to be passive, but to do something and take some further steps. That following week-end two ministers made speeches implying that I was trying to divide the Cabinet and taking me to task for daring to do such a thing. Though I was completely innocent of any such thing, there were all the elements of a row. But the press saw, I think, that it was nonsense, and did not take it up. However, I wrote to the Prime Minister, Anthony Eden, saying that of course there was nothing in this, and that I was astonished that anybody should have suggested that I was trying to divide the Cabinet. Eden replied accepting what I said; but he added that it would be a very good thing if I consulted the minister before making a statement of that kind. I replied that, in fact, I had reported what I proposed to say to the Colonial Secretary the previous Thursday before I spoke on the Tuesday, and it had not seemed to have had any good effect. Well, that was Cyprus.'

Another notable issue upon which the Archbishop found himself ranged against the Government was over Suez. This led, among much else, to a dramatic confrontation in the Lords between the Archbishop and the

[1] The Rev. Kenneth Slack, at that time Secretary of the British Council of Churches.

Lord Chancellor, Lord Kilmuir, which showed an aspect of Fisher rarely seen, that of the formidable and, indeed, ruthless advocate. His own attitude to the Suez question is best given in his own words.

'When Anthony Eden's government decided to take violent action and put troops into Egypt,[1] without any instructions from the United Nations, and when, in fact, they had conspicuously refrained from referring the trouble to the United Nations, I felt that they had not only lost a very good opportunity of doing the right thing, but that they had done the wrong thing. Ever since the end of the second war, there had been very active the great ambition to put an end to force as an instrument of international politics. There was the United Nations appointed to be the means of reconciling quarrels between nations. And here, Great Britain had turned its back on this great movement of history, and this great hope of history; it had chosen to ignore the United Nations and had used force against Egypt, or was in the process of using force against Egypt.

'It seemed to me a dreadful failure to see the creative opportunity. Debates in the House of Lords turned on this matter of referring the dispute to the United Nations. There were magnificent speeches from people like Lord MacNair and other lawyers, urging that it was essential that we, Great Britain, should refer the quarrel to the United Nations for settlement. Other peers maintained that the Charter allowed a nation, in case of emergency, to take action by itself, without referring to the United Nations. There was, indeed, this loophole. But there was, at the same time, Israel advancing into Egypt. We did not know then that there had been collusion between the French, the British and the Israeli governments. But it just looked shocking that we should be proposing to invade from our end, while we could see that Israel was invading from its end. That was the situation. As I say, there were magnificent speeches, saying that it was our duty to go to the United Nations, and on the other side, very strong speeches that here was a violation of international law, that Nasser should be stopped now before he did more damage, and of course it was right for us to invade. The point I remember is that Kilmuir made a great speech in defence of Government policy. At some point he asserted that we were only going into Egypt as a fire-engine

[1] November–December, 1956.

261

to extinguish a blaze. I intervened and asked a question, referring to the fact that the forces of Israel were twenty miles or more inside Egyptian soil. But the Lord Chancellor would not see it, and so I went on trying to make him admit that Great Britain and Israel were both invading Egypt as an act of war. A fierce exchange followed, embalmed now in the pages of *Hansard*.'[1] '*The Lord Archbishop of Canterbury*: My lords, the noble and learned viscount referred to the attacking power against which we have to exercise self-defence. Who is the attacking power?

The Lord Chancellor: My lords, I said that self-defence extended to the protection of nationals on someone else's territory. In that case, we have the right to intervene and use force in that territory to protect our nationals. Then the second point arises—I hope I made this clear; I intended to put it entirely fairly—first we make a peaceful landing; then, if the power into whose territory we are going says that they will resist with all their force, the force which we have the right to use is automatically extended to that sufficient to repulse the force threatened.

The Lord Archbishop of Canterbury: Which is the attacking power in this case?

The Lord Chancellor: In the case I have mentioned, the person who threatens to use force in answer to a proffered peaceful intervention.

The Lord Archbishop of Canterbury: Here is the Canal; here are our Nationals; here is our property. There is an attack upon them which you have to resist. Who is making the attack?

The Lord Chancellor: I see now. The most reverend Primate is asking me a question of fact.

The Lord Archbishop of Canterbury: Yes.

The Lord Chancellor: Then I will deal with that. The threat of force is made by the person who refuses to stop the hostile operations that are threatening the people and the installations. I really must be allowed to continue, perhaps after just one more interruption.

The Lord Archbishop of Canterbury: Who is this attacking power in this case?

The Lord Chancellor: I should have thought the most reverend Primate might have guessed that for himself. It is obviously Egypt who has refused to stop.

[1] House of Lords official report, Vol. 199, No. 137. Thursday, 1 November 1956.

The Lord Archbishop of Canterbury: This is terribly important and perhaps I might ask the Lord Chancellor this. Where does the operational force originate? I should have thought that the attacking force, whether you like it or not, was Israel. Is that not so?

The Lord Chancellor: Yes. I explained the law, and I was going to proceed to the facts. But in applying that to this case, our nationals, our ships, and the Canal itself are in danger from the conflict between Israel and Egypt. We then, with, I believe, complete moral propriety and rightness, asked them both to stop the conflict which is threatening our nationals, our ships and the Canal. The most reverend Primate really must not interrupt again.

Several Noble Lords: Order, order!

The Lord Chancellor: The Israelis agreed to stop hostilities and to retire, but Egypt refused and indicated that they would use force to prevent the steps which we proposed for a peaceful stoppage of the fighting. That is the sense in which I used it. Perhaps now the most reverend Primate will allow me to continue my speech.

The Lord Archbishop of Canterbury: May I say this? I entirely accept everything that the Lord Chancellor has said. I was not criticising it or attacking it. I was merely asking a question: where did the force originate? That, he says, is Israel; and that is all I want to establish.

A Noble Lord: No; he did not say that.

The Lord Chancellor: The most reverend Primate has, I am sure, entirely unintentionally, sought to confuse two situations. There is the first situation, which attracted our peacemaking intention, which was started when Israel crossed the border. Then there is the second situation, which I have been at some pains to explain, when the Egyptians refused our peaceful measures. I hope that I have now made that clear.

The Lord Archbishop of Canterbury: I merely said that there are two statements, one and two. You omitted one. I have now inserted one.

The Lord Chancellor: I am always happy to have the co-operation of the most reverend Primate in making a speech. I have always said, both in public and privately, that he is one of the best speakers in London, and I am sure that any speech of mine will be greatly improved by his interruptions.'

Afterwards, as Fisher recalled, 'As we went out, Lord Jowett, a former Lord Chancellor, a very able lawyer and a boy at Marlborough, senior to me, said: "Well, Fisher, that's one of the best pieces of cross-examination that I've ever heard", which rather pleased me. But it was pretty brutal, and Lord Kilmuir never forgot it. It was years afterwards when, in the House of Lords, something came up and he mentioned that there had been a time when I had heckled him nine times successively. But it was a dreadful time.'

On balance, the impression given by these encounters with the State over many of the great issues of his time is that the Archbishop was more often against Government policy than for it. He was against the Government in the matter of Independent Television; against it over the introduction of Premium Bonds; against the Colonial Office in pressing the matter of religious freedom in Malta. This in itself forms a curious tale.

'There was,' he recounted, 'in the Maltese constitution a special clause that nobody should suffer any disability from his religion. The fact remained that no Anglican was allowed to appear in clerical robes in public at all. The Colonial Office had almost always given in to Roman prejudice, and refused to use any influence whatsoever to get the Anglican rights asserted. And of course, with us suffered Methodists and others. This was much in my mind and a number of cases occurred when I wanted to take action. I found that when Cyril Garbett had visited Malta, and had robed in a house just a few yards from the Cathedral, and walked across to the Cathedral, he had been reprimanded by the authorities in Malta for having shown himself in public in this way.

'When I visited Malta Cathedral for its reconsecration, after the war, I robed in the vestry, went out at the back door and walked round the Cathedral, inside the surrounding railings, to the main entrance, and so entered it. It was expressly seen that I did not set foot off the territory belonging to the Cathedral; and it was entertaining, that as I walked round inside these guarding railings outside, every window was crammed with Maltese, looking to see me pass, and cheering and waving their hands. It was a most royal procession from one point of view. From the other point of view, I was a wild animal kept behind bars.

'That was the setting. Then came the politics of it. I used, from time to time, to bring the issue up; but we got no further with the Colonial Office on the matter. At last there came a real crisis. The Queen was going to dedicate the War Memorial in Malta. By tradition, such a memorial was dedicated either by the Anglican Bishop, or by the Chaplain-General of the Forces, on behalf of all the chaplains. The Bishop of Gibraltar was, of course, quite ready to do it; but he was told he would not be allowed to. The Chaplain-General was told that he would not be allowed to. And it was made perfectly clear that the Roman authorities would not allow any non-Roman priest to appear on the scene at all, and the civil authorities were bound by Roman canon law. We had to accept this, and instead of any religious ceremony at the unveiling by the Queen, there were services in the Cathedral and in the Methodist Church instead. It was a lamentable thing, but there it was, and it was with these feelings that I approached the fact that there was going to be a new constitution for Malta.

'I pressed on the Government that, of course, we must be given our full freedom in Malta under the new constitution, as (nominally) under the old one. I remember the most extraordinary conversations I ever had in the Houses of Parliament. I went to see the Lord Chancellor and the Colonial Secretary, in the Lord Chancellor's room to discuss this very matter. I told them of the indignity from which we suffered, and insisted that under any new constitution our full liberty must be guaranteed. I could not shake them. I reminded them that we were meeting in a House of Parliament where great battles for principles of religious freedom had been fought. They would not budge, and I think I was there for an hour and a half, labouring away to establish our religious freedom in Malta, until finally the Lord Chancellor said that he would refer the matter to the Law Officers of the Crown. I agreed, and heard no more.'

But if the matter was not settled constitutionally, it was settled on another far broader, far higher, and more spiritual basis. It happened in a moment of time, as did so much else in Anglican-Roman relations after Fisher's visit to Pope John XXIII. 'Bishop Craske, when he was Bishop of Gibraltar,' Fisher said, 'told me that he met the Roman Catholic Archbishop of the area, who stopped his car and got out and talked to Craske for ten minutes on the pavement, in the middle of Malta, to the astonishment of all the Maltese who saw it happening—the two in happy conversation together.'

The Archbishop's contacts with other ministers were numerous and varied, and to look at even a few of them is to bring up voices and memories of the past. There is Hugh Dalton, as Chancellor of the Exchequer, listening patiently to a delegation of churchmen led by Fisher, who had come to see him about the losses the churches would suffer through the reduction in the value of railway shares, but making it plain they would have to take their medicine with the rest—a decision which Fisher thought fair enough, disliking in principle the Church's asking for preferential treatment in anything. And there is Aneurin Bevan, in the early days of the Health Service, similarly listening to a delegation regarding the position of hospital chaplains under the new dispensation, and being found by Fisher 'entirely reasonable. He listened to what we had to say. He recognised the problem, and while he didn't give anything away, he said he would certainly have it looked into, and proposals were made which, to a certain extent, were satisfactory.'

And then there were Prime Ministers: Churchill, with his religion of the Englishman, as has already been told; and Attlee, 'a splendid person to work with. When things occurred, he preferred me to go and talk with him directly, and that I liked. Everything was dealt with speedily, properly, competently, and I knew exactly where I was with him.'

In general, the Archbishop's relations with ministers and politicians on both sides was friendly and genial; but on particular matters of official policy he found neither Eden nor Macmillan easy. The latter was a keen and very well-informed churchman; but *au fond* had a somewhat squire-archical view of the Church. This being so, it was perhaps natural that an Archbishop who intervened so actively and toughly in current affairs, though never claiming more than in his personal capacity he could properly claim—his opposition to Premium Bonds was a case in point—should sometimes have failed to commend his activities to this particular Prime Minister.

There is no doubt that Fisher did, in fact, make his voice heard often and with power in the Lords. Towards the end of his archiepiscopate a singular compliment was paid him as regards this aspect of his manifold activities. 'I remember,' he said, 'right at the end, a remark made by Lord Winterton, who was a father of the House of Commons at one time, and then an elder statesman of the Conservatives in the Lords. He generally spoke against me. But he did once say that, while he very rarely agreed with me, he reckoned that I was the clearest and most concise speaker in the House of Lords, and there was never any doubt about what I was meaning to say. That, I thought, was a testimonial worth having.'

And what happened in the end about the press — that Fourth Estate with which the Archbishop was, at various times, so embroiled? Here is a tale with a pleasant ending, reflecting considerable credit on both sides. 'I was invited,' Fisher recalled, 'to the Press Club in Fleet Street. Before that, I had from time to time crossed swords with John Gordon, once editor of the *Sunday Express*, and then with a column in it. I went to the Press Club, and it was arranged that I should first go round and chat with the members as they had their drinks; then afterwards should speak to them for half an hour. I went round, and afterwards I addressed them. On my right hand was an easy chair with John Gordon at full length in it, and I began by saying that wherever I had gone, round the world, reporters had always been extremely kind to me. Then I added *"exceptis excipiendis"*[1] and said, "In case any of you don't know what that means, it means except for people like John Gordon!" I pointed at him, sitting just beneath me, and there was a great roar of laughter and the speech went down very well, all the better perhaps for this introduction. Afterwards, as far as I know, John Gordon no longer referred to me in his column.'

As Colonel Hornby said: 'I found no one warmer with the press than Fisher. Indeed, once the press had interviewed him, or spoken to him, he created a great bond of friendship and warmth.' That bond held, and was to prove of much importance to the manner in which the final great achievement of Fisher's archiepiscopate, his opening up of contacts with the Roman Catholic Church through his visit to Pope John XXIII, not long after this time, was presented to the world.

[1] 'Making all necessary exceptions.'

XIV

The Final Journeys: Jerusalem, Istanbul, Rome

In many parts of the world, and in contact with many churches, I have felt that a resurrection is at work. I pray that my journey to Jerusalem and from Jerusalem to the head of the Orthodox world, and on to the head of the Roman Catholic world, may in some measure give help and encouragement to all who find in the Ecumenical Movement an authentic voice of the Holy Spirit to the churches of the world.

G.F.F., in a sermon in St. George's Cathedral, Jerusalem,
27 November 1960

• • •

'A kiss of peace is never out of place,' said the Archbishop of Canterbury, Dr. Fisher, after being greeted by the Oecumenical Patriarch, Athenagoras.

The Times, 30 November 1960

• • •

The journey I am engaged on is no ordinary journey. I feel that I am truly walking in the spirit of the apostles in my visits.

G.F.F., in a sermon in Christ Church, Istanbul,
30 November 1960

• • •

Here is, indeed, a day of the Lord, like many days of the Lord, simple, unspectacular, hardly to be observed, a whisper of the still, small voice of the Holy Spirit.

G.F.F., in a sermon at All Saints, Rome, 1 December 1960

• • •

A last question was: 'What is your most vivid memory of your tour?' 'Of a camel which looked at me with most ineffable scorn,' he replied. 'A donkey smiles. Roughly speaking, all humanity is a donkey or a camel.'

G.F.F., interviewed at London Airport, 3 December 1960

B Y 1960 Fisher had been Archbishop for fifteen years and was seventy-three. It was a stage, in any man's life, when the time for new adventures and pioneering actions might have been supposed to be over. Surprise was all the greater, therefore, when the following statement was issued from Lambeth Palace at the end of October:

'The Archbishop of Canterbury plans to leave London on 22 November for Jerusalem, where he will be the guest of the Anglican Archbishop of Jerusalem, the Most Reverend Campbell MacInnes.

'His Grace will visit the holy places and call on the Orthodox Patriarch of Jerusalem and heads of other churches in the Middle East, expressing in person the close friendship which has long existed between Anglican and Eastern Churches.

'On the way back the Archbishop hopes it will prove possible for him to call at Istanbul to visit His All Holiness Athenagoras I, Oecumenical Patriarch of the Orthodox Church.

'After Istanbul, the Archbishop of Canterbury proposes to spend a few days in Rome in the course of which he will pay a visit of courtesy to His Holiness Pope John XXIII.

'The Archbishop will return to this country on 3 December.'

At the same time there came from the Church Information Office the following statement: 'During the past fifty years the Church of England has increasingly come into friendly relationship with many other churches. Among them have been the Church of Scotland and the Free Churches in the United Kingdom, with their sister Churches overseas, the Protestant Churches of Europe and the Orthodox and the other Eastern Churches, with whom there is a long tradition of friendship. All these Churches are members of the World Council of Churches, whose Central Committee met at St. Andrews this summer. At this meeting there were observers from the Roman Catholic Church.'

One of these observers had been Monsignor Willebrands, secretary of the then new Secretariat for Christian Unity, set up under Cardinal Bea by Pope John. It was through him that the Archbishop had ascertained that the Pope would welcome such a visit as was now announced, and it was agreed that this visit was to be referred to as a visit of courtesy, or, in the words of the *Osservatore Romano*, '*una semplice visita di cortesia*'. The Archbishop also stressed the fact that this would be an episode in the tripartite pilgrimage of courtesy which he had in mind. Inevitably, it was far more. It could not help being far more. On the other hand, it was not what it was in some quarters instantly supposed to be: the end product of some kind of plot.

This was a supposition sufficiently dangerous to warrant correction, and Fisher took the opportunity of setting the record straight at a meeting of the Church Assembly shortly before his departure. Replying to speeches of goodwill, he made plain how concerned he was that no suggestion of the secrecy which had been associated with the Malines Conversations[1] should be attached to his visit to Rome. Henceforth, he hoped, representatives of the Anglican and Roman Catholic communions would be able to meet for mutual conversation and education without anyone thinking it at all odd. Years later he said: 'The actual idea came to me all in one flash. I was in my study. I remember I was walking to and fro thinking about one thing and another, and suddenly there came, as a single inspiration, Jerusalem, Istanbul, Rome. It lay in my mind for some little time. I told it to the Secretary of the Council of Foreign Relations and nobody else. A moment came when I had three or four bishops in my study, talking about things concerning Rome; I mentioned this idea and they all took to it. So soundings began to be made in the Vatican. But of course the idea entered my head like that only because a lot of factors had been building up subconsciously before the coming of the flash.'

What were these other factors? In the case of Jerusalem, at least, they were numerous. Over all the years, ever since his elder sister, in 1901, had gone to Palestine as a medical missionary, his attention and interest had been, as he put it, 'largely drawn to the Arab world and the Arab people'. He had always had a special interest in the Jerusalem bishopric, which was directly representative of the Anglican Communion, and in increasing its ecclesiastical dignity by the creation of the Jerusalem archbishopric under Campbell MacInnes. In the case of Istanbul, several strong Anglican links had already existed for many years, and Archbishop Lang in 1939 during the course of a cruise in the Mediterranean after illness, had visited the Oecumenical Patriarch in Istanbul. But Fisher's relationships with the

[1] Arising from the initiative of Lord Halifax, these conversations between Anglican and Roman Catholic theologians took place at Malines under the presidency of Cardinal Mercier between 1921 and 1925. They aroused suspicions on both sides and were virtually terminated by the death of Cardinal Mercier in 1926 and the publication of the encyclical *Mortalium Animos* by Pope Pius XI in 1928, which forbade Roman Catholic participation in reunion movements such as Faith and Order.

Orthodox had also a more personal basis. Of this he said: 'I suppose the first and most active cause of that was the friendship and goodness of heart of Archbishop Germanos, who was the Oecumenical Patriarch's representative in London and whom I got to know extremely well. He was a man of few words, but his heart was always in the right place, and he had great wisdom and patience: he won my deep affection as well as my respect and confidence. Occasionally I would go to Orthodox services and get caught there by the strange attraction of Orthodox worship. And then I had met the Oecumenical Patriarch in the U.S.A. when he was holding office there and we were both at a World Council of Churches meeting, and I had perceived his great qualities as Christian and statesman.'

Such were some of the factors which drew Fisher to Jerusalem and Istanbul. In the case of Rome they were of a different order and owed everything to the advent of one man, Pope John XXIII. Up to that point, the Archbishop's relationships with the Church of Rome had been critical and sometimes difficult. 'I grew up,' he said, 'with an inbred opposition to anything that came from Rome. I objected to their doctrine; I objected to their methods of reasoning; I objected to their methods of operation in this country. So I grew up, and I saw no reason for differing from that opinion as the years went by. When I became Archbishop, I had many connections with them. One of the first things I did was to call together representatives of the chief churches on the British Council of Churches to meet representatives of the Church of Rome to discuss how contact with them might be maintained in the future. I recalled the fact that we had all worked together on a small committee of the British Council of Churches, acting with representatives of the Roman Catholic Sword of the Spirit movement, which had had valuable results. I said that, as Archbishop, I could no longer go on as chairman of that committee. Could the British Council of Churches have some more general small committee, not with the Sword of the Spirit, but directly with the Church of Rome? This was discussed at length. The Roman Catholic representative, a bishop sent by the Cardinal to represent him, said at the end that he thought that would be perfectly possible, and that he would go back and put the proposal to Cardinal Griffin. But time passed and I heard nothing. A month or two later, I met the Cardinal at a party. We sat down together and in the course of conversation I mentioned to him that there had been this proposal. He said that he had some recollection of it and would make enquiries; but again I heard nothing at all, and this suggestion for maintaining a regular contact lapsed. When Cardinal Hinsley was at Westminster, relations with Lambeth were very much warmer. The chillier climate which followed gave rise to constant difficulties.'

.Even at this distance of time, short as it is, this seems extraordinary, so profoundly has the ecumenical atmosphere changed. For instance, as late as 1956 at a great meeting in the Albert Hall to show sympathy with Hungary in its sufferings at the hands of Russia, there was objection from Westminster Cathedral to Fisher's saying of the Lord's Prayer, and giving the blessing in the presence of a Roman archbishop. Fisher suggested that the Roman archbishop should leave before the end, which he did.

A very much larger difficulty arose out of arrangements being made by the War Graves Commission for the dedication of the War Memorial at Alamein. How large a matter this was, Fisher discovered when, returning from an American visit, he found waiting for him a telegram from the General Commanding in Egypt, saying that, if the arrangements went through as proposed, he would not take his troops to the memorial service. There was another telegram from the Anglican bishop in Egypt saying that he would not take part in the service unless ordered to do so from Lambeth. The cause of all this was that, while the arrangements allowed for the Bishop and Chaplain General, representing the Anglicans and Free Churches, to have five minutes allotted to them in the service, and the Moslem representative also to have five minutes allotted to him, authority had by inadvertence allowed to the representatives of the Roman Catholic Church twenty minutes or more, during which they would involve the whole company assembled, military and civil, in witnessing a celebration of a Roman Catholic mass. The Archbishop was quite clear that this could not be tolerated, even though (as he was informed) the Pope had given leave for the mass to be broadcast to Roman Catholics all over the world. The matter had to be settled within forty-eight hours. Very great exertions by the Archbishop were necessary before a new and satisfactory arrangement was made, by which the Roman Catholic mass would follow on after the end of the service and would not be broadcast to those present at the ceremony.

Such incidents, symptomatic of many, added to a lifelong antipathy to Roman doctrines and attitudes, made it, on the face of it, unlikely that Fisher would feel drawn to include Rome as the final stage of his pilgrimage, or to pay a visit of courtesy to the head of that vast communion of which Rome was the centre. What changed him? In his own words it was: 'Without any doubt, the personality of Pope John. It was quite obvious to the world that Pope John was a different kind of Pope, whom I should like to meet, and could meet, on grounds of Christian brotherhood without any kind of ecclesiastical compromise on either side. Of this I felt certain already. And so it was that, in a flash, in my study I thought of this pilgrimage as a whole thing exhibiting in one simple manner the unity of the Churches in the Church Militant already existing. The only place to start such a pilgrimage was obviously in Jerusalem. Next would come Istanbul, the centre of the Churches of the East, where I would renew my trustful friendship with the Oecumenical Patriarch, and then Rome, if the Pope was willing that I should meet him as friend to friend. That is exactly how it happened. Satterthwaite[1] worked out all the details; Willebrands was entirely enthusiastic; Cardinal Bea no doubt recommended it to Pope John as a good idea. And so the thing happened.'

It did indeed, and with enormous and lasting results. Who, then, was this 'different kind of Pope' whose personality, even at secondhand, had worked so warmly upon Fisher's heart and mind? It is easy enough to give his name: Angelo Roncalli. It is easy enough to outline his career, from his peasant family beginnings in Northern Italy, through the seminary at Bergamo, and thence out to a long career in the Diplomatic Service of the Holy See, in Bulgaria, in Turkey, in Greece, in Paris. In 1953 he became a cardinal, and Patriarch of Venice. In 1958, at the age of seventy-seven, he was elected Pope. What is not so easy is to indicate what manner of man he was. Some have said that he was essentially simple. 'Pope John was the old-fashioned "garden-of-the-soul" type of Catholic' was one view.[2]

[1] The Rev. J. R. Satterthwaite, General Secretary of the Church of England Council on Foreign Relations.
[2] Cardinal Heenan, *Westminster Cathedral Chronicle*, July, 1964.

Another was that he was 'a political genius', as Robert Kaiser wrote in his book *Behind the Council.* What is certain is that a man who was clearly supposed to be a transition Pope became one of whose short reign it has been said that 'No four years of Papal history have seen such major policy changes as Pope John made. During his short reign he reversed both the international and the Italian policy of the Papacy. It may be true that he had no blue-print for the reform of the Church; he left that to the Council, after showing the bishops where to look for it. A General Council, not the Pope, is the right body to reform the Church. Pope John's aims were wider. He wanted to give a lead to the world.'[1]

Such, then, was the man whom Fisher was to meet in the first personal encounter between a Pope and an Archbishop of Canterbury since Archbishop Arundel visited the Vatican in 1397. He left to a chorus of comment. Cardinal Godfrey of Westminster was sure that 'the Holy Father would receive the Archbishop with the same sympathetic cordiality as he and his predecessors had extended to many other religious leaders'. The Anglican Bishop of Bristol thought it was 'important to realise that this visit has no great diplomatic significance beyond the obvious desirability of Christian leaders knowing each other personally'. The Moderator of the General Assembly of the Church of Scotland said that he found the announcement interesting; the Moderator of the General Assembly of the Free Church of Scotland gave a warning that any move of this kind would have to be watched very carefully. A deputation from evangelical organisations called at Lambeth to urge the Archbishop to safeguard the principles of the Reformation. He reassured them. That done, and all preparations made, including a massive press operation by Colonel Hornby, he set off on what was to be the most remarkable of all the many journeys of his archiepiscopate. He left London on 22 November, flew to Beirut, where he stayed one night with the British Ambassador and another with an old friend, the Metropolitan of Beirut. On the following day, at ten thirty a.m., he stepped out into the warm sunshine of Jerusalem, the first stop on this three-cornered journey.

. . .

[1] E. E. Y. Hales, *Pope John and His Revolution* (Eyre and Spottiswoode).

274

Daily Express cartoon, 2 November 1960 (*London Express News and Feature Service*).

Many people visit the Holy Land. Many have always done so, making a rough journey of it, like the medieval pilgrims, or an easy one like the modern: but all for the most part drawn by the magic of that strange and ancient place. But Fisher's visit, with its immense ecumenical and political overtones, was in a class apart. To say that he did all the usual things, walking along the Via Dolorosa, visiting the Church of the Holy Sepulchre, the Garden of Gethsemane, the Mount of Olives, Bethlehem, Jericho, Jacob's Well in Samaria, and the like, is merely to give an itinerary which many have followed. To say that he called upon His Beatitude Benedictos, Patriarch of Jerusalem, on the Armenian and Latin Patriarchs, the Custodian of the Holy Places, the Governor of Jerusalem, and on Advent Sunday preached at morning service in St. George's Cathedral, is to give but a monochrome picture of what was in fact an extremely colourful occasion, marked by an astonishing outpouring of Christian love and enthusiasm. Fortunately, the Archbishop kept a small diary at the time, the entries in which give something of this colour, and record something of this love which he experienced.

Thus of Thursday, the day after his arrival, he noted:

'It is really impossible to describe or even to remember the impressions of this day. Moving beyond belief; not merely or chiefly because of the historic scenes of Our Lord's Passion; but because of these events recalled on such hallowed ground in the midst of clergy and people of all sorts and all Churches, and myself in their midst. I went forth at eight fifty-five to make my first call on the Acting Governor, and then on to the Temple area, where I was given the privilege of driving right into it, and being met by the Guardian . . .' Of the Via Dolorosa the Archbishop wrote that 'it passed along streets fascinating, narrow, lined with little shops. The Stations of the Cross are ecclesiastical inventions, the supposed events being placed at convenient places in the streets leading from the Praetorium. One could not think of it as the Via Dolorosa for looking at the people in their little cave-like shops and the whole vista of the Street of the Shoemakers and the like. I did realise how Our Lord must have walked that same sorrowful way through the narrow, crowded streets of people doing their ordinary work, and very likely paying little more than a momentary attention to the procession.

'So up we went to the Church of the Holy Sepulchre. As I approached the doorway, the Latin organ played "God Save the Queen" and the Armenian bells clanged. I cannot describe the church. I hardly saw it. I remember the first place I knelt—a stone on which Our Lord's body was supposed to have rested after being taken down from the cross. Why can I not recall all of this with exactitude? Because throughout, in a strange way, I became mentally passive; feeling a kind of victim with Our Lord. For from the moment I entered the church, I was engulfed in a great crowd of Orthodox monks and Franciscans and others, who surrounded me and, almost literally, carried me from place to place. My arm on the left side was held sometimes by two, sometimes by three of the Orthodox, while my right arm was upheld by a Franciscan, caring for me as a devoted disciple might, keeping tight hold of me most of the way. There were many steps down to the chapels and up to the Sepulchre. I hardly walked; I hardly had a chance to stumble; as I was carried and propelled by Orthodox, Franciscans and Armenians, who cared for me and loved me as they bore me round. At a place I would kneel and feel Our Lord looking at us in this strange mixture of past and present; then be borne on again, this way and that, and feeling lovingly at their mercy. And I felt that somehow like this Our Lord was pulled and hustled and felt at the mercy of his unloving guides. More than that I cannot recall. At intervals the bells would clang again. The whole thing was an astonishing outpouring of every kind of excited motion, all flowing round and over me, not me as a person, but as a kind of centre point of that triumphal showing forth of Christian fellowship.

'The Superior of the Franciscans and others became inseparable friends of mine. And all the brethren let me go about as a brother of them all. In Jerusalem the division of the denominations and their jealousies are intense: their territories are marked out and none must transgress. And yet always, more than anywhere else in the world, I sensed that here the denominations know themselves as one in their diversities. They are all fused together in one, even as they maintain themselves against one another. They struggled for my arm in each place, in order that my arm should be held and myself propelled by the right possessors of that part of the church. A Greek would fade away altogether at one place, and then there would be Franciscans. Franciscans would fade away and on both sides Greeks and Armenians would appear. And then again I was a prisoner between Greeks and Latins. It was amazing. And all equally accepted me as the focus of this demonstration.'

The Archbishop visited the Orthodox Patriarch, the Latin Patriarch, the Armenian Patriarch. His diary continues: 'So to the most notable of these calls, to the Franciscan Custodian of the Holy Places and his brethren. Here was I, sitting in the seat of honour, in an assembly of Franciscans. Their chief had obviously given me the seat which was his in friendship. He said: "There is no barrier between us but language." And I said that if people could laugh together, all barriers were overcome. Then he gave me a scroll and pinned on me a medal for pilgrims which, with Papal authority, the Custodian can present.'

As he left the monks crowded round him, many of them kneeling and kissing his ring. In a footnote to this section, the Archbishop wrote that: 'I have not really given any coherent picture of yesterday; I have not mentioned the little prayers at the altars, here and there, in the Church of the Holy Sepulchre. I was in prayer, rather than praying, and feeling Christ who had suffered all this contradiction of sinners with us. I was almost in tears of spiritual ecstasy and exhaustion.'

Press reports of this visit were numerous and generous. Let one stand for them all, summing up the whole affair. Thus *The Times* on 28 November 1960: 'Dr. Fisher's visit has undoubtedly created a big impression—one that is mutual. After being here he is "enormously encouraged". Much admiration has been expressed for Dr. Fisher's stamina in going through unfalteringly, and almost non-stop, with a programme of calls and visits to shrines which would have exhausted many a pilgrim half his age.'

. . .

Leaving Jerusalem, he arrived at the Hilton Hotel, Istanbul, on 29 November, to be the guest of the Oecumenical Patriarch. Here, he noted in his diary, the weather was cloudy and cold, and he drove to his hotel through thick traffic, having been met by the Consul, three bishops—in lounge suits because no ministers of religion are allowed in the streets in clerical dress. At ten thirty he left the Grand Suite in the hotel (which he noted was reserved for film stars and Patriarchs) and went to the Patriarchal Church. There was an interchange of salutations. The choir sang hymns, after which Fisher was given a cross, and blessed the people with it. Thence across a courtyard he was taken to the Oecumenical Patriarch's office, a very small room, where he greeted the Patriarch, a most impressive figure, tall and stately, and very moved to greet Fisher. They sat and drank coffee and talked. After that, there was a call on the Governor of the city and, after lunch in the vast Embassy, there were the customary visits to Hagia Sophia and the Blue Mosque. Later he called on the Armenian Patriarch, 'a humble, loving little man who was at Lambeth not long before. We had a good talk.' Fisher was asked to look into the church just across the street. Bells clanged as he walked over, and found an open, clean church where he went up to the front and there knelt and prayed. When he turned, he found the church was almost full of people, men, women and children who had heard the bells and had hurried to church to see if it was a service.

Fisher also visited the Apostolic Delegate, who had some interesting remarks to make about Pope John whom Fisher was to see. The Pope had once himself been in Istanbul as Apostolic Delegate. Fisher was told of his friendly common sense and his good relationships with the Orthodox and the Anglicans. He was, however, the Apostolic Delegate said to Fisher, 'no diplomat', but 'a humble, simple, loving person with no kind of inhibitions'. The Apostolic Delegate said that he was sure Fisher and the Pope would get on well.

Wednesday, 30 November, St. Andrew's Day, was a heavy day. The Archbishop celebrated at eight in the chapel in the British Consulate and then went to the Liturgy of St. Andrew at ten. This Liturgy lasted until one fifteen, and he found it most impressive. At the end, the Oecumenical Patriarch came to the throne opposite Fisher and made an address, to which Fisher replied. The Patriarch presented Fisher with a costly present, and Satterthwaite and Freddie Temple, the Archbishop's chaplain, with pectoral crosses. After that, Fisher had his hand kissed by almost the whole congregation, as he noted in his diary. The Oecumenical Patriarch was standing at the top of the steps when Fisher's party left—a fine, lonely figure.

Thus ended this second stage of Fisher's pilgrimage. The following day, after a press conference at nine, he left Istanbul at ten forty, was in Athens by eleven forty-five, where he was met by the British Ambassador and representatives of the Anglican Church. At one p.m. he left Athens and his plane touched down at Ciampino Airport, Rome at one fifty, where he was met by the British Ambassador, Sir Ashley Clark; the British Minister to the Holy See, Sir Peter Scarlett; and the Anglican Chaplain in Rome, Canon D. Wanstall. An extraordinary series of events followed.

. . .

That something highly unusual was taking place, and that the press had been thoroughly alerted to the fact, was indicated by the tumult which greeted the Archbishop at the airport. Thus *The Guardian* of 2 December 1960: 'The Archbishop's arrival at Rome airport, however formal it should have been, was a chaotic, noisy but friendly few minutes. No sooner had he stepped on to the landing steps, dressed in purple cassock and cloak, with his black velvet Canterbury cap resting on his eyebrows, than the official welcomers were almost lost from view in the crowd of journalists who surged forward . . . Dr. Fisher looked at the battery of clicking shutters and said he supposed there were some journalists present, although he could not see them. They were in fact pressing in on him from every side. He spoke briefly into three microphones and from what could be heard above the chatter of the crowd said that this was a quite unspectacular event but a rather historic one. He was looking forward with interest and delight to his conversations with His Holiness the Pope. "I have been asked often what we will talk about, and I reply 'About nothing and about everything'." He turned to the nearest Italian reporter and asked, "Is that all right?" Someone shouted a question but the Archbishop was quickly shielded and hurried away to the Ambassador's car.'

This reception was in marked contrast to what, apparently, had been the intentions of the Roman authorities. As to that Fisher recalled: 'On my way in the plane, I remember I drafted some kind of possible press communiqué, to be issued at the end of the visit. When I got to Scarlett, our Minister with whom I was to stay, I showed this to a member of his staff. He looked at it and said: "I don't think some of this will do," so I revised it. Then I found that Tardini, the Secretary of State, had laid down certain conditions, because Scarlett told me what they were. They were astonishing conditions to be greeted with: (1) There should be no official photograph of me with the Pope. To make sure of this, Tardini had sent away the official photographer on a fortnight's holiday. So that was off. It had never occurred to me that there would or would not be official photographs; but he, Tardini, obviously thought it was important; (2) It was stated that I should not see Cardinal Bea, the Head of the department recently set up by the Pope to foster relations with other Churches. This sounded a preposterous thing, but there it was; (3) There was to be no kind of press release after my meeting with the Pope. That was a little odd, as I had already drafted one; (4) The Minister was not to invite to meet me at meals at his house any of the Vatican officials. Nevertheless, the press communiqué I had written and revised was taken to Tardini. He said it would not do, and it was brought back and I wrote a third, and gave this to the Minister, asking him to see it through Tardini, if possible. It was also arranged that Ashley Clark, an old Repton boy, a great friend of mine, should have a reception at the Embassy to which he would ask Vatican officials and anybody else he wished. This was a very great success, as it turned out, because there I met people like Archbishop Matthew, an old friend, the Head of the English College, and many others from Vatican circles, who welcomed the chance of coming to meet me.'

That reception, of course, took place after Fisher had seen the Pope. It is mentioned here, since it represents one of the ways in which the embargo placed upon the Archbishop's contacts during his visit were overcome. One not overcome was the question of photographs, so that no official pictures of this historic occasion exist. The *Daily Mirror* was one paper which regretted this in its issue of 2 December: 'This is the first meeting between the heads of two of the greatest Christian Churches since the profound split in Christendom more than four hundred years ago . . . but unless there is a last-minute change of mind, this historic occasion will go unrecorded by a single photograph . . . It would be ecclesiastical timidity if it were decided that the momentous meeting between the Archbishop and the Pope should take place — in cloistered secrecy. Millions of Christians would be delighted to see a photograph of these two great figures together.' But that, unfortunately, was not to be.

To return, however, to the sequence of events. Fisher's first engagement was a meeting with four representatives of Italian Protestant Churches, including the Waldensians, before preaching at Evensong in All Saints, the Anglican Church. 'His sermon,' said *The Guardian* of 1 December, 'is awaited with considerable interest. Dr. Fisher is expected to exercise the utmost tact, for among the congregation, besides the Italian Protestants, will be Church of Scotland, Methodists, American Episcopal and Lutheran ministers, as well as Russian and Greek Orthodox priests, a Salvation Army officer, and probably a number of Roman Catholics. His words are also certain to reach the majority of priests in Rome.

In his sermon — the last of the trilogy preached during his pilgrimage — Fisher said that he had come to Rome neither to boast nor to complain, but only to greet the Pope in courtesy of Christian brotherhood. This could only have happened, and he could only have suggested the visit, because the Pope had made clear that he would receive him in a similar spirit. He added that here was indeed a Day of the Lord, like many Days of the Lord simple, unspectacular, hardly to be observed, a whisper of the small voice of the Holy Spirit.

The following day, 2 December, the Archbishop visited Pope John. His diary records that, after an early communion, he got ready and at eleven forty set off. 'I drove round behind St. Peter's,' he wrote, 'into a courtyard, and to a door on the left-hand side. There I was met by a chamberlain and a red carpet. I went by lift to the next floor, through six large, magnificent chambers, each with its own appointed Guard. All the doors were fully open. I went to the ante-room and found a small company there. The Guards and indeed everyone from the Pope downwards had been excused the normal retreat or "Advent exercises" especially for this. From twelve fifteen to one twenty I was with the Pope.'

His account of what happened at this momentous time, as recollected later during his retirement, is much fuller.

'I was received in a most impressive way. From the ante-room, where we waited for a few minutes, I was taken into the Pope's room, which was,

I think, a library. We greeted each other at once in the ordinary, friendly way. We shook hands and smiled at each other, and straightaway we started, as any two friendly people would start, talking about one thing or another, breaking the ice. We were standing by some cases, and he pointed at one or two things in them, and so we went on up the room, to the further end where there was a chair on a low platform, and chairs at each side. The further one the Monsignor who interpreted, used. I sat next to the Pope on the other. He began the conversation with a rather elaborate story, designed, I think, to ease the opening of the conversation. It seemed to me it was going on a long time; so at a convenient moment I broke in by saying: "Yes, Your Holiness, that reminds me of—" something that invited a reply. As soon as he realised that this was a to and fro conversation, going wherever the winds or the Holy Spirit took it, he delightedly played it like that. So we talked as two happy people, who had seen a good deal of the world and of life, and of the Churches, glad to talk together. I cannot remember how the conversation went, except that it flowed without the slightest difficulty.

'There are two parts of it that remain in my mind. One is, that at one point he said: "I should like to read to you a passage from an address that I recently gave." He read, in English, a passage which included a reference to "the time when our separated brethren should return to the Mother Church". I at once said: "Your Holiness, not *return*." He looked puzzled and said, "Not return? Why not?" I said: "None of us can go backwards. We are each now running on parallel courses; we are looking forward, until, in God's good time, our two courses approximate and meet." He said, after a moment's pause, "You are right." From that moment, as far as I know, he and the Vatican never talked about our returning to a past situation, and looking backwards for our objective. That was, in fact, a very notable conversion. Somewhere in the Pope's book *The Journey of a Soul*, I happened to find a rather special passage in which he talked about "the separated brethren returning to the Mother Church". It had, not surprisingly, been always much in his thoughts. This sudden check took him by surprise, but he adapted himself to it at once. This was a notable thing at his age and bore fruit.

'The other thing that I noted was that at one point, as we were talking about how the Christian looks at his personal affairs, the Pope quoted something to me from *The Imitation of Christ* to the effect that, for the Christian, if it were a choice between less or more, the choice is almost always less rather than more. I said, in entire agreement, that St. Paul had taught, as one of the things specially to be guarded against, was "wanting more". Our Lord himself had warned us against covetousness, and Paul placed it twice next door to idolatry. Long afterwards, when I was reading *The Journey of a Soul* I found a passage in which Pope John quoted three maxims of the Christian life, and one of them (they were all from Thomas à Kempis) was that the Christian should always choose the less. That remained in my mind from our conversation, and is a constant reminder of a wonderful and joyful bringing-together of our spiritual thoughts in our meeting.

'Somewhere in our conversation, I thanked the Pope for what he had done in setting up the new department under Cardinal Bea. He then said with a smile and a twinkle, "Yes, and this afternoon you shall see Cardinal Bea." I realised that Tardini had been overruled by the Pope, revealing a little of the breaking of the barriers and of the icy wastes of the Vatican curia.'

So ended this notable interview. It had been much longer than any normal courtesy visit, so simple in nature, so historic and so rich in results. It remained for the two principals to exchange gifts. The Archbishop gave to the Pope a special copy of the Coronation Service, bound in white vellum and bearing a special commemorative inscription. The Pope in return presented the Archbishop with the recently published volumes on the Roman Synod, the addresses delivered by him when Patriarch of Venice, and the first volume of the preparatory acts of the Roman Oecumenical Council. He also gave Fisher a medal.

So, at any rate, said an official statement issued later. The reality was considerably more colourful and animated. As Fisher recalled the matter: 'As they could not be given to me to carry away, the Pope said he would send them down. The next day I went to our Minister's office where the gifts were to be brought by the present Apostolic Delegate to England, dear Cardinale. I said to the Minister: "Why have we got to go there?" He said: "It would be too conspicuous if he came to my own residence. It

would be less conspicuous if he comes to my office." It struck me as odd
that it should matter if it was conspicuous or not, but there it was. I got to
his office and there I found that Cardinale had arrived twenty minutes
before, very secretly, and was upstairs in a room waiting for me. I went
up to him and he was grand, as Cardinale has been ever since. We had a
lovely time, and he gave me not only the Pope's books but also a portfolio
of Raphael's cartoons. The time came when I was to go, and I supposed
that we should go together. But he said that he must let me get away first,
before he appeared, and he suggested I should draw all the reporters after
me away from the Minister's office before he did so. This was a queer and
notable thing.'

It would have seemed less queer, and less notable perhaps, if the Archbishop had known then some of the complications which had beset the
work of his Press Officer, Robert Hornby, throughout the whole affair.
And since it was partly through his labours that the impact of this visit
came to be felt so widely, inasmuch as it was so extensively reported, his
narrative is of importance. It was he, for instance, who had in the first
place recognised the immense press interest which the visit would stir up
throughout the world. It was he who had gone, as he put it, throughout
Fleet Street, interviewing each editor separately, 'telling him of this proposed visit, and giving him the details of when we would make the public
announcement. This, of course,' Hornby said, 'was given on a confidential
basis, that nothing would be published and that no hint would appear in
the press until such time as I made the official release from Lambeth.
There was no leak whatsoever, but this did enable each editor to plan the
issue in which the news would be broken, and to make arrangements for
covering the visit to Rome with special correspondents. I was particularly
grateful, for example, to the late "Tony" Cole, then chief of Reuter's in
London, who immediately saw the significance of this to the world, and
called in one of his top foreign correspondents who had a knowledge of
ecclesiastical affairs, and assigned him to the Archbishop for the entire
visit, so that all that came out of Rome, through Reuter's, would be
authentic and would give the background to the visit.'

It was Hornby who, having left for Rome on the Saturday previous to
the visit, had been able to make extensive preparations at that end also

with the press, being assisted throughout by Mgr. Willebrands of the Secretariat for Christian Unity, whose office was outside the Vatican. It was Hornby again who held a meeting in a correspondent's flat in Rome, to which came all the resident British and Commonwealth correspondents and a number of Italian correspondents. At this meeting he outlined the visit for them so that they would know exactly what was happening. He also had with him, on that occasion, the text of the sermon which the Archbishop was to preach at Evensong in All Saints, and had this ready translated into Italian. This particular piece of foresight, as it happened, was to give him considerable trouble, because, when the Archbishop's plane arrived and Freddie Temple, the Archbishop's chaplain, handed him the final draft of the sermon, Hornby discovered that Fisher had considerably altered it. This necessitated recalling all the copies of the sermon he had distributed and asking a group of Embassy staff to sit round a large table and correct all the original copies, both in Italian and English, so that they could be re-issued! It was Hornby again who had arranged with the commandant of the airport at Rome for the press reception of the Archbishop. He also made arrangements with the British Ambassador for the use of the Embassy for a press conference following the visit to the Pope.

Colonel Hornby's memory of the evening service in the Anglican church at which Fisher preached is vivid. 'By that time, the first television pictures had appeared in Rome, and the Rome "populars" had been startled by the sight of this archiepiscopal figure with his Canterbury cap; and there was already interest stirring in Rome. Italian television cameras were present outside the church, and we had press photographers in the church with a number of seats reserved for the press. At the end of the service, the Archbishop came out of the church—by then it was dark—and stood at the West Door which leads directly onto the Via Babuino, a very narrow street packed with people. He was wearing the Coronation Cope and Mitre. All the television arc lamps were trained on the door, so that he appeared to the people lit up in these magnificent robes. I don't think that they were able to grasp that this was an Anglican archbishop. He blessed the crowd, and I noticed a great many Italians kissing his ring as he left the church. So the arrival was a great success, and the next morning the papers carried extensive reports and pictures of his arrival. And without a doubt, the Archbishop of Canterbury was headline news throughout Italy.'

But there still remained, nonetheless, the problem of the communiqué which was to be issued after the visit to the Pope. Hornby's account continued: 'The plan was that I should go to the Vatican with the Archbishop and chaplain, and go to a separate room to await the official interpreter who, after the interview, would meet me and together we would write in the blank paragraph at the end of the communiqué, which said, in general terms, what the Archbishop and the Pope had discussed. We anticipated that the visit would last about thirty minutes. I arrived at the Vatican in the car following the Archbishop. The two chaplains with the Archbishop walked past the Swiss Guards and I saw the Archbishop disappearing round a corner. Then I was whisked into a lift, went up several floors, was taken down a long corridor and shown into a small room. I waited in this room, or walked about it, for well over an hour, with no communication at all with the outside world. I had no idea whether the Archbishop had already left the Vatican or what was happening. I could find no one to talk to. Eventually, the First Secretary to the Legation, McDermott, arrived and said to me "The visit is over. Mgr. Samore is on his way to see you." Samore duly appeared, opened the door, put his hand on his heart and said: "I cannot speak. I am full of emotion. I must lie down." I said: "We have the world press waiting for this communiqué. You cannot lie down!" Nonetheless, he went, and I said to McDermott that this was too bad because it couldn't wait. Eventually Samore returned, and we sat down together at a small marble-topped table and wrote in what I understood had been the purport of the discussion between the Archbishop and the Pope. So with my paragraph completed, I got into the embassy car and returned. Thus the communiqué was issued to the world.'

One amusing story may end Hornby's narrative: 'We had a number of television interviews, B.B.C. and Independent Television came along. Then the Canadian Broadcasting Corporation arrived with a camera crew, but had lost their interviewer. They beseeched me to find someone, or do something, about interviewing the Archbishop. So I asked the British Ambassador if he would be good enough to sit down in front of the cameras. I doubt if the C.B.C. have ever realised to this day that their commentator in Rome, on that particular afternoon, happened to be the British Ambassador.'

Such were some of the backroom scenes during this astonishing time. An Anglican statement issued afterwards said, 'It was never intended that this should be an occasion for consideration of particular problems or issues, and the meeting retained throughout the character of a visit of courtesy. It was marked by a happy spirit of cordiality and sympathy, such as befitted a notable event in the history of Church relations.' A statement from the Vatican covered much the same ground.

But for Fisher, deeply aware of the spiritual yields of his venture, there remained a great content and thankfulness. 'It had been', he wrote in his diary, 'a wonderful tour for me in every way, crammed with all the best that makes up fullness of life. It seems to have released a real stream of living water in many parts of the world.' And, years later, he said: 'So the visit ended, and the pilgrimage ended; and I am thankful that I did it in just that order: Jerusalem first, Istanbul second, and then Rome, in its own proper place, as the third point in my pilgrimage. How many things have flowed from that! It was the final achievement of my archiepiscopate, without any doubt, and it arose in the simplest of ways, as a simple matter of a simple visit to a simple Pope.'

XV

Resignation

I didn't look forward or try to decide what should happen after my resignation. I merely felt this was the right thing and did it.

G.F.F.

. . .

I am convinced that day by day my wisdom increases, and I am also satisfied that my stock of patience diminishes, and that is why I feel the time has come.

G.F.F. in an address to Convocation, 17 January 1961

. . .

I walk up Compton Hill sometimes, and there I look to Yeovil, looking pleasant in the distance, and then further to the right the spire of Trent Church, and between the two the Mendips and Glastonbury Tor. What could be more eloquent of the glory of England?

G.F.F.

. . .

The Rector has the permanent help of the former Archbishop of Canterbury.

Leaflet in Trent Church

AN announcement from Downing Street on 17 January 1961, startled many people.

'The Archbishop of Canterbury has tendered his resignation to Her Majesty the Queen. The Queen has received this intimation with great regret and on the recommendation of the Prime Minister has appointed by Royal Warrant a commission consisting of the Archbishop of York and the Bishops of London, Durham and Winchester to receive and accept the resignation on her behalf. The see and archbishopric of Canterbury have been declared vacant from 31 May of this year and the declaration is being submitted for confirmation by Her Majesty in council today.

The Queen has been graciously pleased to signify her intention of conferring a barony of the United Kingdom for life upon the Archbishop upon his retirement.'

Why it should have been found so startling it is difficult to understand. 'It was evident,' as one paper described the scene in convocation at Church House, when Fisher made a personal statement on the matter, 'that Dr. Fisher's news came as a surprise to most of those present.' Yet so many of the things he had done over the years had come as surprises, of which his just concluded visit to Rome had been possibly the greatest. Now, on top of a wave of popular regard, he was choosing to bow himself out. Why was this so?

As so often with Fisher, his reasons were cogent, thought out, and eminently reasonable. He described them himself several years later.

'The time came when I began to ask myself, can I go on at full stretch? I think the first time that I got a query in my mind was when I came back from Japan. I had been hard at it: we flew straight back and next day I was in Convocation. I knew that there I was talking too much. I intervened in almost everything, just to say something, and it wasn't really necessary and it was a sign that I was tired. I felt rather sorry that had happened, and it was a warning of a kind to me. Some time later, one of my boldest and bravest and best chaplains had a talk with me, in which he said that I was becoming, in Bishops' Meetings, almost intolerable, endlessly talking. That pulled me up. I did not feel domineering; but I was quite sure that I might, at any time, be too dominating. So when my chaplain told me that he thought I was becoming like this, I did not take it amiss. I only wondered how far it was a real case against me. That, I think, was leading up to a decision. Then came the idea of going on pilgrimage to Jerusalem, Istanbul and Rome. It was, I think, some time during our autumn holiday in Scotland before this pilgrimage, that the idea of resignation took positive shape in my mind.

'What else was in my mind? I am perfectly clear. I began to feel that I could not put myself again wholeheartedly into certain things. There was the Assembly of the World Council of Churches in New Delhi, which was looming heavily. I enjoyed these great World Council Assemblies; but found the endless pressure of discussion and of trying to steer people clear of mis-statements or exaggerations in our resolutions very exhausting. This was going to be a particularly heavy one, and I felt very reluctant to throw myself into all the preparations for it.

'At the same time, there was the Anglican Congress in Toronto looming up. Already I was being consulted about its business and I felt that I could not go through all the heavy tasks of keeping an eye on its affairs and taking part in its direction.

'There was also another thing. Henry Sherrill, who had helped so greatly to make the Minneapolis Congress such a splendid thing, would not be at Toronto, and without Henry Sherrill I should have felt I was carrying too heavy a load, without his vitality and forthright friendliness to help me and unite all of us. There were also other considerations. All my time it had been laid on me to lead the Church as far as I could along a very difficult road in order that it might recover a proper sense of co-operative authority. I thought that now we had got to a point where the brow of the hill had been topped, and that I could without injury to the cause leave the task for others to complete. Those were the three special reasons in my mind. And above all I was beginning to feel that I could not go on at my fullest speed, in which case, in such a position, I could not see myself going on at all. If I continued I should only be losing momentum year by year. This therefore was a good time, especially because it would give my successor the opportunity of beginning his reign with New Delhi and Toronto, where he would put himself into the middle of World Council affairs, and right into the middle of the life of the Anglican Communion. That I felt to be so right that it carried me to the final decision that I must resign. That autumn I gave Macmillan warning that I should be resigning soon: then I went on the tour of Jerusalem, Istanbul and Rome. When I came back, I told Macmillan that I was ready.'

And so he went, quietly and without apparent emotion. He said: 'Polite things were said about me; but I've never been happy with vale-dictory encomiums. I had none when I left Repton. As a matter of fact William Temple came to my last Speech Day and my wife was expecting him to hold forth upon the excellence of my period as headmaster and so forth; but William Temple (just like him, and it didn't worry me at all) merely said that I had been there for eighteen years and it had been a very notable reign. He then started, at once, to talk about something which interested him of an educational kind. I knew that was just the right thing. I never much liked farewell speeches; I didn't want any when I resigned as Archbishop, though there were some, and very moving and touching they were.'

There were indeed. There was also a sense of loss. One member of the Standing Committee of the Canterbury Diocesan Conference, for instance, remembered how, the Archbishop having announced his decision, 'the Standing Committee of the Diocesan Conference took tea with the Archbishop and Mrs. Fisher at the Old Palace at Canterbury for the last time. It seemed that the place could never be the same again.'

It was characteristic of Fisher to play all this down into a minor key. 'I am happy to think,' he commented in after times, 'that I've never been the kind of person who can raise funds, or attract gifts and visible forms of expression of that sort. I've never been out for them; I've never wanted them. I've always been rather embarrassed when I got them. What did satisfy me was that some people thought, for various reasons, that I'd done a good thing in resigning; many people were sorry and were not quite sure what the future would be like without me. And that ended that.'

.   .   .

There remained a period of several moves before a final place of retirement was found: first to a cottage in Exmoor, then to other temporary places in the same area, after that, for eleven months, to a small house in the country town of Sherborne in Dorset. Finally, through the generosity of the diocese of Bath and Wells, came the offer of Trent Rectory. It was a happy landing, the last of many. He said: 'If we'd searched England, we couldn't have found any place at all which would have suited us better. All is just what it should be: true country and a pure country village. Both Rosamond and I were born in the country and our heart is always there. We are near Sherborne, which is a country town. All this is coming back into our lives at last. And there is also the beauty of the church, and of the surroundings, which are exquisite. And so we came here, and the house itself is just what anybody who cares for the history of England, and the history of English domestic life, would want. It is comely; it is half the old rectory, just a little bit short of space, but what does that matter? The staircase, which is often a great test, has low rises so that as one's legs get more feeble it is still easy to mount the staircase. The rooms are beautifully proportioned, and there and in the church one feels one is in the quiet, graceful atmosphere of the Church of England as it has grown through the seventeenth and eighteenth and nineteenth centuries and is now, in the twentieth century, changing its image and its relation to the world, but always its strong and splendid self.

'I have been wonderfully blessed in the whole thing. I'm allowed to take services, two or it may be three every Sunday, in our own church, or in Nether Compton, or Over Compton. That is a joy. The other thing I've discovered is that the fact of having no responsibility gives one a completely new and happy approach to people in the village and elsewhere.'

Happy is the word, although it would scarcely be true to a portrait of Fisher to represent him as fading, in retirement, to a life of bucolic obscurity. On the contrary, the same vivid interest in the affairs of the world and the Church, always a part of him, continues unabated to this moment, and his letters to the press and other writings have, from time to time made no small stir.

Even so, three final glimpses, three final touches to this attempt at a portrait of Fisher may not be out of place. The first shows him in relation to the country town near which it has been his destiny to settle: the second shows him in relation to the Church in which he serves: the third shows him in relation to the village which he loves, and which loves him.

Miss Diana Reader-Harris, Headmistress of Sherborne School for Girls, had this to say: 'Since Lord Fisher retired we have seen quite a bit of him in Sherborne because, for his first year after retirement, he lived in the town itself, and then went to Trent, which is only a few miles away. The comment that so many people, including the girls at school, have made is of his wonderful friendliness when they meet him in the street, or when people meet him in shops. He always stops and asks them who they are, what they've been doing and so forth. At Trent church itself, girls from the school go cycling over to attend his morning services, again not only to hear his sermons, which are friendly and full of reminiscences of the past, but also in order to hear him talk to them, coming out of the church. He seems to enjoy the young. In the school here, when we have plays, he comes regularly each year and is a wonderful member of the audience because, if the play is in any sense moving or sad, he shows emotion very easily, and blows his nose hard. Lady Fisher apologises because he shows emotion too readily. He laughs and does it again, and the cast is delighted because at least one member of the audience is really appreciating their performance.'

As to the village church, let one glimpse suffice. The Archbishop had been deputed to take Evensong at Nether Compton, one of the churches of the parish. It was a very beautiful June evening, with the countryside in full bloom. The village was quiet. The small, plain church was cool and there was a view of fields and cows through the open door. There were eleven people present as the single bell tolled. Eventually a car was heard to draw up and, after a while, the Archbishop, wearing Canterbury cap, rochet and chimere, doctor's scarlet hood and a decoration or two on his scarf, came slowly into the church, leaning heavily on his stick. He read an introduction to explain the Old Testament lesson. The second lesson he read in his own personal translation. His sermon lasted fifteen minutes, and was on the collect for the fourth Sunday after Trinity: 'Increase and multiply upon us thy mercy; that, thou being our ruler and guide, we may so pass through things temporal, that we finally lose not the things eternal.' When the service was over, he greeted everybody, shook hands, consulted a churchwarden over a swarm of bees which had descended upon his house, and then was driven through the winding Dorset lanes back to Trent.

Finally, the village. The golden wedding of Archbishop Lord Fisher of Lambeth and Lady Fisher occurred on 12 April 1967. There were many celebrations in connection with this, two of them far away from Trent. There was a banquet at Lambeth Palace. The Archbishop and Lady Fisher were also asked to stay with the Queen at Windsor, on 11 April. The Queen presented them with a pair of golden candlesticks before dinner. As the party dispersed after midnight, the Queen and the Duke came over the room and said that the golden wedding day had already dawned and gave them their personal best wishes.

But Trent village also celebrated the occasion in style. The church bells were rung: the following Sunday Ian White-Thomson, Dean of Canterbury and chaplain in his time to both Temple and Fisher, was the preacher at Matins. On the following 5 May, the Archbishop's eightieth birthday, the church bells were again rung and there was a reception in the village hall. This was the occasion for the first public performance of 'The Ballad of Trent', locally written, and celebrating the fact that the village once sheltered Charles II and later had an archbishop for its curate. The company sang its many verses, of which these are a few:

> Now this is the Ballad of Trent,
> Which all of us join to present,
> The big and the small, the short and the tall,
> *To please you, and that's our intent.*

> O Trent is a place of renown,
> Though we cannot match London Town,
> Yet we sheltered a king, and of this we may sing,
> *When others are getting us down.*

> But more wonderful still's the event
> Of which we shall never repent,
> Which gives us as curate, long may he endure it,
> *Lord Fisher of Lambeth in Trent.*

> He's won all our hearts. Every one
> Takes pride in old Trent's greatest son,
> The youngest, the oldest, the warmest, the coldest,
> *And so let our ballad be done.*

> Lord Fisher, the night is far spent,
> So all of your neighbours in Trent,
> The big and the small, the short and the tall,
> *Wish both of you every content.*

Index

U

297

Ecumenical Movement, 18, 122, 152, 183 n., 187, 189, 192, 197
Eden, Anthony, 260, 261, 266
Edinburgh Conference, 1910, 18
Edinburgh, Duke of, *see* Philip
Edward VII, King, 239, 250
Edward VIII, King, 166, 242, 247, 250
Egypt, 261, 262, 263, 272
Eisenhower, President, 211–12
Eley, Stanley, 91, 102, 127, 149, 158, 165, 170, 179, 180
Eliot, George, 27
Eliot, T. S., 75, 100, 152
Eliot, W. H., 75
Elizabeth I, Queen, 241, 248
Elizabeth II, Queen, 70, 135, 181, 236, 238, 240, 241, 242, 244, 248–9, 250, 265, 289, 290, 294; as Princess Elizabeth, 128, 132–3, 169, 170, 171, 236
Elizabeth, Queen (The Queen Mother), 128, 129, 135, 237, 240, 243, 249, 250
Encyclical Letter, 1948, 180; 1958, 195, 196
English Public School, the, 37, 38, 39–40, 41, 48, 53
EOKA, 257
Ethiopia, Church of, 192
Evangelicals, 151, 152–3, 208, 274
Evangelism, 67, 77
Evanston, 178
Evening Standard, 17
Exeter College, Oxford, 44, 46, 47
Exchequer, Chancellor of, 181, 215, 216, 266

Fairbairn, Rev., 103
Faith and Order, Council for, 188
Movement, 18, 189, 270 n.
Family in Contemporary Society, The, 195, 197
Family Planning, Report on, 197–8
Faribault Cathedral, Minnesota, 194
Farrar, 39
Federal Council of Churches in U.S.A., 175
Federal Council of Evangelical Free Churches, 150, 158; Congress of, 151; General Purposes Committee of, 157
Festival of Britain, 137–8
Ffoulkes, Mrs., 77

Fisher, Charles (son), 59
Fisher, Edith (sister), 28
Fisher, Francis (son), 59, 82
Fisher, Geoffrey Francis, CHILDHOOD AND SCHOOLDAYS; his clerical ancestors, 27; childhood at Higham, 28, 31, 32, 36; his family, 28–9; father, 29–30, 32, 33; mother, 30–1, 32, 34; and the village community, 29, 32; at the village school, 32; at Lindley Lodge prep. school, 32, 34–5, 36, 221; foundations of character, 32–3, 34; sense of history, 33–4; regard for authority, 35, 36, 38, 40; and the English Public school, 37–8; at Marlborough, 36, 37, 38, 40–4, 46, 80–1; discipline at Marlborough, 38, 43–4, 49–50; and the Prefects' Roll, 43; and the influence of Frank Fletcher, 41–2, 43, 44, 50; and the school chapel, 44; at Oxford, 44–8, 189–90, 200, 223; and smoking, 45; faith of, 44–5, 49, 66; and doctrine, 46–7, 77; religion of, 48; and personalities of Oxford, 47; and the S.C.M., 47; a master at Marlborough, 48–51, 81; ordination of, 49. HEADMASTER OF REPTON, 20, 26, 37, 38, 51, 52–64, 200, 239, 288, 291–2; and discipline, 35, 38, 54–5, 80; and the Somervell-Gollancz row, 55–7; statesmanship of, 55, 57; marriage of, 57, 58; wife of, 37, 57–8; and family, 58–9, 69, 82, 117; sons of, 37, 117; and changes at Repton, 59–60; interest in boys, 60–2, 64; and school chapel services, 44, 62–3, 239; preaching of, 63; and William Temple, 26, 51, 63, 68, 72, 98, 102, 190. BISHOP OF CHESTER, 20, 35–6, 37; accepts bishopric, 63; at Chester, 65–78; and Anglo-Methodist relations, 66, 158–60; consecration of, 67–8; friendliness of 64, 69–70, 94, 128; family life of, 69; popularity of, 69, 94; interest in people, 70; in Church Assembly, 70–1; at Bishops' Meetings, 71; in Convocation, 70, 71–2, 73; and Chester College, 71; and Industrial Christian Fellowship Missions, 75–6; and evangelism, 67, 77; other refs., 88,